Hayti
Or, The Black Republic

by
Sir Spenser St. John

Hayti
Or, The Black Republic
by Sir Spenser St. John

Copyright © 2024

All Rights reserved.

No part of this publication may be reproduced, stored in a retrieval system, or transmitted in any form or by any means, electronic, mechanical, photocopying or Otherwise, without the written permission of the publisher.
The author/editor asserts the moral right to be identified as the author/editor of this work.

ISBN: 978-93-62763-97-6

Published by

DOUBLE 9 BOOKS
2/13-B, Ansari Road
Daryaganj, New Delhi – 110002
info@double9books.com
www.double9books.com
Tel. 011-40042856

This book is under public domain

ABOUT THE AUTHOR

Sir Spenser St. John was the British Consul in Brunei in the mid-nineteenth century. On September 20, 1827, Spenser was christened at St Pancras Old Church. In 1847, St. John's father, journalist James Augustus St. John, introduced him to James Brooke. The following year, he traveled to Sarawak to serve as Brooke's private secretary, launching his diplomatic career. He served as the British Consul General in Brunei beginning in 1856, and in 1858 he climbed Mount Kinabalu twice with Hugh Low. Mount Kinabalu's "St John's Peak" is named in his honor. St John was appointed British charge d'affaires in Haiti in 1863, and again in the Dominican Republic in 1871. He was appointed Minister in Haiti late in 1872, then charge d'affaires in Lima and Minister in Peru from 1874 to 1883, during which time he received the KCMG. While in Peru, he amassed a ceramic collection that is currently housed in the British Museum. In 1884, St John released Hayti: Or, The Black Republic, a chronicle of his adventures in Haiti that sparked public indignation with exaggerated accounts of cannibalism in the Vodou faith.

CONTENTS

INTRODUCTION..7

CHAPTER I
GENERAL DESCRIPTION OF HAYTI...13

CHAPTER II
HISTORY BEFORE INDEPENDENCE...26

CHAPTER III
HISTORY SINCE INDEPENDENCE...51

CHAPTER IV
THE POPULATION OF HAYTI...80

CHAPTER V
VAUDOUX WORSHIP AND CANNIBALISM..................................110

CHAPTER VI
THE GOVERNMENT..135

CHAPTER VII
RELIGION, EDUCATION, AND JUSTICE.......................................145

CHAPTER VIII
ARMY AND POLICE..161

CHAPTER IX
LANGUAGE AND LITERATURE...174

CHAPTER X
AGRICULTURE, COMMERCE, AND FINANCE............................186

FOOTNOTES:...205

INTRODUCTION

Whilst in Port-au-Prince, a Spanish colleague once remarked to me, "*Mon ami*, if we could return to Hayti fifty years hence, we should find the negresses cooking their bananas on the site of these warehouses." Although this judgment is severe, yet from what we have seen passing under the present Administration, it is more than probable—unless in the meantime influenced by some higher civilisation—that this prophecy will come true. The negresses are in fact already cooking their bananas amid the ruins of the best houses of the capital. My own impression, after personally knowing the country above twenty years, is, that it is a country in a state of rapid decadence. The revolution of 1843 that upset President Boyer commenced the era of troubles which have continued to the present day. The country has since been steadily falling to the rear in the race of civilisation.

The long civil war (1868-1869) under President Salnave destroyed a vast amount of property, and rendered living in the country districts less secure, so that there has been ever since a tendency for the more civilised inhabitants to agglomerate in the towns, and leave the rural districts to fetish worship and cannibalism. Fires, most of them incendiary, have swept over the cities; in the commercial quarters of Port-au-Prince, it would be difficult to find any houses which existed in 1863, and the fortunes of all have naturally greatly suffered.

When I reached Hayti in January 1863, the capital possessed several respectable public buildings. The palace, without any architectural beauty, was large and commodious, and well suited to the climate; the Senate, the House of Representatives, the dwellings occupied by several of the Ministers, the pretty little theatre, were all features which have now entirely disappeared.

The town of Pétionville or La Coupe, the summer and health resort of the capital, where the best families sought a little country life during the great heats, was almost entirely destroyed during the revolution of 1868, and nothing has taken its place. People are still too poor to afford to rebuild.

Society also has completely changed. I saw at balls given in the palace in 1863 a hundred well-dressed prosperous families of all colours; now political dissensions would prevent such gatherings, even if there were a building in the city which could receive them, and poverty has laid its heavy hand more or less on all. It is the same in a greater or lesser degree in every other town of the republic.

Agriculture in the plains is also deteriorating, and the estates produce much less than formerly, though their staple produce is rum, to stupefy and brutalise the barbarous lower orders.

Foreigners, nearly ruined by their losses during the constant civil disturbances, are withdrawing from the republic, and capital is following them; and with their withdrawal the country must sink still lower. The best of the coloured people are also leaving, as they shun the fate reserved for them by those who have already slaughtered the most prominent mulattoes.

In fact, the mulatto element, which is the civilising element in Hayti, is daily becoming of less importance; internal party strife has injured their political standing, and constant intermarriage is causing the race to breed back to the more numerous type, and in a few years the mulatto element will have made disastrous approaches to the negro. The only thing which could have saved the mulatto would have been to encourage the whites to settle in their country; yet this step the coloured men have blindly resisted.

In spite of all the civilising elements around them, there is a distinct tendency to sink into the state of an African tribe. It is naturally impossible to foretell the effect of all the influences which are now at work in the world, and which seem to foreshadow many changes. We appear standing on the threshold of a period of great discoveries, which may modify many things, but not man's nature. The mass of the negroes of Hayti live in the country districts, which are rarely or ever visited by civilised people; there are few Christian priests to give them a notion of true religion; no superior local officers to prevent them practising their worst fetish ceremonies.

In treating of the Black and the Mulatto as they appeared to me during my residence among them, I fear that I shall be considered by some to judge harshly. Such, however, is not my intention. Brought up under Sir James Brooke, whose enlarged sympathies could endure no prejudice of race or colour, I do not remember ever to have felt any repugnance to my fellow-creatures on account of a difference of complexion.

I have dwelt above thirty-five years among coloured people of various races, and am sensible of no prejudice against them. For twelve years I lived in familiar and kindly intercourse with Haytians of all ranks and shades of colour, and the most frequent and not least-honoured guests at my table were of the black and coloured races.

All who knew me in Hayti know that I had no prejudice of colour; and if I place the Haytian in general in an unenviable light, it is from a strong conviction that it is necessary to describe the people as they are, and not as one would wish them to be. The band of black and coloured friends who gathered round me during my long residence in Port-au-Prince were not free from many of the faults which I have been obliged to censure in describing these different sections of the population, but they had them in a lesser degree, or, as I was really attached to them, I perhaps saw them in a dimmer light.

The most difficult chapter to write was that on "Vaudoux Worship and Cannibalism." I have endeavoured to paint it in the least sombre colours, and none who know the country will think that I have exaggerated; in fact, had I listened to the testimony of many experienced residents, I should have described rites at which dozens of human victims were sacrificed at a time. Everything I have related has been founded on evidence collected in Hayti, from Haytian official documents, from trustworthy officers of the Haytian Government, my foreign colleagues, and from respectable residents—principally, however, from Haytian sources.

It may be suggested that I am referring to the past. On the contrary, I am informed that at present cannibalism is more rampant than ever. A black Government dares not greatly interfere, as its power is founded on the good-will of the masses, ignorant and deeply tainted with fetish worship. A Haytian writer recently remarked in print, "On se plaisit beaucoup de ce que le Vaudoux a reparu grandiose et sérieux." The fetish dances were forbidden by decree under the Government of President Boisrond-Canal. That decree has been since repealed, and high officers now attend these meetings, and distribute money and applaud the most frantic excesses.

President Salomon, who is now in power, lived for eighteen years in Europe, married a white, and knows what civilisation is. He probably, on his first advent to the Presidency, possessed sufficient influence in the country to have checked the open manifestations of this barbarous worship; but the fate of those of his predecessors who attempted to grapple with the evil was not encouraging. It was hoped, however, that he would make the attempt, and that, grasping the nettle with resolution, he might suffer no evil results; but many doubted not only his courage to undertake the task, but even the will; and they, I fear, have judged correctly. Whenever all the documents which exist on this subject are published, my chapter on Cannibalism will be looked upon but as a pale reflection of the reality.

With regard to the history of the country, materials abound for writing a very full one, but I do not think it would prove interesting to the general reader. It is but a series of plots and revolutions, followed by barbarous military executions. A destructive and exhausting war with Santo Domingo, and civil strife during the Presidency of General Salnave, did more to ruin the resources of the country than any amount of bad government. The enforced abandonment of work by the people called to arms by the contending parties, introduced habits of idleness and rapine which have continued to the present day; and the material losses, by the destruction of the best estates and the burning of towns and villages, have never been fully repaired.

From the overthrow of President Geffrard in 1867 the country has been more rapidly going to ruin. The fall was slightly checked during the quiet Presidency of Nissage-Saget; but the Government of General Domingue amply made up for lost time, and was one of the worst, if not the worst, that Hayti has ever seen. With the sectaries of the Vaudoux in power, nothing else could have been expected.

I have brought my sketch of the history of Hayti down to the fall of President Boisrond-Canal in 1879, and shall not touch on the rule of the present President of Hayti, General Salomon. I may say, however, that he is the determined enemy of the coloured section of the community; is credited with having been the chief adviser of the Emperor Soulouque in all his most disastrous measures; and the country is said to have sunk into the lowest depths of misery. The civil war, which by last accounts was still raging in Hayti, has been marked by more savage excesses than any previously known in Haytian history, the black authorities, hesitating at no step to gain their object, which is utterly to destroy the educated coloured class. They care not for the others; as they say, "Mulatte pauvre, li negue."

A few words as to the origin of this book. In 1867 I was living in the country near Port-au-Prince, and having some leisure, I began to collect materials and write rough drafts of the principal chapters. I was interrupted by the civil war, and did not resume work until after I had left the country. It may be the modifying effect of time, but on looking over the chapters as I originally wrote them, I thought that I had been too severe in my judgments on whole classes, and have therefore somewhat softened the opinions I then expressed; and the greater experience which a further residence of seven years gave me enabled me to study the people more and avoid too sweeping condemnations.

I have not attempted to describe the present condition of the republic of Santo Domingo, but from all I can hear it is making progress. The Dominicans have few prejudices of colour, and eagerly welcome foreign capitalists who arrive to develop the resources of their country. Already there are numerous sugar estates in operation, as well as manufactories of dyes, and efforts are being successfully made to rework the old goldmines. The tobacco cultivation is already large, and only requires hands to develop it to meet any demand. I hear of a railway having been commenced, to traverse the magnificent plain which stretches from the Bay of Samana almost to the frontiers of Hayti.

After having written the chapter on Vaudoux Worship, my attention was called to a communication which appeared in *Vanity Fair* of August 13, 1881, by a reply published in a Haytian journal. It is evident that the writer in *Vanity Fair* was a naval officer or a passing traveller in the West Indies, and he probably carefully noted the information given him. He was, however, too inclined to believe what he heard, as he gravely states that a Haytian told him that the kidneys of a child were first-rate eating, adding that he had tried them himself; and the writer remarks that the Haytian did not seem to think it strange or out of the way that he had done so. No Haytian would have ever stated seriously that he had eaten human flesh. Probably, amused by the eagerness of the inquirer, he told the story to test his powers of belief, and must have been diverted when he found his statement was credited. Cannibalism is the one thing of which Haytians are thoroughly ashamed.

This communication makes mention of the herb-poisonings and their antidotes; of the midwives who render new born-babes insensible, that are buried, dug up, restored to life, and then eaten. In May 1879 a midwife and another were caught near Port-au-Prince eating a female baby that had been thus treated; he adds that a Haytian of good position was discovered with his family eating a child. In the former case the criminals were condemned to six weeks' imprisonment, in the latter to one month. (I may notice that I never heard of a respectable Haytian being connected with the cannibals.) The light punishments inflicted were due to the fear inspired by the Vaudoux priests. In January 1881 eight people were fined for disinterring and eating corpses. An English medical man purchased and identified the neck and shoulders of a human being in the market at Port-au-Prince. In February 1881, at St. Marc, a cask of so-called pork was sold to a foreign ship. In it were discovered fingers and finger-nails, and all the flesh proved to be that of human beings. An English coloured clergyman at Cap Haïtien said that the Vaudoux did away with all the effect of his ministry; and that his wife was nearly purchasing in the market human flesh instead of pork. Four people were fined in that town for eating corpses. When the writer arrived at Jacmel he found two men in prison for eating corpses, and on the day of his arrival a man was caught eating a child. Near the same town nine thousand people met at Christmas to celebrate Vaudoux rites. At Les Cayes a child of English parents was stolen, and on the thieves being pursued, they threw it into a well and killed it.

These are the statements made by the writer in *Vanity Fair*, and nearly all are probable. If correct, the open practice of Vaudoux worship and cannibalism must have made great strides since I left Hayti, and shows how little a black Government can do, or will do, to suppress them. The digging up and eating of corpses was not known during my residence there.

This communication to *Vanity Fair* provoked a reply in a journal published at Port-au-Prince called *L'Œil*, October 1, 1881. It denies everything, even to the serious existence and power of the Vaudoux priests, and spends all its energies in abuse. The article is quite worthy of the editor,[1] who was one of the most active supporters of President Salnave, whose connection with the Vaudoux was notorious. It is in this angry spirit that the Haytians generally treat any public reference to their peculiar institution.

Mexico, *January 1884.*

CHAPTER I
GENERAL DESCRIPTION OF HAYTI

Standing on one of the lofty mountains of Hayti, and looking towards the interior, I was struck with the pertinence of the saying of the Admiral, who, crumpling a sheet of paper in his hand, threw it on the table before George III., saying, "Sire, Hayti looks like that." The country appears a confused agglomeration of mountain, hill, and valley, most irregular in form; precipices, deep hollows, vales apparently without an outlet; water occasionally glistening far below; cottages scattered here and there, with groves of fruit-trees and bananas clustering round the rude dwellings. Gradually, however, the eye becomes accustomed to the scene; the mountains separate into distinct ranges, the hills are but the attendant buttresses, and the valleys assume their regular forms as the watersheds of the system, and the streams can be traced meandering gradually towards the ocean.

If you then turn towards the sea, you notice that the valleys have expanded into plains, and the rushing torrents have become broad though shallow rivers, and the mountains that bound the flat, open country push their buttresses almost into the sea. This grand variety of magnificent scenery can be well observed from a point near Kenskoff, about ten miles in the interior from the capital, as well as from the great citadel built on the summit of La Ferrière in the northern province. Before entering into particulars, however, let me give a general idea of the country.

The island of Santo Domingo is situated in the West Indies between 18° and 20° north latitude and 68° 20' and 74° 30' west longitude. Its greatest length is four hundred miles, its greatest breadth one hundred and thirty-five miles, and is calculated to be about the size of Ireland. Hayti occupies about a third of the island—the western portion—and, pushing two great promontories into the sea, it has a very large extent of coast-line. It is bounded on the north by the Atlantic Ocean, on the east by the republic of Santo Domingo, on the south by the Caribbean Sea, and on the west by the passage which separates it from Cuba and Jamaica.

Its most noted mountain-ranges are La Selle, which lies on the south-eastern frontier of Hayti; La Hotte, near Les Cayes; and the Black Mountains in the northern province; but throughout the whole extent of the republic the open valleys are bounded by lofty elevations. In fact, on approaching the island from any direction, it appears so mountainous that it is difficult to imagine that so many smiling, fertile plains are to be met with in every department. They are, however, numerous. The most extensive are the Cul-de-Sac, near Port-au-Prince, the plains of Gonaives, the Artibonite, Arcahaye, Port Margot, Leogâne, that of Les Cayes, and those that follow the northern coast.

Hayti has the advantage of being well watered, though this source of riches is greatly neglected. The principal river is the Artibonite, which is navigable for small craft for a short distance; the other streams have more the character of mountain torrents, full to overflowing during the rainy season, whilst during the dry they are but rivulets running over broad pebbly beds.

The lakes lying at the head of the plain of Cul-de-Sac are a marked feature in the landscape as viewed from the neighbouring hills. They are but little visited, as their shores are marshy, very unhealthy, and uninhabitable on that account, while the swarms of mosquitoes render even a temporary stay highly disagreeable. The waters of one of them are brackish, which would appear to indicate more salt deposits in the neighbourhood.

There are a few islands attached to Hayti, the principal, La Tortue, on the north, Gonaives on the west, and L'Isle-à-Vache on the south coast. Some attempts have been made to develop their natural riches, but as yet with but slight success. The first two named are famous for their mahogany trees.

The principal towns of the republic are Port-au-Prince, the capital, Cap Haïtien in the north, and Les Cayes in the south. Jacmel, Jérémie, Miragoâne, St. Marc, and Gonaives are also commercial ports.

Port-au-Prince is situated at the bottom of a deep bay, which runs so far into the western coast as almost to divide Hayti in two. It contains about 20,000 inhabitants, and was carefully laid out by the French. It possesses every natural advantage that a capital could require. Little use, however, is made of these advantages, and the place is one of the most unpleasant residences imaginable. I was one day talking to a French naval officer, and he observed, "I was here as a midshipman forty years ago." "Do you notice any change?" I asked. "Well, it is perhaps dirtier than before." Its dirt is its great drawback, and appears ever to have been so, as Moreau de St. Méry complained of the same thing during the last century. However, there are degrees of dirt, and he would probably be astonished to see it at the present day. The above paragraph was first written in 1867; since that it has become worse, and when I last landed (1877), I found the streets heaped up with filth.

The capital is well laid out, with lines of streets running parallel to the sea, whilst others cross at right angles, dividing the town into numerous islets or blocks. The streets are broad, but utterly neglected. Every one throws out his refuse before his door, so that heaps of manure, broken bottles, crockery, and every species of rubbish encumber the way, and render both riding and walking dangerous. Building materials are permitted occasionally to accumulate to so great an extent as completely to block up the streets and seriously impede the traffic. Mackenzie, in his notes on Hayti, remarks on the impassable state of the streets in 1826; torn up by tropical rains, they were mended with refuse (generally stable dung to fill up the holes, and a thin layer of earth thrown over), only to be again destroyed by the first storm. Ask Haytians why they do not mend their streets and roads, they answer, "Bon Dieu, gâté li; bon Dieu, paré li" (God spoilt them, and God will mend them). Then, as now, the roads were in such a state in wet weather that only a waggon with a team of oxen could get through the muddy slough.

On first entering the town, you are struck with the utter shabbiness of the buildings, mean cottages and grovelling huts by the side of the few decent-looking dwellings. Most of the houses are constructed of wood, badly built with very perishable materials, imported from the United States or our Northern colonies. The idea that originally prevailed in the construction of the private houses was admirable; before each was a broad verandah, open to all passers, so that from one end of the town to the other it was intended that there should be cool, shady walks. But the intolerable stupidity of the inhabitants has spoilt this plan; in most streets the level of the verandahs of each house is of a different height, and frequently separated by a marshy spot, the receptacle of every species of filth; so that you must either walk in the sun or perform in the shade a series of gymnastic exercises exceedingly inconvenient in a tropical climate.

On either side of the street was a paved gutter, but now, instead of aiding the drainage, it is another cause of the accumulation of filth. The stones which formerly rendered the watercourses even are either removed or displaced, and the rains collecting before the houses form fetid pools, into which the servants pour all that in other countries is carried off by the sewers. In a few of the more commercial streets, where foreigners reside, more attention is paid to cleanliness, but still Port-au-Prince may bear the palm away of being the most foul-smelling, dirty, and consequently fever-stricken city in the world.

The port is well protected, but is gradually filling up, as the rains wash into it not only the silt from the mountains, but the refuse of the city, and no effort is made to keep it open. As there is but little tide, the accumulations of every species of vegetable and animal matter render the water fetid, and when the sea-breeze blows gently over these turbid waves, an effluvia is borne into the town sickening to all but native nostrils.

The most remarkable edifice of Port-au-Prince was the palace, a long, low, wooden building of one storey, supported on brick walls: it contained several fine rooms, and two halls which might have been rendered admirable for receptions; but everything around it was shabby—the stables, the guard-houses, the untended garden, the courtyard overrun with grass and weeds, and the surrounding walls partially in ruins. This spacious presidential residence was burnt down during the revolutionary attack on Port-au-Prince in December 1869, and no attempt has been made to rebuild it.

The church is a large wooden building, an overgrown shed, disfigured by numerous wretched paintings which cover its walls; and, as an unworthy concession to local prejudice, our Saviour is occasionally represented by an ill-drawn negro.

The senate-house was the building with the most architectural pretensions, but its outer walls only remained when I last saw it, fire having destroyed the roof and the interior wood-work. There is no other edifice worthy of remark; and the private houses, with perhaps a score of exceptions, are of the commonest order.

The market-places are large and well situated, but ill-tended and dirty, and in the wet season muddy in the extreme. They are fairly supplied with provisions. I may notice that in those of Port-au-Prince very superior meat is often met with, and good supplies of vegetables, including excellent European kinds, brought from the mountain gardens near Fort Jaques.

The supply of water is very defective. During the reign of the Emperor Soulouque a luminous idea occurred to some one, that instead of repairing the old French aqueduct, iron pipes should be laid down. The Emperor had the sagacity to see the advantage of the plan, and gave orders for the work to be done. As an exception to the general rule, the idea was to a certain extent well carried out, and remains the only durable monument of a most inglorious reign. Had the iron pipes been entirely substituted for the old French work, the inhabitants would have enjoyed the benefit of pure water; but when I left in 1877, the people in the suburbs were still breaking open the old stone-work to obtain a source of supply near their dwellings; and pigs, children, and washerwomen congregated round these spots and defiled the stream.

The amount of water introduced into the town is still most inadequate; and though numerous springs, and one delightful stream, La Rivière Froide, are within easy distance of the port, no effort has been made to increase the supply. La Rivière Froide—name redolent of pleasant reminiscences in a tropical climate—could easily fill a canal, which would not only afford an inexhaustible supply for the wants of the town and shipping, but, by creating an outward current, would carry off the floating matter which pollutes the port. Since my departure a Mr. Stephens commenced some works to afford the town a constant supply of water, but these, I understand, have as yet only been partially carried out. If ever finished, they will afford to the inhabitants a great boon.

The cemetery is situated outside the town. I never entered it except when compelled to attend a funeral, and hastened to leave it as soon as possible, on account of an unpleasant odour which pervades it. It is not kept in good order, though many families carefully attend to the graves of their relatives, and there are several striking tombs. People of all religions are buried here; but it is on record that a brawling Irish priest once attempted to disinter a Protestant child. His brawling subsequently led to his banishment.

I noticed on my first arrival in Port-au-Prince two marble coffins, very handsome, lying neglected on the ground outside the palace. I was told they had been brought from abroad in order that the remains of Pétion and Boyer, two of their best Presidents, should repose in them; but for many years I saw them lying empty on the same spot, and I never heard what became of them.

The curse of Port-au-Prince is fire. Every few years immense conflagrations consume whole quarters of the town. Nothing can stop the flames but one of the few brick-houses, against which the quick-burning fire is powerless. During my residence in Port-au-Prince five awful fires devastated the town. On each occasion from two to five hundred houses were destroyed. And yet the inhabitants go on building wretched wooden match-boxes, and even elaborate houses of the most inflammable materials. Companies should be careful how they insure property in Port-au-Prince, as there are some very well-authenticated stories of frauds practised on them both by Europeans and natives.

Port-au-Prince, on my first arrival in 1863, was governed by a municipality, over which presided a very honest man, a Monsieur Rivière, one of those Protestants to whom I have referred in my chapter on religion. As a new arrival, I thought the town sufficiently neglected, but I had reason to change my opinion. It was a pattern of cleanliness to what it subsequently became. The municipality, when one exists, has for its principal duties the performance or neglect of the registration of all acts relating to the "état civil," and to divide among its members and friends, for work never carried out, whatever funds they can collect from the city.

At the back of the capital, at a distance of about five miles, was the village of La Coupe, the summer residence of the wealthier families. As it was situated about 1200 feet above the level of the sea and was open to every breeze, it afforded a delightful change from the hot, damp town; but during the civil war of 1868 the best houses were destroyed and never reconstructed. There is a natural bath there, the most picturesque feature of the place; it is situated under lofty trees, that cast a deep shade over the spot, and during the hottest day it is charmingly cool.

Cap Haïtien is the most picturesque town in Hayti; it is beautifully situated on a most commodious harbour. As you enter it, passing Fort Picolet, you are struck by its safe position—a narrow entrance so easily defended. My first visit was in H.M.S. "Galatea," Captain Macguire; and as we expected that we might very possibly be received by the fire of all the batteries, our own crew were at their guns, keeping them steadily trained on Fort Picolet, whose artillery was distant about a couple of hundred yards. Having slowly steamed past forts and sunken batteries, we found ourselves in front of the town, with its ruins overgrown with creepers, and in the background the rich vegetation sweeping gracefully up to the summit of the beautiful hill which overshadows Cap Haïtien.

Cap Haïtien never recovered from the effects of the fearful earthquake of 1842, when several thousands of its inhabitants perished. To this day they talk of that awful event, and never forget to relate how the country-people rushed in to plunder the place, and how none lent a helping-hand to aid their half-buried countrymen. Captain Macguire and myself used to wander about the ruins, and we could not but feel how little energy remained in a people who could leave their property in such a state. It was perhaps cheaper to build a trumpery house elsewhere.

One of those who suffered the most during that visitation wrote before the earth had ceased trembling, "Against the acts of God Almighty no one complains," and then proceeded to relate how the dread earthquake shook down or seriously injured almost every house; how two-thirds of the inhabitants were buried beneath the fallen masonry; how the bands of blacks rushed in from mountain and plain, not to aid in saving their wretched countrymen, whose cries and groans could be heard for two or three days, but to plunder the stores replete with goods; and—what he did complain of—how the officers and men of the garrison, instead of attempting to keep order, joined in plundering the small remnants of what the rest of the inhabitants could save from the tottering ruins. What a people!

The most striking objects near Cap Haïtien are the remains of the palace of Sans Souci, and of the citadel constructed by King Christophe, called La

Ferrière. It requires a visit to induce one to believe that so elaborate, and, I may add, so handsome a structure, could exist in such a place as Hayti, or that a fortification such as the citadel could ever have been constructed on the summit of a lofty mountain, five thousand feet, I believe, above the level of the sea. Some of the walls are eighty feet in height, and sixteen feet in thickness, where the heavy batteries of English guns still remain in position. All is of the most solid masonry, and covering the whole peak of the mountain.

We were really lost in amazement as we threaded gallery after gallery where heavy fifty-six and thirty-two pounders guarded every approach to what was intended to be the last asylum of Haytian independence. Years of the labour of toiling thousands were spent to prepare this citadel, which the trembling earth laid in ruins in a few minutes. What energy did this black king possess to rear so great a monument? but the reverse of the medal states that every stone in that wonderful building cost a human life.

It is a popular idea in Hayti that the superiority of the northern department, and the greater industry of its inhabitants, date from the time of Christophe, and some express a belief that his iron system was suitable to the country; but the fact is that Moreau de St. Méry, writing in the last century, insists on the superior advantages of the northern province, its greater fertility, the abundance of rain, and consequently the number of rivers, as well as the superior intelligence and industry of the inhabitants, and their greater sociability and polish. They are certainly more sociable than in the capital, and people still seek northern men to work on their estates. As for Christophe's system, no amount of increase in produce could compensate for its brutality.

Gonaives is a poor-looking town, constantly devastated by revolutions and fires, with a few broad, unfinished streets, and some good houses among the crowds of poor-looking buildings. This neighbourhood is famous for what are called white truffles. They are dried and sent to the different parts of the republic.

St. Marc, though not so scattered as Gonaives, is a small place. It was formerly built of stone; a few specimens of this kind of building still remain. Jacmel has a very unsafe harbour, but possesses importance as one of the ports at which the royal mail steamers call, and has a large export trade in coffee. Les Cayes, Jérémie, and other smaller ports I have only seen at a distance, but I hear they are much like the other cities and towns of the republic. Mackenzie says that the city and environs of Les Cayes are described as "très riante," and that in his time it was kept in better order than the capital. This is said still to be the case.

My last long ride in Hayti was from Cap Haïtien to Gonaives, and nestling in the hills I found some very pretty villages, planted in lovely sites, with fresh, babbling streams, and fruit groves hiding the inferior-looking houses. The place I most admired was, I think, called Plaisance. There was a freshness, a brightness, a repose about the village that made me regret it was situated so far from the capital.

Wherever you may ride in the mountains, you cannot fail to remark that there is scarcely a decent-looking house out of the towns. The whole of the country is abandoned to the small cultivators, whose inferior cottages are met with at every turn, and, as might be expected from such a population, very dirty and devoid of every comfort, rarely any furniture beyond an old chair, a rickety table, a few sleeping-mats, and some cooking utensils. There is no rule, however, without an exception, and I remember being much struck by seeing at Kenskoff, a small hamlet about ten or twelve miles direct from Port-au-Prince, a good house, where there were some chairs, tables, and bedsteads, and around this dwelling several huts, in which the wives of our host lived separately.

Now and then a peasant will build a larger house than usual; we met with one, the last we slept in on our ride to the mountain, La Selle, whose proprietor had really some ideas of comfort, and before whose dwelling coffee-plants were growing, trimmed to the height of six feet, planted separate from one another, perfectly clean, and covered with indications of an abundant crop. They had been planted there in former days by an intelligent proprietor, and the peasant had the merit of not neglecting them.

The plain of Cul-de-Sac, adjoining the north side of Port-au-Prince, was one of the richest and most cultivated during the time of the French; and as all regular cultivation depends on the amount of water, their engineers had constructed the most careful system for the storage and distribution of the supplies. Properly managed, all the large estates could receive the quantity necessary for their lands, but for many years the stone-work was neglected, and the grand barrage was becoming useless, when President Geffrard placed the affair in the hands of an able French engineer, Mons. Ricard, who efficiently restored the main work, but had not funds to complete the canals for distributing the waters. As usual in all enterprises in that country, the money voted had to pass through so many hands, that before it reached the engineer it had diminished to less than half.

The soil of the plain is most fertile, and only appears to require water to give the most promising crops of sugar-cane. There are some very extensive estates that could afford work for a large population, but the ever-increasing disturbances in the country render Capital shy of venturing there.

As might readily be supposed, the roads are greatly neglected, and during the rainy season are almost impassable. They are composed simply of the surrounding soil, with a few branches thrown into the most dangerous holes. The bridges are generally avoided; it is a saying in Hayti, that you should go round a bridge, but never cross it, and the advice is generally to be followed. For the main streams there are fords. An attempt was once made to bridge over La Grande Rivière du Cul de Sac, but the first freshet washed away all the preliminary work.

In the mountains there are only bridle-paths, though occasionally I came across the remains of old French roads and good paths. On the way to Kenskoff there is a place called L'Escalier, to escalade the steepest side of the mountain. The horses that are used to it manage well, but those from the plains find the steps awkward. On the road from Gonaives to the northern province there is a very remarkable paved way, the work so well done that it has resisted the rain during a hundred years of neglect. Some of the bridle-paths in the north are exceedingly good, and are admirably carried up the sides of hills, so as to avoid the most difficult spots.

In the range above Tourjeau I came across a very pretty grassy bridle-path, and near I found the remains of a large French country-house, evidently the residence of some great proprietor. The tradition in the neighbourhood is that there was an indigo factory adjoining, but I could scarcely imagine the site suitable. Wherever you may go in Hayti you come across signs of decadence, not only from the exceptional prosperity of the French period, but even of comparatively recent years. After the plundering and destruction of 1868 and 1869, few care to keep up or restore their devastated houses, and it is now a hand-to-mouth system.

Cul-de-Sac is a glorious plain, and in good hands would be a fountain of riches; and the same may be said of the other splendid plains that abound throughout the island. Every tropical production grows freely, so that there would be no limit to production should the country ever abandon revolutions to turn its attention to industry. About three-fourths of the surface of the plains are occupied by wood or prickly acacia, that invades every uncultivated spot.

The mountains that bound these plains and extend to the far interior present magnificent sites for pleasant residences; but no civilised being could occupy them on account of the difficulty of communication and the doubtful character of the population. Up to the time of the fall of President Geffrard it was possible; now it would be highly imprudent. In one of the most smiling valleys that I have ever seen, lying to the left whilst riding to the east of Kenskoff, a friend of mine possessed a very extensive property.

The place looked so beautiful that I proposed to him a lengthened visit, to which he acceded. Delay after delay occurred, and then the civil war of 1865 prevented our leaving Port-au-Prince. In 1869 there were arrested in that valley a dozen of the worst cannibals of the Vaudoux sect, and the police declared that the whole population of that lovely garden of the country was given up to fetish worship. It was probably a knowledge of this that made my friend so long defer our proposed visit, as the residence of a white man among them might have been looked upon with an evil eye.

I have travelled in almost every quarter of the globe, and I may say that, taken as a whole, there is not a finer island than that of Santo Domingo. No country possesses greater capabilities, or a better geographical position, or more variety of soil, of climate, or of production; with magnificent scenery of every description, and hill-sides where the pleasantest of health-resorts might be established. And yet it is now the country to be most avoided, ruined as it has been by a succession of self-seeking politicians, without honesty or patriotism, content to let the people sink to the condition of an African tribe, that their own selfish passions may be gratified.

The climate of Hayti is of the ordinary tropical character, and the temperature naturally varies according to the position of the towns. Cap Haïtien, being exposed to the cooling influence of the breezes from the north, is much more agreeable as a residence than Port-au-Prince, which is situated at the bottom of a deep bay.

In summer, that is, during the months of June, July, August, and September, the heat is very oppressive. The registered degrees give one an idea of the disagreeableness of the climate. In my house at Tourjeau, near Port-au-Prince, 600 feet above the level of the sea, I have noted a registering thermometer marking 97° in the drawing-room at 2 p.m. in July, and 95° in the dining-room on the ground-floor; and in a room off a court in the town I have heard of 103°—no doubt from refraction.[2] At the Petit Séminaire the priests keep a register, and I notice that rarely is the heat marked as 95°, generally 93.2° is the maximum; but the thermometer must be kept in the coolest part of the college, and is no criterion of what is felt in ordinary rooms. The nights also are oppressively warm, and for days I have noticed the thermometer seldom marking less than 80° during the night. In August the heat is even greater than in July, rising to 97° at the Petit Séminaire, whilst in September the maximum is registered as 91.5°; and this heat continues well on into November, the maximum being the same. I have not the complete returns, but generally the heats of September are nearly equal to those of August. In what may be called winter, the thermometer rarely marks over 84°, and the nights are cool and pleasant. In fact, I have been assured of the thermometer having fallen as low as 58° during the night, but

I never saw it myself below 60°. It is a curious fact that foreigners generally suffer from the heat, and get ill in consequence, whilst the natives complain of the bitter cold of the winter, and have their season of illness then.

Port-au-Prince is essentially unhealthy, and yellow fever too often decimates the crews of the ships of war that visit its harbour. In 1869, on account of the civil convulsion, French and English ships remained months in harbour. The former suffered dreadfully; the "Limier," out of a crew of 106 men and eight officers, lost fifty-four men and four officers, whilst the "D'Estrés" and another had to mourn their captains and many of their crew. Who that ever knew him can forget and not cherish the memory of Captain De Varannes of the "D'Estrés," one of the most sympathetic of men, a brilliant officer, and a steady upholder of the French and English alliance? De Varannes was an Imperialist, an aide-de-camp of the Empress, and thoroughly devoted to the family that had made his fortune. When the medical men announced to him that he had not above two hours to live, he asked the French agent if he had any portraits of the Imperial family; they were brought and placed at the foot of the bed where he could see them. He asked then to be left alone, and an hour after, when a friend crept in, he found poor De Varannes dead, with his eyes open, and apparently fixed on the portraits before him. I should add that both these vessels brought the fever to Port-au-Prince from Havana and Martinique.

The English ships suffered less, as our officers are not bound by the rigid rules that regulate the French commanders, who would not leave the harbour without express orders from their Admiral, though their men were dying by dozens. Captain Hunter of the "Vestal" and Captain Salmon of the "Defence" knew their duty to their crews too well to keep them in the pestilential harbour, and as soon as yellow fever appeared on board, steamed away; and the latter went five hundred miles due north till he fell in with cool weather, and thus only lost three men. A French officer told me that when the sailors on board the "Limier" saw the "Defence" steam out of harbour, they were depressed even to tears, and said, "See how the English officers are mindful of the health of their men, whilst ours let us die like flies." Captain Hunter of the "Vestal" never had due credit given him for his devotion to his crew whilst suffering from yellow fever. He made a hospital of his cabin, and knew no rest till he had reached the cool harbours of the north.

Merchant seamen in certain years have suffered dreadfully from this scourge, both in Port-au-Prince and in the neighbouring port of Miragoâne. Two-thirds of the crews have often died, and every now and then there is a season in which few ships escape without loss.

Yellow fever rarely appears on shore, as the natives do not take it, and the foreign population is small and mostly acclimatised. The other diseases from which people suffer are ordinary tropical fevers, agues, small-pox, and the other ills to which humanity is subject; but although Port-au-Prince is the filthiest town I have ever seen, it has not yet been visited by cholera. In the spring of 1882 small-pox broke out in so virulent a form that the deaths rose to a hundred a day. This dreadful visitation continued several months, and it is calculated carried off above 5000 people in the city and its neighbourhood.

If Hayti ever becomes civilised, and if ever roads are made, there are near Port-au-Prince summer health-resorts which are perfectly European in their climate. Even La Coupe, or, as it is officially called, Pétionville, about five miles from the capital, at an altitude of 1200 feet, is from ten to twelve degrees cooler during the day, and the nights are delicious; and if you advance to Kenskoff or Furcy, you have the thermometer marking during the greatest heat of the day 75° to 77°, whilst the mornings and evenings are delightfully fresh, with the thermometer at from 57° to 68°, and the nights cold. On several occasions I passed some months at Pétionville, and found the climate most refreshing after the burning heats of the sea-coast.

The regular rainy season commences about Port-au-Prince during the month of April, and continues to the month of September, with rain again in November under the name of "les pluies de la Toussaint." After several months of dry weather one breathes again as the easterly wind brings the welcome rain, which comes with a rush and a force that bends the tallest palm-tree till its branches almost sweep the ground. Sometimes, whilst dried up in the town, we could see for weeks the rain-clouds gathering on the Morne de l'Hôpital within a few miles, and yet not a drop would come to refresh our parched-up gardens.

During the great heats the rain is not only welcome as cooling the atmosphere, but as it comes in torrents, it rushes down the streets and sweeps clean all those that lead to the harbour, and carries before it the accumulated filth of the dry season. In very heavy rains the cross streets are flooded; and one year the water came down so heavily and suddenly that the brooks became rushing rivers. The flood surprised a priest whilst bathing, swept him down to the Champs de Mars, and threw his mangled body by the side of a house I was at that moment visiting.

That evening, as I was already wet, I rode home during the tempest, and never did I see more vivid lightning, hear louder thunder, or feel heavier rain. As we headed the hill, the water rushing down the path appeared almost knee-deep; and to add to the terror of my animal, a white horse, maddened by fear, came rushing down the hill with flowing mane and tail, and swept past us. Seen only during a flash of lightning, it was a most picturesque sight, and I had much difficulty in preventing my frightened horse joining in his wild career.

The rainy season varies in different parts of the island, particularly in the north. I am surprised to observe that the priests have found the annual fall of rain to be only 117 inches. I had thought it more. Perhaps, however, that was during an exceptionally dry year.

The great plain of Cul-de-Sac is considered healthy, although occasionally intensely warm. It is, however, freely exposed not only to the refreshing sea-breezes, but to the cooling land-winds that come down from the mountains that surround it. There is but little marsh, except near La Rivière Blanche, which runs near the mountains to the north and is lost in the sands.

On the sugar-cane plantations, where much irrigation takes place, the negro workmen suffer somewhat from fever and ague, but probably more from the copious libations of new rum, which they assert are rendered necessary by the thirsty nature of the climate.

I had often read of a clap of thunder in a clear sky, but never heard anything like the one that shook our house near Port-au-Prince. We were sitting, a large party, in our broad verandah, about eight in the evening, with a beautiful starlight night,—the stars, in fact, shining so brightly that you could almost read by their light,—when a clap of thunder, which appeared to burst just over our roof, took our breath away. It was awful in its suddenness and in its strength. No one spoke for a minute or two, when, by a common impulse, we left the house and looked up into a perfectly clear sky. At a distance, however, on the summits of the mountains, was a gathering of black clouds, which warned my friends to mount their horses, and they could scarcely have reached the town when one of the heaviest storms I have known commenced, with thunder worthy of the clap that had startled us. Though all of us were seasoned to the tropics, we had never been so impressed before.

In the wet season the rain, as a rule, comes on at regular hours and lasts a given time, though occasionally it will continue through a night and longer, though rarely does it last above twenty-four hours without a gleam of sunshine intervening.

CHAPTER II
HISTORY BEFORE INDEPENDENCE

I do not doubt but the discovery of America by Columbus was good in its results to mankind; but when we read the history of early Spanish colonisation, the predominant feeling is disgust at the barbarities and fanaticism recorded in almost every page. We generally overlook much of this, being dazzled by pictures of heroic deeds, as set forth in the works of Prescott and Robertson—heroic deeds of steel-clad warriors massacring crowds of gentle, almost unresisting natives, until despair, lending energy to their timid natures, forced them occasionally to turn on their savage persecutors.

In no country were the Spaniards more notorious for their cruelty than in the first land in America on which Columbus established a settlement. The population was then variously estimated, the numbers given varying between 800,000 and 2,000,000, the former calculation being the more probable. They were indeed a primitive people, the men moving about entirely naked, the women wearing a short petticoat. They are said to have been good-looking, which, if true, would mark them as a people distinct from any other in America, as the Indians, who still remain by millions in South America and Mexico, are as a race the most ill-favoured natives I have seen in any portion of the globe. That was my impression when I travelled among them, though I have seen among the young women who followed the Indian regiments to Lima a few who might almost be considered handsome, but these by their appearance were probably of mixed breed.

Columbus only stayed two months in Santo Domingo, but left behind him forty of his companions in an entrenched position. They now began to commit excesses; and hearing that a cacique in the interior had a large store of gold, they penetrated to his town and robbed him of his riches. This roused the population against them; they were pursued and killed in detail.

In the meantime Columbus had revisited Spain, been received with honour, and seventeen vessels, laden with every kind of store and domestic animal, as well as a large force, were placed at his disposal. On his arrival his first thoughts were for gold, and he marched in search of the mines, which, being pointed out to him, were soon in full work, the Indians by force being compelled to this task. The conduct of these white men appears to have been so wantonly cruel, that the population rose *en masse*, and a hundred thousand Indians are said to have marched to attack the Spaniards, two hundred and twenty of whom put this crowd to flight without the loss of a single man. These are the heroic deeds we are called upon to admire. It has often been declared impossible that such, on one side, bloodless encounters could take place; but I am well assured that two hundred well-armed Englishmen could in the present day march through any number of the Land Dyaks of Borneo, and defeat them without loss.

It is not necessary to trace in detail the history of the island; but I may notice that in 1507 the population was estimated at 60,000, which shows that the original reckoning must have been greatly exaggerated, as not even these early apostles of the religion of charity could have thus wiped out the population by millions. The story of what one called the early exploits of the Spaniards in Santo Domingo has been so often related that it is useless to tell it over again, especially as it would present but a sequence of sickening events, of murders, executions, robbery, and lust, with but few traits of generosity and virtue to record.

These foreign settlers soon saw that the island would be useless to them without population, so they early began to introduce negroes from Africa, as well as families from the neighbouring isles. The Coral Indians were not spared, and the Spanish historians themselves are the chroniclers of this record of infamy. Now not a descendant of an Indian remains.

Santo Domingo, deprived of population, with its mineral wealth, for want of hands, no longer available, and agriculture neglected, rapidly degenerated, and little was left but the city of Santo Domingo and in the interior a population of herdsmen. Then the famous buccaneers appeared to inflict on the Spaniards some of the misery they had worked on the Indians. Notwithstanding every effort to prevent them, the French adventurers gradually spread through the western end of the island, and began to form towns and settlements.

In 1640 Levasseur was sent from France as Governor of these irregularly-acquired possessions, and from that time the French may be said to have established themselves firmly in the western part of Santo Domingo—which hereafter I may call by its present name, Hayti, to simplify the narrative—but their rule was not recognised by Spain until the year 1697.

From this date to the breaking out of the French Revolution the colony increased in prosperity, until it became, for its extent, probably the richest in the world. Negroes were imported by thousands from the coast of Africa, and were subjected to as harsh a slavery as ever disgraced the worst system of servitude.

Two events occurred during this period of prosperity which were worthy of being noted: First, the fearful earthquake which destroyed Port-au-Prince in 1770, when for fifteen days the earth trembled under repeated shocks, and left the city a heap of ruins.[3] The second was the war in which France engaged to aid our colonists to acquire their independence. To increase their forces the French commanders permitted the free blacks and mulattoes to enlist, and they did good service; and when they returned to their country, they spread widely a spirit of disaffection, which no ordinances could destroy.

When England in 1785 was forced to acknowledge the independence of the United States, how despotic France and Spain rejoiced over the downfall of the only country where liberty was known! The results were, for France, the Revolution, which, with all its crimes, did unspeakable good, and deprived her of the finest colony that any country ever possessed. To Spain it brought the loss of world-wide possessions, and a fall in power and prestige which to this day she shows but few signs of recovering.

On the eve of the great Revolution, France possessed, as I have said, the finest colony in the world. Her historians are never weary of enumerating the amount of its products, the great trade, the warehouses full of sugar, cotton, coffee, indigo, and cocoa; its plains covered with splendid estates, its hill-sides dotted with noble houses; a white population, rich, refined, enjoying life as only a luxurious colonial society can enjoy it; the only dark spot, then scarcely noticed, the ignorant, discontented mass of black slavery, and the more enlightened disaffection of the free mulattoes and negroes.

It has often been a subject of inquiry how it was that the Spaniards, who were the cruellest of the cruel towards the Indians, should have established negro slavery in a form which robbed it of half its terrors, whilst the French, usually less severe than their southern neighbours, should have founded a system of servitude unsurpassed for severity, cruelty, nay, ferocity.

To this day the barbarous conduct of the Marquis of Caradeux is cited as a justification for the savage retaliation of the insurgent negroes. I think that the explanation of the different conduct of the Spanish and French slave-owner may be, that the former is indolent and satisfied with less, whilst the latter, in his fierce struggle to be rich, cared not how he became so, and worked his negroes beyond human endurance, and then, to keep down the inevitable discontent, sought to terrorise his slaves by barbarous punishments.

The true history of Hayti commences with the French Revolution, when, amid the flood of impracticable and practicable schemes, a few statesmen turned their generous thoughts towards the down-trodden African, and firing assembled France with their enthusiasm, passed laws and issued decrees granting freedom to the black; but before these had any practical effect, Hayti had to pass through scenes which have left blood-stains that nothing can wash away.

When reading the different accounts which have been written of the state of Hayti when France was upsetting the accumulated wrongs of ages, I have often desired to disbelieve them, and place to exaggerated feelings of sympathy the descriptions of the prejudices of the planters and the atrocities committed under their influence. But I have lived long in the West Indies, and know that there are many whites born in our colonies, who not only look upon the negro as of an inferior species—which he may be—but as fit only for servitude, and quite unworthy of freedom, and on an alliance with a coloured person as a disgrace which affects a whole family. They speak of a mulatto as they would of one affected with leprosy. If in these days such sentiments exist, we can readily believe that they existed even in a greater degree before, awakened to a feeling of justice, most European nations formally abolished slavery, and let the black and the coloured man have an equal chance in the struggle of life.

For some years before the meeting of the States-General, philanthropists who had inquired into the condition of the slave had had their compassion aroused, and to give direction to their efforts to ameliorate it, had founded in Paris a society called "The Friends of the Blacks."

The summoning of the States-General in France created much enthusiasm throughout Hayti; the planters now reckoned that justice would be done, and that a share would be accorded them in the government of the colony; the lower class of whites had a vague idea that their position must be improved, and hailed the movement as the promise of better times—though in truth these two classes had little of which to complain; the former were rolling in wealth, and the latter were never in want of high-paid employment. Another class felt even greater interest—that of the free black and coloured men; they thought that no change could occur which would not better their condition, which was one of simple toleration; they might work and get rich, have their children educated in France, but they had no political rights, and the meanest white considered himself, and was treated, as their superior. The slaves, although discontented, were only formidable from their numbers.

Exaggerated expectations were naturally followed by disappointment. The planters, finding that the French Government had no intention of employing them to administer the colony, began to think of independence; whilst the lower whites, passionately attached to the dream of equality, thought that that should commence by an apportionment among them of the estates of the rich. A third party consisted of the Government employés, whose chiefs were Royalists under the leadership of Penier, the Governor-General, and Mauduit, colonel of the regiment of Port-au-Prince.

The Colonial party, or rather that of the planters, in order to increase their power, which had hitherto been disseminated in local assemblies, determined to have the law carried out which authorised a General Assembly. This was elected, and held its first meetings in St. Marc in March 1790. The leaders soon commenced to quarrel with the Government authorities, and dissensions rose to such a height that both parties began to arm; and on the Assembly decreeing the substitution of another Governor for Penier, he was roused to resistance, and in a brief struggle he forced the General Assembly to dissolve, a portion of the members seeking refuge on board of a ship of war, whose crew they had induced to mutiny and sail with them to France.

The white population thus set the example of internal strife, and in their struggle for mastery called in the aid of the freedmen, and then after victory insulted them. These, however, began gradually to understand the advantages they possessed in being able to support the climate, and the persecutions and cruelties of the French made them feel that those who would be free themselves must strike the blow.

Among the educated and intelligent mulattoes who had gone to France to urge on the National Assembly the rights of their colour was Ogé. He naturally thought that the time had arrived for justice to be done, when the President of the "Constituant" had declared that "aucune partie de la nation ne réclamera vainement ses droits auprès de l'assemblée des représentants du peuple français." He visited the Club Massiac, where the planters held supreme sway, and endeavoured to enlist their sympathy, but he was coldly received. He then determined to return to Hayti to support the rights of his caste, which, though ambiguously, had been recognised by the legislature; but unexpected obstacles were thrown in his way by the Colonial party, and an order to arrest him was issued should he venture to embark for his native land. By passing through England and the United States he eluded these precautions, and landed privately at Cap Haïtien. When the news of his arrival on his property at Dondon reached the authorities, they endeavoured to capture him; then he, with a few hundreds of his colour, rose in arms, but after a few skirmishes they dispersed, and Ogé was forced to seek refuge in the Spanish settlement of Santo Domingo. There he was arrested, and, on the demand of the Governor of the French colony, handed over to his enemies. He was tried as a rebel and broken on the wheel, together with three companions; others were hung, the rest sent to the galleys.

Ogé's armed resistance had encouraged the men of colour in the south to demand their rights; but they were easily dispersed, and their chief, Rigaud, taken prisoner. These isolated and irresolute outbreaks rendered the division between the coloured and the white population more marked than ever; the latter despised the former for their wretched resistance, while the coloured men were indignant at the cruel and unsparing executions which marked the close of Ogé's career.

Monsieur Blanchelande was then Governor, a weak man at the head of the Royalist party, who had not the courage to follow the energetic counsels of Colonel Mauduit. By his vacillation all discipline was lost both in the army and in the fleet, and the revolutionary party rose in arms in Port-au-Prince, murdered Colonel Mauduit, and drove the pusillanimous Governor to seek refuge in the plain of Cul-de-Sac. Thus the whites were everywhere divided, but were still strong enough to disperse any assembly of the freedmen.

The news of the troubles in Hayti produced a great effect in Paris, and the Constituent Assembly determined to send three commissioners to restore tranquillity; but they prefaced this measure by decreeing (May 15, 1791) that every man of colour born of free parents should enjoy equal political rights with the whites. On the planters declaring that this would bring about civil war and the loss of the colony, the famous phrase was uttered, "Perish the colonies rather than a principle," which phrase has not been forgotten by those amongst us who would sacrifice India to the perverse idea of abandoning our high political status in the world.

When the substance of this decree reached Hayti, it roused to fury the passions of the whites; all sections united in declaring that they would oppose its execution even by force of arms, and a strong party was formed either to declare the independence of the colony, or, if that were not possible, to invite England to take possession. The coloured men, on the other hand, determined to assert their rights, and held secret meetings to bring about an accord among all the members of their party; and when they heard that Governor Blanchelande had declared he would not execute the decree, they summoned their followers to meet at Mirebalais in the western department.

The whites in the meantime determined that the second Colonial Assembly should be elected before the official text of the dreaded decree of the 15th May should arrive; and so rapidly did they act, that on the 1st August 1791 the Assembly met at Leogâne, and was opened under the presidency of the Marquis de Cadusch, a Royalist. They called Governor Blanchelande to the bar of the House, and made him swear that he would not carry into effect the law giving equal rights to the freedmen. As Cap Haïtien had become in reality the capital of the colony, both the Governor and the Assembly soon removed there.

The Royalist party, headed by the Governor, found their influence gradually declining, and, to strengthen their hands against both the Colonial Assembly with its traitorous projects and the violence of the lower part of the white population, are accused of having first thought of enlisting the blacks to further their schemes and to strengthen their party. It is said that they proposed to Toussaint, a slave on the Breda estates, to raise the negroes in revolt in the name of the King. This account I believe to be a pure invention of the coloured historians, and the conduct of the blacks clearly proved that they were not moved by French officers. Whoever was the instigator, it is certain that the negroes in the northern province rose in insurrection, put to death every white that fell into their hands, began to burn the factories, and then rushed *en masse* to pillage the town of Cap Haïtien. Here, however, their numbers availed them little against the arms and discipline of the French troops, and they were driven back with great slaughter, and many then retired to the mountains. It would naturally be suspected that the coloured people were the instigators of this movement, were it not certain that they were as much opposed to the freedom of the blacks as the most impassioned white planter.

The insurgent slaves called themselves "Les Gens du Roi," declaring that he was their friend, and was persecuted for their sake; they hoisted the white flag, and placed an ignorant negro, Jean François, at their head. The second in command was a Papaloi or priest of the Vaudoux, named Biassou. He encouraged his followers to carry on the rites of their African religion, and when under its wildest influence, he dashed his bands to the attack of their civilised enemies, to meet their death in Hayti, but to rise again free in their beloved Africa. The ferocity of the negro nature had now full swing, and the whites who fell into their hands felt its effects. Prisoners were placed between planks and sawn in two, or were skinned alive and slowly roasted, the girls violated and then murdered. Unhappily some of these blacks had seen their companions thus tortured, though probably in very exceptional cases. Descriptions of these horrors fill pages in every Haytian history, but it is needless to dwell on them. On either side there was but little mercy.

The Governor at length collected 3000 white troops, who, after various skirmishes, dispersed these bands with much slaughter; but as this success was not followed up, Jean François and Biassou soon rallied their followers.

In the meantime the coloured men at Mirebalais, under the leadership of Pinchinat, began to arouse their brethren; and having freed nine hundred slaves, commenced forming the nucleus of an army, that, under the leadership of a very intelligent mulatto named Bauvais, gained some successes over the undisciplined forces in Port-au-Prince, commanded by an Italian adventurer, Praloto. The Royalists, who had been driven from the city by the mob, had assembled at "La Croix des Bouquets" in the plains, and to strengthen, their party entered into an alliance with the freedmen. This alarmed the inhabitants of Port-au-Prince, and they also recognised the existence of Pinchinat and his party by entering into a regular treaty with them. The Haytians, as I may call the coloured races, began now to understand that their position must depend on their own courage and conduct.

When everything had been settled between the chiefs of the two parties, the Haytians returned to Port-au-Prince, and were received with every demonstration of joy; they then agreed to a plan which showed how little they cared for the liberty of others, so that they themselves obtained their rights. Among those who had fought valiantly at their side were the freed slaves previously referred to. For fear these men should incite ideas of liberty among those blacks who were still working on the estates, the coloured officers consented that they should be deported from the country. In the end they were placed as prisoners on board a pontoon in Mole St. Nicolas, and at night were for the most part butchered by unknown assassins. And Bauvais and Pinchinat, the leaders and the most intelligent of the freedmen, were those that agreed to this deportation of their brethren-in-arms who had the misfortune to be lately slaves! I doubt if the blacks ever forgot this incident.

The coloured men gained little by this breach of faith, as shortly after news arrived that the French Assembly had reversed the decree of May 15, which gave equal rights to the freedmen; and then dissensions broke out, and the coloured men were again driven from Port-au-Prince with heavy loss. This was the signal for disorders throughout the whole country, and the whites and the freedmen were skirmishing in every district. Praloto and the rabble reigned supreme in Port-au-Prince, and soon made the rich merchants and shopkeepers feel the effects of their internal divisions. They set fire to the town, and during the confusion plundered the stores, and exercised their private vengeance on their enemies.

The whole country was in the greatest disorder when the three commissioners sent by the French Government arrived in Hayti. The Colonial Assembly was still sitting at Cap Haïtien, and the insurgent negroes were encamped at no great distance. They immediately endeavoured to enter into negotiations with them, which had little result, on account of the obstinacy of the planters. The three commissioners were Mirbeck, St. Leger, and Roume. Finding that their influence was as nought, the former two returned to France, whilst Roume went ultimately to Santo Domingo.

The state of the colony may be imagined when it is remembered that the whites were divided into three distinct sections. The coloured men, jealous of each other, did not combine, but were ready to come to blows on the least pretext; while the blacks, under Jean François, were massacring every white that fell into their hands, and selling to the Spaniard every negro or coloured man accused of siding with the French. The planters wanted independence or subjection to England; the poorer whites anything which would give them the property of others; the coloured were still faithful to France; whilst the blacks cared only to be free from work; yet among them was Toussaint, who already had fermenting in his brain the project of a free black State.

It would interest few to enter into the details of this history of horrors, where it is difficult to feel sympathy for any party. They were alike steeped in blood, and ready to commit any crime to further their ends. Murder, torture, violation, pillage, bad faith, and treachery meet you on all sides; and although a few names arise occasionally in whom you feel a momentary interest, they are sure soon to disgust you by their utter incapacity or besotted personal ambition.

The National Assembly in Paris, finding that their first commissioners had accomplished nothing, sent three others, two of whom, Sonthonax and Polvérel, are well known in Haytian history. They had full powers, and even secret instructions, to do all they could to give freedom to the slaves.

These two commissioners were of the very worst kind of revolutionists, talked of little but guillotining the aristocrats, and were in every way unsuited to their task; they dissolved the Colonial Assembly, and substituted for it a commission, consisting of six whites of the stamp suited to them, and six freedmen. They decided to crush the respectable classes, whom they called Royalists, because they would not join in revolutionary excesses, and the massacre commenced at the Cape.

Polvérel appears to have had some idea of the responsibility of his position, though both cruel and faithless; but Sonthonax was but a blatant babbler, with some talent, but overwhelmed by vanity. He caused more bloodshed than any other man, first setting the lower white against the rich, then the mulatto against the white, and then the black against both. Well might the French orator declare on Sonthonax's return to France that "il puait de sang." The third commissioner, Aillaud, thinking, very justly, that his companions were a couple of scoundrels whom he could not control, embarked secretly and left for home. Whilst these commissioners were employed in destroying the fairest colony in the world, France, in a moment of excited fury, declared war against the rest of Europe, and a new era opened for Hayti.

Many of the more influential and respectable inhabitants of all colours, utterly disgusted by the conduct of the different parties, thought that the war between England and France would give them some chance of rest from the excesses of the insurgent blacks; and the factious freedmen, supported by that *fou furieux*, Sonthonax, sent to Jamaica to invite the Governor to interfere and take possession of the colony.

England did interfere, but in her usual way, with small expeditions, and thus frittered away her strength; but the resistance made was in general so contemptible, that with little effort we succeeded in taking Jérémie in the south, and then St. Marc, and subsequently Port-au-Prince. Had we sent a large army, it is equally possible that we should not have succeeded, as the intention was to reimpose slavery. As the garrison of Jamaica could only furnish detachments, the British authorities began to enlist all who wished to serve irrespective of colour, and being supported by those who were weary of anarchy and revolutionary fury, were soon able to present a very respectable force in the field. The Spaniards, aided by the bands of revolted negroes, overran most of the northern province; in this they were greatly aided by Toussaint L'Ouverture, who now began to come to the front. Sonthonax, whose idea of energy was simply to massacre and destroy, ordered that every place his partisans were forced to evacuate should be burnt. At the same time he thought that a little terror might be of service, so he erected a guillotine in Port-au-Prince; and having at hand a Frenchman accused of being a Royalist, he thought he would try the experiment on him. An immense crowd of Haytians assembled to witness the execution; but when they saw the bright blade descend and the head roll at their feet, they were horror-stricken, and rushing on the guillotine, tore it to pieces, and no other has ever again been erected in Hayti.

Curious people! they who never hesitated to destroy the whites, guilty or innocent, or massacre, simply because they were white, women and children, down to the very babe at the breast, who invented every species of torture to render death more hideous, were horrified because a man's head was chopped off, instead of his being destroyed in a fashion to which they were accustomed, and this at a time when white, coloured, and black were vying with each other in arts of bloodthirsty cruelty!

The whole country was in terrible confusion; the French had not one man who had the talent or influence to dominate their divided factions; the coloured were represented by such respectabilities as Pinchinat, Bauvais, and Rigaud, but without one of incontestable superiority; the blacks were as yet led by such men as Jean François and Biassou, who must even make the respectable negroes blush to acknowledge that they were of the same race; yet, as I have said, there was one man coming to the front who was to dominate all.

Amid the many heroes whose actions the Haytians love to commemorate, Toussaint L'Ouverture does not hold a high rank. And yet the conduct of this black was so remarkable as almost to confound those who declare the negro an inferior creature incapable of rising to genius. History, wearied with dwelling on the petty passions of the other founders of Haytian independence, may well turn to the one grand figure of this cruel war. Toussaint was born on the Breda estate in the northern department, and was a slave from birth; it has been doubted whether he was of pure negro race. His grandfather was an African prince, but if we may judge from the portraits, he was not of the pure negro type. Whether pure negro or not, there is no doubt of the intelligence and energy of the man. Though but a puny child, by constant exercise and a vigorous will he became as wiry and active as any of his companions, and, moreover, gave up much of his leisure time to study. He learnt to read French, and, it is said, in order to understand the Prayer-Book, a little Latin; but he never quite mastered the art of writing. He was evidently trusted and kindly treated by his master's agent, who gave him charge of the sugar-mills. There is an accusation constantly brought against Toussaint, that of being a religious hypocrite, but his early life shows that it is unfounded. Whilst still a slave, his principles would not allow him to follow the custom of his companions and live in concubinage; he determined to marry, though the woman he chose had already an illegitimate son named Placide, whom he adopted. It is pleasing to read of the happy domestic life of Toussaint, and it is another proof of that affectionate disposition which made those who served him devoted to him.

When the insurrection broke out in the northern province, Toussaint remained faithful to his master, and prevented any destruction on the estate; but finding ultimately that he could not stem the tide, he sent his master's family for safety into Cap Haïtien, and joined the insurgents. He was at first appointed surgeon to the army, as among his other accomplishments was a knowledge of *simples*, which had given him great influence on the estate, and was now to do so in the insurgent forces. He liked this employment, as it kept him free from the savage excesses of his companions, who were acting with more than ordinary barbarity.

The three leaders of the insurgents were then Jean François, a negro, about whom opinions differ. St. Remy says he was intellectual, though the general idea is more probable, that he was an energetic savage. Biassou was sensual and violent, as cruel as man could be and an avowed leader of the Vaudoux sect, and apparently a Papaloi; but the vilest of the three was Jeannot. He loved to torture his white prisoners, and drank their blood mixed with rum; but he was as cowardly as he was cruel, and the scene at his execution, when he clung to the priest in frantic terror, must have afforded satisfaction to the friends of those whom he had pitilessly murdered. Jeannot was also a great proficient in Vaudoux practices, and thus gained much influence with the ignorant slaves; it was this influence, not his cruelties, which roused the anger of Jean François, who seized and summarily shot him.

It is curious to read of the projects of these negro leaders. They had no idea of demanding liberty for the slaves; they only wanted liberty for themselves. In some abortive negotiations with the French, Jean François demanded that 300 of the leaders should be declared free, whilst Toussaint would only have bargained for fifty. The mulatto leaders, however, were most anxious to preserve their own slaves, and, as I have related, gave up to death those blacks who had aided them in supporting their position; and a French writer records that up to Le Clerc's expedition, the mulattoes had fought against the blacks with all the zeal that the interests of property could inspire.

The blind infatuation of the planters prevented their accepting Jean François' proposition; they even rejected it with insult, and savagely persecuted the negroes who were living in Cap Haïtien. Biassou then ordered all his white prisoners to be put to death; but Toussaint, by his eloquent remonstrances, saved them. Other negotiations having failed, Biassou attacked the French lines, and carried them as far as the ramparts of the town. The planters had brave words, but not brave deeds, with which to meet their revolted bondsmen. All the black prisoners taken by the insurgents were sent over the frontiers and sold as slaves to the Spaniards. Toussaint remonstrated against this vile traffic, but never shared in it. The new Governor, Laveaux, at this time nearly stifled the insurrection, dispersing all the insurgent forces; but, as usual, not following up his successes, allowed the negroes again to concentrate. No strength of position as yet enabled the blacks successfully to resist the white troops.

When the negro chiefs heard of the death of Louis XVI., they thought they had lost a friend, and openly joined the Spaniards in their war on the French Republic.

At this time Sonthonax and Polvérel acted as if they intended to betray their own country, by removing the chief white officers from command and entrusting these important posts to mulattoes. It was not, however, treachery, but jealousy, as such a man as General Galbaud could not be made a docile instrument in their hands. Then finding that power was slipping from them, they proclaimed (1793) the liberty of all those slaves who would fight for the Republic.

In the meantime Toussaint was steadily gaining influence among his troops, and gradually freeing himself from the control of Biassou, whose proceedings had always shocked him; and some successful expeditions, as the taking of Dondon, added to his prestige. Whilst fighting was going on throughout the northern provinces, Sonthonax and Polvérel were solemnising pompous *fêtes* to celebrate the anniversary of the taking of the Bastile. It is singular what a passion they had for these childish amusements.

Rigaud, a mulatto, in future days the rival of Toussaint, now appears prominently upon the scene, being appointed by the commissioners as chief of the northern department.

Toussaint continued his successes, and finding that nothing could be done with the estates without the whites, appeared anxious to induce them to return to superintend their cultivation, and he succeeded in inducing many hundreds to reside in their devastated homes.

Alarmed by the continued successes of Toussaint, Sonthonax proclaimed in August 29, 1793, the liberty of all, which, under the circumstances, may be considered the only wise act of his administration.

The people of the north-west, however, were weary of the tyranny of the commissioners, and, being probably privately informed of Toussaint's intentions, surrendered Gonaives to him, and the rest of the neighbouring districts followed. A new enemy, however, now appeared in the shape of the English, who took possession of St. Marc with seventy-five men,—so like our system! In June 1794 Port-au-Prince surrendered to the English after a faint resistance, the commissioners retiring to Jacmel, from whence they embarked for France, to answer for their conduct. At that time Port-au-Prince was in a fair state for defence; but Captain Daniel of the 41st took the famous fort of Bizoton by storm with sixty men, and then the English advanced on the town. The effect of having replaced the French officers by untrained mulattoes was here apparent: though everything had been prepared to blow up the forts, nothing was done; the garrison fled, leaving 131 cannon, twenty-two laden vessels, with 7000 tons more in ballast, and all their stores and ammunition.

At this time Jean François became suspicious of Toussaint and arrested him, but he was delivered by Biassou. Toussaint had for some time been meditating a bold stroke. The proclamation by Sonthonax of the freedom of the blacks probably worked on him, and he determined to abandon the party of the king of Spain, which was that of slavery, and join the French Republic. He did so, proclaiming at the same time the freedom of the slaves. His soldiers sullied the change by massacring two hundred white planters, who, confiding in the word of Toussaint, had returned to their estates.

The new General of the republic now acted with energy against Jean François, drove him from the plains, and forced him to take refuge with his followers in the Black Mountains. Success followed success, until Toussaint found himself opposite St. Marc; but his attack on that town was easily repulsed by its garrison in English pay. His activity was incessant, and he kept up constant skirmishes with all his enemies. He appeared ever unwearied, whatever might be the fatigue of his companions.

Toussaint had naturally observed, that however his men might succeed against the undisciplined hordes of Jean François, they could do nothing against a disciplined force. He therefore, in 1795, formed four regiments of 2000 men each, whom he had daily drilled by French soldiers, his former prisoners; and, I may notice here, with such success, that English officers were subsequently surprised at their proficiency.

Rigaud had, in the meantime, with his usual jactancy, marched on Port-au-Prince to expel the English, but was repulsed. Toussaint assembled all his army for another attack on St. Marc, and for three days, from the 25th to 27th July 1795, tried by repeated assaults to capture the town; but English discipline prevailed, and the small garrison foiled every attempt.

It is noticed by St. Remy that Toussaint, when once he gave his word, never broke it, which was a new experience among these unprincipled leaders; and it is added, that he never had any prejudice of colour.

An important event for the French in 1795 was the peace made between France and Spain, by which Santo Domingo was ceded to the former.

The year 1796 was ushered in by various English expeditions and skirmishes, and their failure to take Leogâne. Some of the Haytian accounts are amusing. Pétion defended the fort of Ça-ira against the whole English fleet until the fortifications were demolished. Fifteen thousand English bullets were showered into the place, and yet only seven Haytians were killed. It looks as if the garrison had quietly retired and left us to batter away at the earthworks.

One is often surprised, in reading Haytian accounts of the war, at the defeats of the English, which make one wonder what could have become of the proverbial courage and steadiness of our men; but a little closer inquiry shows that in most of these instances there were few or no English present, only black and coloured men in our pay, or planters who had taken our side in the war, none of whom were more than half-hearted in our cause.

The French were also weakened by internal dissensions. General Vilatte, a mulatto, incited a revolt in the town of Cap Haïtien, arrested the French governor, Laveaux, and threw him into prison. The latter called on Toussaint to aid him, and the black general had the supreme satisfaction of marching into the town and freeing the white governor. With what curious sensations must Toussaint have performed this act of authority in a place that had only known him as a slave! Laveaux received him with enthusiasm, and promoted him from the grade of General of Brigade, in which the French Government had confirmed him, to be Lieutenant-General of the Government, April 1, 1796. This successful movement confirmed the ascendancy of the blacks in the north, and Vilatte had shortly to sail for France, from whence he returned with the expedition sent to enslave his countrymen.

Sonthonax and a new commission now arrived at Cap Haïtien, to find Rigaud almost independent in the south, and Toussaint master in the north. Both Laveaux and Sonthonax are accused of endeavouring to set the blacks against the mulattoes. Laveaux having returned to France as deputy for the colony, Sonthonax remained at the head of affairs, and one of his first acts was to name Toussaint General of Division.

Toussaint was in the meantime organising his army and working hard at its drill; he then started to the attack of Mirebalais, a port occupied by a French planter in our service, the Count de Bruges, who appears to have retired, with numerous forces, without much resistance. He probably could scarcely trust his raw levies. Sonthonax was so pleased with this important success that he named Toussaint Commander-in-Chief of the army in Santo Domingo, which step displeased Rigaud, who was thus placed under the orders of a black general.

Toussaint appears to have felt a justifiable distrust of Sonthonax. He saw that he desired to set black against coloured, that he was even talking of the independence of the island, perhaps only to test Toussaint's fidelity; but he had no difficulty in assuring himself that wherever Sonthonax was, mischief was sure to be brewing. He therefore had him elected deputy, and sent him to follow Laveaux. Sonthonax did not like this step, and made some show of opposition, but Toussaint informed him that if he did not embark immediately he would fall on Cap Haïtien with 20,000 men. This irresistible argument made Sonthonax give way. As he went down to the boat that was to take him on board, the streets were lined by crowds of all colours; but not one said, "God bless him," as he had betrayed every party in turn; and his one wise act of proclaiming the liberty of the slaves was simply a political expedient, wrung from him by the circumstances of the hour. He was a boasting, bad man, whose history is written in the blood of thousands of every colour.

The Directory, alarmed at the growing influence of Toussaint, sent out General Hédouville as pacificator of the island, and, to produce harmony, gave him power to defeat Rigaud. On his arrival at Cap Haïtien he summoned the rivals to confer with him, and Rigaud and Toussaint, meeting at Gonaives, went together to the capital. Hédouville, jealous of the power of the latter, gave all his attention to the former, whilst the newly-arrived French officers laughed at the negro and his surroundings. Toussaint, suspecting a plot to arrest him and send him off to France, and probably very jealous of the superior treatment of his rival, withdrew from the city and returned to his army.

The English had now become convinced that it was useless to attempt to conquer the island; their losses from sickness were enormous, and the influence of the planters was of no avail. Their black and coloured mercenaries were faithless, and ready to betray them, as at St. Marc, where the English governor had to shoot a number of traitorous mulattoes who would have betrayed the town into the hands of the blacks. They therefore determined to treat with Toussaint, and evacuated St. Marc, Port-au-Prince, and L'Arcahaye. He thus gained at one stroke what no amount of force could have procured for him.

Toussaint, with a greatness of mind which was really remarkable, agreed to allow those French colonists who had sided with us to remain, and promised to respect their properties; and as it was known that this magnanimous black ever kept his word, no important exodus followed our retreat. Admiral Maitland had arranged for the surrender of the mole with General Hédouville, but on finding his hostility to the French planters, whom he insisted on Toussaint expelling the country, our naval chief made a new settlement with the black general and handed the mole over to him. Maitland invited Toussaint to visit him, and reviewed before him the English army collected from the rest of the country. He was exceedingly pleased by the treatment he received from our people, and ever after showed a kindly feeling towards them.

One can scarcely understand why the English gave up the mole, which a small garrison could have defended, and the importance of the position in naval warfare is indisputable. If we wanted to gain Toussaint and induce him to declare the island independent, we should have held it until that desirable event had happened.[4]

Toussaint treated the old colonists with distinction, and left many of them in the commands they had held under the English. Hédouville protested against this good treatment of his own countrymen, and annoyed Toussaint so much that he began to consider whether it would not be prudent to send Hédouville to follow Sonthonax.

Hédouville was not the only one who objected to the good treatment of the planters; his opinion was shared by the black general, Moïse, then commanding in the northern department. To show his displeasure at Toussaint's humanity, he caused some white colonists to be murdered in the plains near Cap Haïtien. Hédouville, frightened by the practical result of his teaching, summoned Toussaint to his aid; but doubtful of his general, he escaped on board a vessel in harbour. In order to do all the mischief he could before leaving, he wrote to Rigaud, saying he was no longer to obey Toussaint, but consider himself the governor of the southern department, adding that Toussaint was sold to the English and the *émigrés*.

It was Hédouville who thus laid the foundation of that civil war which degenerated into a struggle of caste. The agents sent by France proved each worse than the other. Rigaud, with the true spirit of a mulatto, also wrote to Toussaint to drive out the white planters. When his teaching had incited his soldiers to murder his white countrymen, all Rigaud could say was, "Mon Dieu, qu'est que le peuple en fureur?"

On the departure of Hédouville, Toussaint invited Roume to leave Santo Domingo and come and reside at Port-au-Prince, where they met in January 1799. Roume appears to have had a profound admiration for Toussaint. We find him writing to General Kerverseau as early as February 1795, and describing the negro chief as a philosopher, a legislator, a general, and a good citizen.

Roume had a difficult part to play. He was most anxious to bring about concord among the different generals, and therefore invited Rigaud and Bauvais to meet Toussaint on the *fête* of the 4th of February to commemorate the memorable day when the National Convention proclaimed full liberty to the slaves. A little outward concord was obtained, but soon after, Toussaint, suspecting a plot, arrested some mulattoes. A slight disturbance among the negroes taking place at Corail, thirty were captured and died in prison, from "the effect of the gas created by white-washing the prison." This remarkable excuse did not satisfy Toussaint, who believed the men to have been assassinated by Rigaud's officers.

Toussaint and Roume had in the meantime left for Cap Haïtien, where they appear to have negotiated a commercial treaty with the Americans, and some arrangement was also, it is said, made with Admiral Maitland.

It was during this year that Captain Rainsford visited Cap Haïtien. As we were at war with France, our officer passed as an American, and soon after landing was met by Toussaint in the street, who came up to him to ask the news. He next saw him at a restaurant where all classes dined, and he sat down at a long table with a drummer-boy next him and the general not far off. The latter used to say that except on service he did not see the necessity of making distinctions. In the evening Captain Rainsford played billiards with Toussaint at the public tables.

Rainsford appears to have been as much struck with Toussaint as Roume. He says he was constrained to admire him as a man, a governor, and a general. He describes him as a perfect black, then about fifty-five years of age, of a venerable appearance, and possessed of uncommon discernment and great suavity of manners. He enters fully into a description of his dress. The general wore as a uniform a kind of blue spencer, with a large red cape falling over his shoulders, and red cuffs, with eight rows of lace on the arms, and a pair of huge gold epaulettes, a scarlet waistcoat, pantaloons and half-boots, a round hat with red feather and national cockade, and an extremely large sword was suspended from his side. Rainsford adds: "He receives a voluntary respect from every description of his countrymen, which is more than returned by the affability of his behaviour and the goodness of his heart." The vessel in which Rainsford was a passenger was next driven by stress of weather into Fort Liberté. Arrested as a spy, he was condemned to death; but Toussaint would not permit the sentence to be carried out. He dismissed him with a caution not to return without passports.

There is much exaggeration in the account given by Rainsford of what he saw and heard at Cap Haïtien. He talks of 62,000 inhabitants leaving the city after the great fire, and of Toussaint reviewing his army of 60,000 men and 2000 officers. He was a better judge probably of their manœuvres. He says that the soldiers went through their exercises with a degree of expertness he had seldom before witnessed. At the signal of a whistle, a whole brigade ran three or four hundred yards, and then separating, threw themselves on the ground, keeping up a heavy fire from every kind of position. The complete subordination and discipline astonished him.

Rigaud having evidently decided to carry out General Hédouville's instructions and defy both Toussaint and Roume, it became necessary to subdue him. Ten thousand men were collected at Port-au-Prince, whilst Rigaud concentrated his army at Miragoâne, and commenced the war by seizing Petit Goave, and there, without the slightest excuse, murdered all the white inhabitants. It is singular to contrast the conduct of the two generals: Toussaint, without the slightest prejudice of colour, and Rigaud, the mulatto, the son of a Frenchman, showing "how he hated his father and despised his mother" by murdering the whites and refusing to obey a black.

Roume published a proclamation, calling on the north and west to march against the south to restore unity of command; but before entering on the campaign, Toussaint had to return to the north to repress some movements, and on his journey back almost fell into two ambuscades, from which he was saved by the fleetness of his horse. Toussaint shot those who were concerned in these conspiracies, whether black or coloured; but the stories told by St. Remy of his ordering 180 young mulatto children to be drowned at L'Arcahaye, is so contrary to everything we know of his character, that we may set this fable down to caste hatred. That he was severe with his enemies is no doubt true.

Then began the wearisome civil war in the south by Dessalines driving back Rigaud's army, and by the siege of Jacmel, which lasted four months. Pétion greatly distinguished himself in the defence, and conducted the evacuation. It appears unaccountable that while the main body of Toussaint's army was thus engaged, Rigaud remained passive; it can only be explained by mean jealousy, which was his characteristic to the last year of his life. But his principal fault was jactancy, shown by his proclamation, saying, "Let the enemy appear and I'll slay them," which was answered by another from Toussaint offering pardon and peace.

Toussaint's army in the south was commanded by Dessalines and Christophe, or, in other words, by two ferocious blacks, to whom pity was unknown. Dessalines soon forced the strong position near Miragoâne, and defeated Rigaud and Pétion, driving them before him towards Les Cayes. Rigaud ordered his officers to burn and destroy everything in their retreat, which naturally roused the inhabitants against these measures of defence, and they became clamorous for peace.

In the meantime the Consular Government at Paris sent out officers to Hayti, among whom was Colonel Vincent. Toussaint was confirmed in his position as General-in-Chief, but the war in the south was disapproved. Colonel Vincent was enabled to tell him of all the changes that had taken place in France, but the black chief could readily see that he was suspected by the French Government. He, however, sent Vincent and other officers to Les Cayes to offer peace. It is amusing to read the account given of Rigaud. He went to see the French officers, a blunderbuss on his shoulder, pistols in his belt, a sword on one side and a dagger on the other. On hearing that his conduct did not meet with the support of the French Government, he drew his dagger as if to stab himself, but did not do so: he preferred making a truce and embarking for France, together with his principal officers.

Toussaint entered Les Cayes on the 1st August 1800, and showed the grandeur of his character by implicitly carrying out his original proclamation. He again proclaimed union and peace, and pardoned all those who had been led into rebellion against him; and, to the astonishment of his enemies, he kept his word and behaved with great magnanimity. Even his worst opponents were then constrained to allow that, when once given, he never broke his word.

If Toussaint was clement, Dessalines was the reverse; and the mulattoes declare that he killed upwards of ten thousand of their caste, which is probably more of that colour than the southern province ever contained.

Whilst this campaign was at its height, Roume committed the indiscretion of trying to raise a revolt in Jamaica. His agents were taken and hung; and as a punishment the English captured one of Toussaint's convoys destined for Jacmel. The General, very angry with Roume, sent for him; he refused to come, upon which Toussaint went to Cap Haïtien, and after reproaching him, insisted on his giving him an order to invade the eastern end of the island. He refused at first, but ultimately yielded to the menaces of General Moïse.

When the southern campaign was over, Toussaint began to prepare for the occupation of Santo Domingo, but finding that Roume was inclined to withdraw his permission, he arrested him and sent him back to France. Toussaint's prestige was now so great in the island, that little resistance was made, and he occupied the city of Santo Domingo almost without a shot being fired, and established his brother Paul as governor.

The whole of the island being now under one chief, Toussaint decided to put into execution a constitution which he had already promulgated. It was certainly a model of liberality. It placed all colours equal before the law; employments might be held by black, white, or coloured; as much freedom of trade as possible; a governor to be named for five years, but on account of the eminent services of Toussaint, he was to occupy that post for life, with power to name his successor. He sent this constitution to

Buonaparte for approval; but evidently it was too much or too little. Had he boldly proclaimed the independence of the island, he might have saved the country from great misfortunes.

Peace being now re-established over all the island, Toussaint began his civil administration. All accounts are unanimous in declaring that he himself governed admirably, but the instruments he had to employ were too often utterly unworthy. He organised the country into districts, and appointed inspectors to see that all returned to their work, and decreed that a fifth of the produce should be given to the labourers. Dessalines was appointed inspector-in-chief; and if a man without any sentiment of humanity was required for that post, surely Dessalines was a good choice, as he was ready to beat to death any man, woman, or child whom he chose to accuse of idleness. Toussaint, looking to difficulties ahead, continued to pay the greatest attention to his army, organised it with care, and preserved the strictest discipline. The stick appears to have been as popular in that day as it is now.

Toussaint was very friendly to the whites, and was most anxious to encourage them to aid in developing the country. This excited the jealousy of some of his generals; among others, of Moïse, his nephew, who to thwart his uncle's projects incited a movement in the north to massacre the French. Several having fallen victims, Toussaint hastened to the spot, and finding that Moïse was the real instigator of the murders, sent him before a court-martial. He was sentenced to death, and very properly shot on the 26th November 1800. Had Toussaint connived at these crimes, he would have upset all confidence in his trusted word.

All was now progressing on the island; the government was regularly administered, the finances were getting into order, and agriculture was beginning to raise its head, when Buonaparte, having secured peace in Europe, determined to recover the Queen of the Antilles and restore slavery. The story of this attempt may be told in a few words. General Leclerc started with 30,000 men to subdue the island, and although the evident intention of the French Government was to restore slavery, the principal mulatto officers accompanied him, chief among whom were Rigaud, Pétion, and Vilatte. It is true the mulattoes had not yet frankly accepted the full freedom of the blacks.

General Leclerc did all he could to cause an armed resistance, as a peaceful solution would have given him no military glory; therefore, instead of sending Toussaint his children and the letter he bore from Buonaparte, he tried to surprise Cap Haïtien. But General Christophe, before retiring with its garrison, set fire to the town and almost destroyed it; and Toussaint sent instructions to his other generals to follow this example. Leclerc, mortified by the result of his first attempt, now thought of writing to Toussaint, and sent him his two boys. Toussaint behaved with great nobility of character, and asked naturally, "Why words of peace but acts of war?" Finding that he could not circumvent his black opponent, Leclerc published a decree in February 1802 placing both Toussaint and Christophe "hors la loi." This was followed by the burning of the towns of St. Marc and Gonaives, and a retreat of the black troops towards the interior.

Whenever you see a fortress in Hayti, you are sure to be told that it was built by the English; among others thus known was La Crête à Pierrot. The French general Debelle, treating with contempt these negro troops, attacked this fort with an inefficient force and was beaten; then Leclerc made an assault in person, but he also was beaten, and was forced to lay siege to it. The attack and defence were conducted with singular courage, particularly the latter, considering the quality of the men, who had never before been measured with real white troops: however, after having repulsed several assaults, the garrison evacuated the forts. Pétion commanded a portion of the French artillery in this attack on his countrymen struggling for freedom. If he loved France but little, he hated Toussaint more.

Even the enemies of the great black general are full of admiration of the courage displayed by him during all this important struggle, and especially dwell on his devotion to his wounded officers. I may here remark that the French general Rochambeau distinguished himself for his cruelties, and shot every prisoner that fell into his hands; which fully justified the retaliation of the Haytians.

Discouraged by a series of reverses which followed the loss of La Crête à Pierrot, where it was amply proved that the negro soldiers, even among their mountains, were no match for the disciplined troops of France, some of the black generals, as Christophe, began to make terms with the French; and Toussaint, finding himself thus abandoned, wrote to Leclerc offering submission. As it was accepted, he went to Cap Haïtien to meet the commander-in-chief, and was received and treated with much distinction. He then returned to the village of Marmalade, and there issued orders to all his officers to cease opposition and acknowledge the French authorities, and peace was established throughout the island.

General Leclerc was but temporising with these black leaders; his secret orders were, not only to arrest Toussaint, Dessalines, and Christophe, but to re-establish slavery. He found, however, the last two so zealous in carrying out his instructions to disarm the population, that he preserved them in their commands.

Toussaint himself, having ever kept his word, could not believe that the French commander-in-chief would not keep his, and therefore, in spite of all warnings that treachery was meditated, stayed quietly on his estate at Ennery. He there received a letter from General Brunet, asking for an interview at a certain spot; Toussaint went, and was immediately arrested under circumstances of the greatest treachery. He was bound with ropes and embarked on board the French ship "Creole;" then put on board the "Héros" with all his family and sent to France. When received on board by Savary, Chef de Division, he said to him, "En me renversant on n'a abattu à Saint Domingue que le tronc de l'arbre de la liberté des noirs; il repoussera, parceque les racines en sont profondes et nombreuses." When reading this account of the capture of Toussaint, we can scarcely credit that we are recording the acts of French officers, whose plighted word was thus broken. [5]

On Toussaint's arrival in France he wrote to the French Chief Consul; but he might as well have written to Dessalines as expect either mercy or justice from the despot who then ruled France. He was separated from his family and hurried off to the Château de Joux in the Alps, where his rival Rigaud was already confined. Here he died from cold and neglect, under circumstances which raised the suspicion that the close of this illustrious life was hastened by unfair means. It is some satisfaction to think that his executioner died also a prisoner in exile, though surrounded by every comfort that the generous English Government could afford him.

We have all heard or read something of Toussaint L'Ouverture, and been taught to think well of him: I was therefore the more surprised, on my arrival at Port-au-Prince, to hear his memory so depreciated. I do not remember any Haytian having voluntarily spoken of him, though they never wearied of talking of Dessalines, Christophe, and Rigaud. I at first thought that Toussaint never having unnecessarily shed white blood, whilst the others may be said to have rejoiced at the sight of it, was one of the chief causes; but the real reason why the historians and biographers of Hayti would lower Toussaint's memory is the energy with which he acted against the rebellious mulattoes, and his firm determination that all colours should be equally respected by the law, and that all should have equal rights.

It is impossible not to be struck with almost the unanimous opinion favourable to Toussaint which has been recorded by all parties, even by his enemies. The Marquis d'Hermonas says that "God in this terrestrial globe could not commune with a purer spirit;" the French general Pamphile Lacroix records that "Nul n'osait l'aborder sans crainte, et nul ne le quittait sans respect." We have seen the opinion of Roume and Rainsford, that

Toussaint was "a philosopher, a legislator, a general, and a good citizen," and that the latter was compelled to admire him as "a man, a governor, and a general."

He was personally brave, and being a splendid rider, loving from his earliest childhood to be on horseback, he never appeared fatigued even after the greatest exertions. As a general he is thought to have shown much skill; and, what proves his sense, but does not add to his popularity among Haytians, he did not believe that his men were fitted to cope with the trained bands of France. He constantly said that they must trust to climate and yellow fever as their best allies. As an administrator he had much capacity, and his influence being unbounded, he would probably have restored its old prosperity to Hayti, had not Leclerc's expedition arrived to throw the whole island into confusion.

Toussaint's personal qualities appear to have been equal to his public: his word was sacred, he was humane on most occasions, yet with a firmness and decision which astonished his enemies. In his family relations he showed the most tender affection for wife and children; his fine nature was apparent on all occasions in his solicitude for his wounded officers and soldiers, and the thoughtful care of the prisoners that fell into his hands. His affectionate treatment of animals was also greatly noticed, and whenever he came upon fugitive women and children of any colour, his first thought was for their comfort.

Our Consul-General Mackenzie (1827) often talked to the black officers of Toussaint; they described him as stern and unbending, but just, and intimately acquainted with the habits of the people and the best interests of his country.

The one mistake of his life appears to have been his refusal, when urged to do so by England, to declare the independence of Hayti. Had he accepted the English proposals and entered into a treaty with us and with the Americans, it is not likely that Buonaparte would have ever attempted an expedition against him, and the history of Hayti might have been happier.

There is one fact which strikes the reader of the histories of these times, and that is, the soldiers are described as veritable *sans-culottes*, without pay and without proper uniforms, and yet all the chiefs, as Toussaint, Dessalines, and Christophe, were living in splendid houses in the greatest luxury. Toussaint is recorded to have lent the French Treasury 600,000 livres, an enormous sum for a slave to possess after a few years of freedom. Gragnon-Lacoste, who published a Life of Toussaint L'Ouverture in 1877, founded on family papers, says that this general had a marble house in Cap

Haïtien, elegantly furnished, and that he kept up the same style in all his plantations. His descendants in late years claimed about the fourth of Hayti as the estates of the black general.[6]

Toussaint was also a fervent Roman Catholic, and was greatly attached to the priesthood; he did all he could to repress the Vaudoux, and he published a strong proclamation forbidding all fetish rites.[7]

The treachery of Leclerc towards Toussaint had its reward; it could not but excite suspicion among the black leaders, as the previous deportation of Rigaud had done among the mulattoes. And now the most fearful epidemic of yellow fever fell upon the French army, and almost annihilated it. Forty thousand are reported to have been lost during the years 1802 and 1803: among the victims were Leclerc and twenty other French generals. The Haytians saw their opportunity, and Dessalines, Christophe, and Pétion abandoned the invaders, and roused their countrymen to expel the weak remnants of the French army. War had now been declared between France and England, and our fleets were soon off the coasts. The French were driven from every point, and forced to concentrate in Cap Haïtien. Rochambeau, who had succeeded Leclerc, did all that man could do to save his army; but besieged by the blacks to the number of 30,000, and blockaded by our fleet, pinched by hunger, and seeing no hopes of reinforcements, he surrendered to the English and embarked for Europe.

Thus ended one of the most disastrous expeditions ever undertaken by France, and ended as it deserved to end. Its history was sullied by every species of treachery, cruelty, and crime; but we cannot but admire the splendid bravery of the troops under every discouragement, in a tropical climate, where the heat is so great that the European is unfitted for continued exertion, but where yellow fever and death follow constant exposure.

CHAPTER III
HISTORY SINCE INDEPENDENCE

"Que deviendra notre pays quand il sera livré à la vanité et à l'ignorance," exclaimed Bauvais, one of the leaders of the mulatto party. I am afraid this sketch of the history of Hayti since the war of independence will show what are the results to a country when governed by vanity and ignorance.

Having driven out the French by deeds of unquestioned valour and energy, and with a cruelty which the infamous conduct of Rochambeau could palliate, if not justify, the Haytians determined to throw off all allegiance to France and establish an independent government.

At Gonaives, on the 1st January 1804, General Dessalines assembled all his military chiefs around him and had read to them the Act of Independence, which terminated with the words, "for ever to renounce France, and to die rather than live under her dominion." In a proclamation, Dessalines was careful to declare that it was not their mission to disturb the tranquillity of neighbouring islands, but in unmistakable language he called upon them to put to death every Frenchman who remained in the island. This was followed by a declaration signed by the chief generals choosing Dessalines as Governor-General of Hayti for life, with power to name his successor, and to make peace or war. He was thus invested with arbitrary power, and proceeded to exercise it.

His first act was the one on which his fame rests, and which endears his memory to the Haytians. He in fact decreed that all the French who were convicted or suspected of having connived at the acts of the expelled army, with the exception of certain classes, as priests and doctors, should be massacred; and this applied not only to those suspected of guilt, but to all their wives and children. Fearing that some of his generals, from interest or humanity, might not fully carry out his decree, he made a *tournée* through the different departments, and pitilessly massacred every French man, woman, or child that fell in his way. One can imagine the saturnalia of these liberated slaves enjoying the luxury of shedding the blood of those in whose presence they had formerly trembled; and this without danger; for what resistance could those helpless men, women, and children offer to their savage executioners? Even now one cannot read unmoved the records of those days of horror.

Dessalines, like most of those who surrounded him, was in every way corrupt; he is said to have spared no man in his anger or woman in his lust. He was avaricious, but at the same time he permitted his friends to share in the public income by every illicit means. His government was indeed so corrupt, that even the native historians allow that the administration was distinguished "for plunder, theft, cheating, and smuggling." Dessalines, when he appointed an employé, used to say, "Plumez la poule, mais prenez garde qu'elle ne crie,"—the rule by which the Government service is still regulated.

The tyranny exercised by Dessalines and his generals on all classes made even the former slaves feel that they had changed for the worse. There were no courts to mitigate the cruelty of the hard taskmasters, who on the slightest pretext would order a man or woman to be beaten to death.

In the month of August 1804 news arrived that Buonaparte had raised himself to the imperial throne; Dessalines determined not to be behindhand, and immediately had himself crowned Emperor. His generals were eager that a nobility should be created, but he answered, "I am the only noble in Hayti." As the eastern portion of the island was still occupied by the French, he determined to drive them out; but he was unable to take the city of Santo Domingo, and retired again to the west.

In June 1805 he published a constitution, which was worked out without consulting his generals, and created discontent among them. A conspiracy was organised; a rising in the south followed a visit from Dessalines, where he had given full scope to his brutality, and the insurgents marched forward and seized Port-au-Prince. When the Emperor heard of this movement, he hastened to the capital, fell into an ambuscade, and was shot at Pont Rouge, about half a mile from the city.

The only good quality that Dessalines possessed was a sort of brute courage: in all else he was but an African savage, distinguished even among his countrymen for his superior ferocity and perfidy. He was incapable as an administrator, and treated the public revenue as his own private income. He had concubines in every city, who were entitled to draw on the treasury to meet their extravagance; in fact, the native historians are in truth utterly ashamed of the conduct and civil administration of their national hero.

The death of Dessalines proved the signal of a long civil war. A National Assembly met at Port-au-Prince, voted a constitution prepared by

General Pétion, by which the power of the chief of the state was reduced to a minimum, and then elected Christophe as first President of the republic. He in some respects was another Dessalines, and resented this effort to restrain his authority. He marched on the capital of the west with twelve thousand men, but after various combats failed to capture the city; then retired to Cap Haïtien, and there had a constitution voted which proclaimed him President of Hayti.

The Senate again met in Port-au-Prince in 1806 to elect a President, and their choice fell on Pétion, who, of all the influential men in the west and south, certainly appeared the most deserving. He had scarcely been installed, when his generals began to conspire against him, and the war with Christophe absorbed most of the resources of the country. No event, however, of any great importance occurred till the year 1810, when Rigaud, having escaped from France, arrived in Hayti, and was received with much enthusiasm. Pétion apparently shared this feeling for his old chief, and imprudently gave him the command of the southern department. Rigaud was too vain to remain under the authority of Pétion, his former subordinate, and therefore separated the south from the west. The President would not attempt to prevent this by war, and accepted the situation, so that the island was divided into five states,—Christophe in the north, the old Spanish colony in the east, Pétion in the west, Rigaud in the south, and Goman, a petty African chief, in the extreme west of the southern department.

Christophe in 1811 proclaimed himself King and created a nobility. Rigaud died, and soon after the south rejoined the west, which was menaced by a new invasion from the north. In 1812 Christopher's army advanced to besiege Port-au-Prince; but finding their attacks frustrated, the soldiers, weary of the war, began to desert to Pétion, and had not the King hastened to raise the siege, it is probable his army would have gone over to the enemy.

King Henry I., as he was called, appears then to have abandoned himself to his savage temper, and his cruelties might be compared to those of Dessalines, and prepared the way for that union of the whole island which followed. Pétion, though rather an incapable ruler, was not cruel, and attached the people to his government.

In 1814, the fall of Napoleon brought about peace in Europe, and the French Government hastened to send agents to Hayti to claim submission to the mother country. Pétion refused, whilst offering an indemnity to the colonists; but Christophe, having secured the secret instructions of the French agent, did not hesitate to execute them. These proceedings of the French made the rival chiefs forget their own dissensions and prepare to receive another French expedition. Orders were given that on its appearance off the coast every town and village should be burnt down, and that the inhabitants should retire to the mountains. The old planters were urging their Government to destroy all the inhabitants of Hayti and repeople it from Africa; but a discovery of their projects produced so great an effect in England, that public opinion forced the Congress of Vienna to declare that the slave-trade was for ever abolished.

In 1816 Pétion named a commission to revise the constitution; the principal alterations were to elect a President for life and to add to the Senate a Chamber of Deputies. Pétion, however, did not long enjoy his new dignity; he died in 1818, at the early age of forty-eight, it is said of fever, but the opinion is still prevalent in Hayti that he died of weariness of life, brought on by the loss of all his illusions and the constant public and private annoyances to which he was subject. During his illness he is said to have refused all restoratives, and even to have rejected food. Pétion, though not a great man, sincerely loved his country, and devoted his energies to govern it well; but he was feeble in his measures, and from love of popularity allowed every kind of abuse to flourish in the financial administration. M. Robin, however, says truly that he was "the most popular and humane chief that Hayti ever possessed."

Boyer, through the energetic intervention of the military, was unanimously chosen by the Senate President of the republic, and commenced his long career as chief of the state in March 1818. Though he committed many faults, he appears to have been the most energetic and honest of the series of Haytian rulers. His first care was to establish order in the finances; and if his only errors were not to have erected a statue to his predecessor or founded an hospital for beggars, with which M. Robin appears to reproach him, his friends may still be permitted to admire him. Fortune, or rather his energy, everywhere favoured him. In 1819 he put down the long-neglected insurrection of Goman in the far west, and then prepared to move against King Henry, whose savage rule had alienated the affection even of his own guards. Struck down by apoplexy, the chief of the northern department was deserted by all, and sought refuge from anticipated indignities in suicide.

The north almost unanimously determined to rejoin the rest of the republic, and Boyer marched on Cap Haïtien, to be received there with enthusiasm as the first President of United Hayti.

Christophe was no doubt a very remarkable man, with indomitable energy, who saw the necessity of developing his country, but whose despotic nature cared not for the means, so that the end were attained. In spite of many admitted atrocities, however, there is no doubt he acquired a marked ascendancy over the minds of the people, which even to this day is not completely lost. Discussions still continue as to the rival systems of Pétion and Christophe, but if to secure the greatest happiness to the greatest number be the object of government, the *laisser-aller* system of the former was more suited to Haytian nature than the severity of the latter. As far as material prosperity was concerned, there was no comparison between the two departments, though the productiveness of the north was founded on the liberal application of the stick. On many of the large estates, a certain number of lashes was served out every morning as regularly as the rations.

Boyer's fortune continued. In 1822 Santo Domingo separated from Spain and placed herself under the command of the President of Hayti, who was welcomed in the Dominican capital with every demonstration of joy.

In the next important event of his Presidency, Boyer was not so fortunate. From the year 1814 France had been continually tormenting the Governments of Hayti with the claims of her colonists, and negotiations were carried on by the two parties without much success till 1825, when Baron de Mackau was sent with a fleet to enforce the acceptance of French terms. Though the wording of the royal ordinance was mortifying to the Haytians, and the indemnity demanded (£6,000,000) out of the power of that little country to pay, yet Boyer and the senate thought it better to acquiesce, to avoid the evils of a blockade which would have followed refusal. The indemnity was so enormous, that although it was subsequently reduced to £3,600,000, it has not yet been completely discharged. The terms of the royal ordinance created great indignation amongst the people, and the French Government acting evasively added to the excitement, and a plot was formed to overthrow Boyer. But he showed his usual energy; arrested four conspirators and sent them before a court-martial, which, with thorough Haytian disregard of justice, allowed no defence, as a pure waste of time, and condemned them to death. They were shot under circumstances of even unusual barbarity.

These negotiations with France continued to unsettle the country until 1838. M. Dupetit Thomars had come to Port-au-Prince, and being convinced that Hayti was really unable to pay this great indemnity, induced his Government to reconsider the matter; and a fresh mission was sent, consisting of Baron de Lascases and Captain Baudin. Two treaties were negotiated— one political, by which France acknowledged the complete independence of the republic; the second financial, by which the balance to be paid of the indemnity was reduced to £2,400,000. As thirty years were allowed for this payment, in annual instalments on an average of £80,000, no doubt Hayti could have paid it had the country remained quiet. The acknowledgment of this debt, however, was seized on by the political enemies of Boyer to undermine his position, and the cry was raised that he had sold the country to the whites. The continued necessity of sending French naval expeditions to enforce the payment of the arrears of this debt has been injurious to the interests of all Europeans, has increased the unpopularity of foreigners, and helped to support the policy of those who wish to keep the white man out of the country. Among the people, the popular song

"Blancs français viennent demander l'argent"

implies that they have unfairly made use of their naval power in order to extract money which was not due to them from a people incapable of effectual resistance. This wretched debt to France has been the cause of half the misfortunes of Hayti.

The Government of General Boyer had certainly the merit of preserving tranquillity, and if ever population should have increased in Hayti, it was during this tranquil epoch, when for above twenty years no blood was shed in warlike operations, and very little in repressing conspiracies. In 1825 England formally acknowledged the republic of Hayti by entering into relations with her, sending Mr. Mackenzie as Consul-General. His reports and writings drew considerable attention to the country.

In March 1836 Dr. England negotiated a concordat by which the Pope was acknowledged head of the Haytian Church, with the power of confirming the nomination of bishops. However, this arrangement had little practical effect, as the clergy remained without control, and were a scandal to every true Catholic.

I am quite unable to reconcile the reports made of the state of affairs in Hayti at this time. After a twenty years' peace, the country is described as in a state of ruin, without trade or resources of any kind; with peculation and jobbery paramount in all the public offices; an army supposed to consist of 45,000 men, according to the budget; in reality few soldiers, but many officers, among whom the appropriations were divided. I feel as if I were reading of more modern times instead of the halcyon days of Haytian history.

Another of the evils which arose from the indemnity question was the special position which it gave to French agents, who, even after the independence of the republic had been recognised, affected to treat Hayti as a dependency until all the debt should have been paid. The most pretentious of these agents at this time threw the whole country into commotion on account of an article in a newspaper, and continued to harass the Government on every possible occasion with his absurd pretensions.

The close of Boyer's career was as unfortunate as its commencement had been the reverse. To the humiliations inflicted by the French Consul-General was now added the necessity of saluting the Spanish flag under threat of bombardment. Throughout Haytian history these affairs are continually recurring; no people are more ready to insult foreigners, nor more humiliated by the necessary reparation.

The greatest calamity, however, was the earthquake of 1842, which injured every city in the northern department, and almost annihilated Cap Haïtien. I have referred to this event in a previous chapter, when the peasantry from the plains and mountains, and the officers and soldiers of the garrison, vied with each other in plundering the city, whilst 5000 of their countrymen were buried in the ruins, the cries of many of whom could for days be heard imploring that help which could readily have been afforded, but whose supplications were unheeded by the brutal populace.

This calamity in the north was followed by another in Port-au-Prince, where a large portion of the city was burnt down. These extensive fires appear to be incendiary, as they almost always occur at moments of political disturbance.

The humiliations inflicted on President Boyer by the French and Spaniards, and the discontent that followed the great losses in the northern department, encouraged the ill-affected, and early in 1843 an insurrection broke out under Hérard-Rivière, a fair mulatto. After a brief show of resistance, Boyer abdicated in March, thus closing a Presidency of twenty-five years.

General Boyer showed considerable talent during his administration, but he was essentially narrow-minded, and full of prejudice against foreigners. During the last ten years of his rule he had conceived the project of expelling them from Hayti in a legal manner by refusing any fresh licenses to trade; but though he in some measure succeeded, he increased the discontent against him, as his countrymen are only capable of conducting with success a retail business, and require foreigners for the larger operations of commerce. Boyer had the rare quality of being honest, and left in the treasury, on his departure, the sum of £200,000, the first and last chief who was ever guilty of so unaccountable a weakness. His time is still remembered as one of repose, and the troubles which followed his departure soon made even his enemies regret his fall. Her Majesty's corvette "Scylla" had the honour of conducting General Boyer and his family to Jamaica. It will be noticed hereafter that almost every President has died prematurely, or claimed the hospitality of a foreign ship of war to bear him into exile.

When the popular army entered Port-au-Prince, it was hailed as the precursor of better days, but scarcely had a Provisional Government been organised than the blacks began to conspire, as they wanted a President of their own colour. General Dalzon went so far as to propose that they should put to death every mulatto. However, the latter had now the upper hand, and the general was taken, and disappeared from the scene.

The most serious result of the overthrow of General Boyer was the separation of the eastern end of the island and its formation into a distinct republic. The brutality of the Haytian officers and soldiers who garrisoned that part of the country no doubt hastened this secession. I have often listened to President Geffrard when he was describing his own conduct and that of others towards the Dominicans, and my only wonder is that they did not separate before.

On December 30, 1843, the Constituent Assembly finished their new constitution, and then elected General Hérard-Rivière President of Hayti; contemporary accounts say "with much enthusiasm." He soon found it was not a bed of roses. M. Barrot arrived with the object of obtaining a monopoly of the Haytian trade for France, by relieving the Government of the immediate payment of the instalments due on the indemnity. But the President was more anxious to subdue the Dominicans than to negotiate, and on their proclaiming their independence in February 1844, he collected an army, it is said of from 24,000 to 30,000 men, and marched to attack them. The numbers must be greatly exaggerated; but whatever they were, they did nothing, and after many skirmishes they only penetrated as far as Azua, and there the President halted, complaining that he was harassed by French intrigues in favour of the Dominicans.

How Boyer must have smiled when he heard, within a twelvemonth of his departure, that the Government of his successor was considered more arbitrary and was more unpopular than his own. In April, after four short months of power, Hérard-Rivière was deposed, amidst even greater enthusiasm than marked his accession, and banished. General Guerrier was elected in his place, and died after a twelvemonth of debauchery. In his political acts he appears to have managed fairly well, and he had to contend against the French agents, who were working for either a protectorate, or, if that were not possible, commercial advantages for their country. They made themselves so unpopular that their officers and men were insulted in the streets, and their almost open support of the Dominican revolt rendered them obnoxious to the Government.

As the popular wish for a black President had been unmistakably expressed at the election of Guerrier, an incapable black of the name of

Pierrot was chosen to succeed him; but his Government was upset in less than a twelvemonth, and President Riché, another black, was chosen by the troops at St. Marc, who did not wish to march against the Dominicans (March 1, 1846). In almost every encounter the Haytian troops were defeated by a handful of their enemies; they had no heart in the war, and the exaggerated stories of the peculiarly objectionable mutilations from which their prisoners suffered, and the arrival of some of these unfortunates, spread a panic in the Haytian army, and they would not march!

Riché has left a very good reputation as a President, which may partly be accounted for by his judicious choice of ministers. He had Celigny-Ardruin and Dupuy among them, and both these men were considered capable administrators, and both will again appear upon the scene.

The black mob in the south rose in arms against Riché, but after some resistance the movement was suppressed. Unfortunately for the country, this Presidency did not last a twelvemonth, as Riché died on the 27th February 1847. He was sincerely regretted, as, although an ignorant man, he was capable of choosing good advisers. He left the country perfectly tranquil, with reduced expenditure, order in the finances, and his firm hand had been felt throughout the republic. He protected foreigners, without whom he saw there was no prosperity possible. During the time of Guerrier and Pierrot there was a perfect mania for public employment, and every officer appeared to wish to live in luxury at the expense of the state; but Riché's prudent management checked this infatuation. His Government restored the constitution of 1816, which, though it included Article 7, directed against foreigners acquiring real property, yet assured freedom of worship. He too is said to have died at an advanced age from the effects of debauchery.

On March 2 the enlightened Ministers of the late General Riché chose as President of the republic a black captain of the guards of the name of Soulouque. He was an ignorant, stupid man, completely unfit for any public employment, but it is said that he was chosen as an instrument that could be easily handled by his Ministers. He was known to be given up to fetish worship, and soon after his election he began to fear that some *wanga* or poison might be given him. He put aside Riché's Ministers, to supply their place with nonentities, and advanced to the first rank the most ignorant blacks of the army. He excited hatred against the men of colour, whom he feared for their intelligence; but, alarmed by his growing unpopularity, he dismissed his incapables and restored Dupuy and others to power.

Soulouque had placed in command of his guards a general of the name of Similien, who was the black the most notorious for his hatred of the mulattoes that he could find. During the absence of the President in the north, this man refused to obey the orders of the Government, seized the palace, and threatened to massacre the mulattoes, but this result was deferred for a short time.

A curious affair occurred towards the end of 1847. A senator of the name of Courtois had written an article in a newspaper at which the President took offence; though Courtois was a scurrilous writer who had been previously tried for an insolent article, but who had been triumphantly acquitted when it was found he only insulted the foreign community, and had on this last occasion written some reasonable comments on the attitude assumed by General Similien and his followers. The Senate, to please the President, sentenced Courtois to a month's imprisonment. But when Soulouque heard of this, he went into one of his ungovernable passions, assembled his generals, called out his troops, and condemned Courtois to death, and ordered the immediate execution of the culprit. The sentence would certainly have been carried into effect had not our agents, Consul Ussher, Vice-Consul Wyke, and the French Consul-General Raybaud interfered, and persuaded Soulouque to pardon him; he was, however, banished. And Senator Courtois, who owed his life to foreigners, had spent his best energies in abusing them!

Throughout the spring of 1848 an uneasy feeling appears to have pervaded the country that some calamity was about to take place. On the 9th April the rabble assembled round the palace and demanded that the respectable Ministry then in power should be dismissed. As this movement was evidently encouraged by Soulouque, they resigned; but all were assembled at the palace on the 16th April, when suddenly the guards, who had been drawn up before it, opened fire upon the crowd in the galleries and rooms, and a *sauve qui peut* followed. General Dupuy told me that in a moment he comprehended that a massacre of the mulattoes was meant; he sprang on a horse, and dashed for the high iron railings that surrounded the palace gardens, jumped down, and although closely pursued, managed to get over these high rails, how he knew not, and escaped. Celigny-Ardruin, less fortunate, was severely wounded, and as he lay on a sofa was reviled by the President, who said he should be shot. Consul Ussher was present in the palace during this scene, and acted admirably, with his colleague of France, in trying to save those who had not been able to put themselves under their direct protection. He ran the greatest personal dangers, and narrowly escaped being shot by the excited soldiery.

From the palace the massacring passed on to the town, where every mulatto who showed himself was shot; many assembled in groups to defend themselves, but only hastened their fate, whilst hundreds ran for refuge to the Consulates. The news spread to the southern department, and murder and plunder followed in every district, and the property of the mulattoes was given to the flames. A few black generals who tried to preserve order were shot as accomplices of the mulattoes in their supposed conspiracy. The President was delighted with the energy of his supporters in the south, and went in person to thank them. On his return he pardoned six innocent men, and thus gained a little popularity among his cowed adversaries. It is pleasant to know how our acting Consul Wyke worked to save those menaced with death. But even he had little influence over the faithless President, who would grant a pardon at his intercession, and then shoot the pardoned prisoner. After General Desmaril and Edmond Felix had been executed in 1849 in the market-place, and died after receiving twenty discharges, Soulouque went with his staff to inspect their mangled bodies and gloat over the scene. Naturally Celigny-Ardruin did not escape; he was shot, but Wyke was enabled to save many others and send them out of the country. In fact, the chiefs of the mulatto party who escaped death had all to go into exile.

In January 1849, I may notice, Soulouque had abolished the Ministry and named as Secretary-General Dufrène, and as Minister of Finance Salomon, the present President of Hayti; and in April, invigorated by his massacre of the mulattoes, invaded Santo Domingo with a numerous army. He had some success at Azua and St. Jean, but he was surprised at Ocoa by General Santana, and the whole Haytian army fled before 500 Dominicans. And these were the descendants of the men who fought so bravely against the French. It was after this defeat that Soulouque returned to his capital, and, full of anger at his discomfiture, committed the judicial murders previously recorded.

All black chiefs have a hankering after the forms as well as the substance of despotic power, and Soulouque was no exception to the rule. He therefore decided to follow in the footsteps of Dessalines, and was elected Emperor, August 26, 1849. A fresh constitution was naturally required, and this was a strange medley of republican and aristocratic institutions. Soulouque did not disappoint his generals, and created a nobility: four princes and fifty-nine dukes headed the list, to be followed by innumerable marquises, counts, and barons. This contented the chiefs, and quiet reigned for a short time.

In 1850, England, France, and the United States united to oppose diplomatically the war with Santo Domingo; during these long negotiations the Haytian Government appeared influenced by the conviction that to concede independence to Santo Domingo would introduce the foreign element into the island, and, by the development of the eastern province, end in robbing Hayti of its independence. A year's truce was obtained, however, in October 1851. The negotiations were admirably conducted by our agent, Consul-General Ussher. One of the difficulties against which the diplomatists had to contend was the personal feelings of the Emperor, which had been outraged by the Dominicans calling him a *rey de farsa*, an *opera bouffé* king. There is no doubt but that they really did look for assistance abroad, owing to the poverty of the country arising from their eight years' war with Hayti, and the internal dissensions which always follow national financial pressure.

On the 18th April 1852 Soulouque was crowned Emperor under the title of Faustin I. He had no fear of exciting discontent by lavish expenditure. He paid £2000 for his crown, and spent £30,000 for the rest of the paraphernalia. He was liberal to his nobility, and had few internal troubles after he shot his Grand Judge Francisque and four companions for supposed conspiracy, and had condemned Prince Bobo for some imprudent words.

Soulouque, it is fair to say, gained the good opinion of many of our countrymen on account of the protection which he generally accorded to foreigners, and a supposed predilection for the English, which the manly and conciliatory conduct of our agents had greatly fostered, and which contrasted with that of the French agents, who brought a fleet to Port-au-Prince under Admiral Duquesne to threaten to bombard the capital (1853). No events occurred worthy of record, except the interminable negotiations to induce the Emperor to conclude peace with Santo Domingo, which occupied 1853 and 1854.

The year 1855 was enlivened by a very comic quarrel between the Haytian Government and the Spanish agent. The Emperor had decided that every one that passed the palace should show his respect for his office by raising his hat. It appears that a Spanish employé did not observe this formality, and was stopped by the guard, who insisted on his complying with it. The Emperor, attracted by the altercation, put his head out of a window of the palace and cried, "Qui moun-ça sacré f— — blanc qui veut pas saluer mon palais, f— —?" The Spaniard had a long discussion with the Haytian Foreign Office, and would not accept the denial by the Emperor of his having used these words—in fact, there was much ado about nothing.

In spite of all the efforts of the foreign agents, Soulouque in December 1855 marched with all his forces to attack the Dominicans—those under his personal command numbering, it is said, 15,000 men. But in January 1856 he was disgracefully beaten by the enemy. His troops fled at the first volley, and losing their way in the woods, fell into the hands of their enemies, who did not spare them. The Emperor, furious at his defeat, shot several superior officers for treachery or cowardice, and then returned with the remains of his army to his capital, where he was received in mournful silence, amid the scarcely-concealed murmurs of the people; the muttered curses of the women at the loss of their relatives being particularly remarked.

This dissatisfaction could not escape the notice of the Emperor, and to assuage his outraged feelings he shot sixteen men in Les Cayes, amid such circumstances of barbarity that even Haytians of all classes were moved by feelings of indignation and disgust. But Soulouque cared not; he shot three more and condemned above fifty to his dungeons, where little more was heard of them; in fact, they are said to have been beaten or starved to death.

After renewed efforts on the part of foreign agents, a truce of two years was negotiated with Santo Domingo. The fall of the empire was now a mere matter of time. The people were disgusted with the losses incurred during the last invasion of the eastern province, which had been more disastrous than all the former attacks; the finances were in the greatest disorder; peculation and pillage were the order of the day; a great incendiary fire in Port-au-Prince occurred in 1857, and in 1858 heavy commercial failures followed a wild speculation in bills and coffee. Discontent was rife, and all turned their eyes to General Geffrard as the only man that could rescue them from this disastrous condition of affairs. He had gained great popularity in the army during the last invasion, when he commanded the rear-guard, and it was acknowledged that his bravery and devotion had saved the remnants of the troops from destruction. The Haytians had had four black rulers in succession, and thought they could not be less prosperous under the rule of an intelligent mulatto.

The Emperor kept a watch on Geffrard, but he behaved with so much prudence that there was no excuse to imprison him. At last, in December 1858, the order for his arrest was given; but warned by a friend, he embarked during the night in an open boat with a few followers, and on his arrival at the town of Gonaives proclaimed the deposition of the Emperor and the re-establishment of the republic. He was received "with enthusiasm," and in a few days all the north and north-west adhered to the revolution, and he began his march on Port-au-Prince with an army of about 6000 men.

On hearing of this insurrection, the Emperor moved out to meet his opponent, but with only 3000 discontented men, who, after a skirmish with the insurgents, retreated, and Soulouque re-entered Port-au-Prince with his forces reduced by desertion to 1500. Finding that the whole country had declared against him, the Emperor abdicated on the 15th January 1859, and retired for safety to the French Legation.

On his first arrival on the 10th, Soulouque, furious with his rival, ordered Madame Geffrard and her daughters to be put to death, but yielded to the intercession of our agents. However, the populace of all colours were so united against the ex-Emperor and some of his chiefs, that fears were entertained that they would break into the French Legation and kill all the refugees. The attitude of the tumultuous crowd became so menacing, and the indifference of the Haytian guard so marked, that M. Mellines appealed to our acting Consul-General Byron for protection.

Hearing of the danger to which all foreigners were exposed in Port-au-Prince, the captain of an English transport, the "Melbourne," with the consent of Captain M'Crea, who commanded a detachment of artillery on board, steered for the capital and arrived at a critical moment. Seeing that the French Legation was about to be invaded, Byron took the bold resolution of calling on Captain M'Crea to land his artillerymen and protect the refugees. This they did, and, strange to say, the mob, instead of resenting this armed interference, were delighted at the magnificent appearance of the men and their perfect discipline, and cheered them more than ever they cheered one of their own regiments. This movement saved the Emperor; he and his followers were subsequently embarked on board the "Melbourne," and followed Boyer and Hérard-Rivière to Jamaica.

Too much credit cannot be given to this bold proceeding of Mr. Byron and of Captain M'Crea; it had an admirable effect, and for years after, the landing of these fine men was a subject of conversation among the people. All felt that more had been saved than the French Legation and the lives of the refugees, as once pillage had commenced it would have been difficult to prevent it spreading through the town.

Thus closed the ignoble reign of Soulouque, one of the most contemptible that ever existed even in Hayti. Peculation on the one hand, and cruelty and cowardice on the other, marked almost every event of these disastrous twelve years of misgovernment.

When ignorance ceased to govern, vanity appeared to follow. Judging after the events, it seems clear that General Geffrard might have avoided many of the difficulties of his Presidency, had he called good men to his councils and listened to their advice. He, however, would do all himself, and treated his Ministers as if they were but head clerks. He really thought he knew more than any of those who surrounded him, and perhaps he did.

The revolution was conducted with exemplary moderation, and the great and small plunderers of the preceding reign succeeded in securing their ill-gotten wealth; for though the properties of certain persons were sequestrated, it had little practical effect. I have seen a trustworthy paper of the amounts taken by the Emperor and his followers, and they were so enormous as to surpass belief.

Geffrard's difficulties were great, as he had to conciliate the black party and appoint as Ministers certain foremost generals of that colour, and their ignorance and stupidity were almost beyond anything that can be conceived; and this is the President's best excuse for having tried to govern himself. And yet the extreme section of the party was not satisfied, and soon after Geffrard's advent to power began to conspire against him, and to raise the cry that he was about to sell the country to the whites. As soon as a coloured chief shows the slightest desire to modify any legislation hostile to foreigners, this cry is raised, and prevents many improvements.

To show of what a negro conspirator is capable, I must enter into a few particulars of what was called the conspiracy of General Prophète. In September of 1859, the year of Geffrard's advent to power, a section of the blacks determined to murder him. They knew that he was a most affectionate father, and accustomed to visit every evening Madame Blanfort, his newly-married daughter; they therefore laid an ambush for him behind a ruined wall that skirted the street that led to her house. The usual hour having passed for the evening visit, the conspirators began to fear that their project might fail that night and be discovered, so they moved quietly towards Madame Blanfort's residence, and looking through the window, saw the young bride seated reading, evidently awaiting her father's arrival. The conspirators held a hurried consultation, and decided to murder the daughter, in the expectation that Geffrard, on hearing what had occurred, would rush out. They therefore returned to the window, and a negro named Sarron raised his blunderbuss, fired at the girl, and killed her on the spot. Geffrard heard the shot, and rushing to the palace door, would have fallen into the ambush had not some friends seized and detained him.

Fortunately these conspirators were as stupid as they were brutal, and the whole of them were taken. The chief of the political conspiracy was allowed to depart, whilst the others, to the number of sixteen, were shot. It was stated at the time that too many suffered, but they were all equally guilty, for although all had not been consulted as to murdering the daughter, all meant to assassinate the father. These conspirators were most of them aides-de-camp to the President, and belonged to what are called the best families of the capital. What is a President to do with such people?

In March 1860 a concordat was signed with the See of Rome, an account of which as amended is given in another chapter. In September there was a fresh conspiracy to murder Geffrard, in which a man named Florosin was implicated, and therefore the plot was called after him. In the following year Hayti reaped the fruit of her obstinacy in refusing to acknowledge the independence of the eastern province. Discouraged by the continual state of tension in their relations with the black republic, the Dominicans decided to return to their allegiance to Spain, and in March 1861 Santo Domingo was declared a Spanish colony, with the Dominican General Santana as first Governor-General. Geffrard thus found himself face to face with a new danger, as every question remained unsettled, including the important one of boundaries.

The annexation to Spain had been brought about by Santana and his party, but was opposed by another faction, who crossed over into Hayti, and there being secretly furnished with arms and money by the authorities, invaded the Spanish colony and commenced a guerilla warfare. They were beaten, and twenty-one being taken, were summarily shot by Santana.

Proofs having then been obtained of the complicity of the Haytian Government in this movement, Spain determined to punish these intermeddlers. A fleet was sent to Port-au-Prince, with orders to demand an indemnity of £40,000, to be paid in forty-eight hours, and a salute which was not to be returned. The money was not to be had at so short a notice, and the discontented blacks threatened to upset the Government and massacre the whites if a salute were fired first.

At that time the chief representative of the foreign powers was Mr. Byron, our acting Consul-General, and on him fell the sole responsibility of effecting an amicable arrangement and preventing the threatened bombardment. He saw the Spanish admiral Rubalcava, of whom he ever spoke in the highest terms, explained the difficulties of Geffrard's position, and obtained important concessions—first, as to the payment of the indemnity, which was ultimately reduced to £5000, and, second, that the Haytian salute should be returned. He then went to the palace, smiled at the fears of the rabble, and gave the resolute advice to brave them and fire the salute. This was done, and all passed off as well as he had predicted. Throughout their history, the Haytians have been thus beholden to the agents of England and France.

In November 1861, General Legros *père* conspired to upset the Government, but these mild plotters were only banished or imprisoned. This abortive movement was followed (1862) by an attempted insurrection of the Salomon family in the south. This conspiracy, the third in which they were accused of being engaged, was a complete fiasco, but it cost the lives of fourteen of their members.

One of the promises made by the new Government was a reform in the finances and a reduction of useless expenditure; but Geffrard's incapable or corrupt Ministers had not fulfilled that promise. The Chambers were naturally curious as to the disappearance of millions of dollars without any explanation being forthcoming, and forced two incapables to resign, and General Dupuy, the Minister of Riché, was summoned from London to take charge of the finances. He was a very intelligent man, quite worthy of the post, and his appointment inspired confidence; but the Opposition in the Chambers continued their attacks on the Government, and at last Geffrard was forced to dissolve and order fresh elections. There can be no doubt that so many abuses were protected as to justify much discontent, but the Opposition might have been more moderate considering the difficulties of the situation, the insurrection in the east against the Spaniards, and the continued conspiracies of the blacks.

Geffrard and Dupuy were both anxious to modify Article 7 of the constitution, aimed against foreigners, but the proposition was so badly received that it was withdrawn.

Another rising (May 1863) of the Legros family followed in Gonaives. As they had been the principal instruments of the revolution in favour of Geffrard, their defection can only be accounted for by unsatisfied ambition and the desire to secure the spoils of office. It failed, and eight were shot.

In September 1863 Monseigneur Testard de Cosquer was named Archbishop of Port-au-Prince. He was one of the most agreeable men I have ever met, remarkably eloquent, and of fine presence; he did not, however, arrive at the capital until June of the following year. Disgusted with what was passing in his country, General Dupuy resigned his position as Minister of Finance and Foreign Affairs, and was succeeded by M. Auguste Elie, than whom a better choice could not have been made.

The year 1864 was distinguished for its conspiracies. In May a Colonel Narcisse denounced four coloured men of the best position in the capital as being engaged in a plot. The proofs of an active conspiracy were wanting. As I have given details of the trial in another chapter, I need only say that they were condemned to death, but their sentence was commuted at the intercession of the diplomatic corps. In July there was a conspiracy at Cap Haïtien by General Longuefosse, but the people not joining, he was taken and shot, with three of his companions. This was followed by another, in which Salnave, afterwards a revolutionary President of Hayti, first made his appearance in rather an interesting manner. General Philippeaux, Minister of War, had been sent by Geffrard to Cap Haïtien to restore order after Longuefosse's abortive plot, when a conspiracy was formed in an artillery corps to murder Philippeaux, and Salnave was chosen to carry it into execution. One evening the Minister of War was sitting playing cards in a verandah, when Salnave, ensconced behind a neighbouring tree, raised his carbine and fired at him; the ball struck Philippeaux above the temple and glanced off. Not even the solid skull of a black could have resisted the bullet, had not the Minister, at the moment when Salnave fired, slightly turned his head.

I may notice that in 1865 Spain abandoned Santo Domingo, and the Dominican republic was restored. If ever the true history be written of that temporary resuscitation of a colony, Spaniards themselves will be astonished at the revelations of iniquity and fraud that brought about the revolution against them.

The year 1865 was an unfortunate one for Hayti. First a great fire burnt down three hundred and fifty houses in the best part of the capital; then there was a movement in the south; then one in the north, where Salnave, invading that department from Santo Domingo, found all ready to receive him. The regiments joined him or dispersed; but the rapid movement of Geffrard's troops under Generals Morisset and Barthélemy, both of whom were killed fighting, disconcerted the conspirators, and they were soon driven from the country districts and forced to take refuge in Cap Haïtien. Had not many of the chiefs of Geffrard's army been traitors to his cause, the whole affair might have been over in a month. A siege commenced, which appeared likely to endure long, when an incident occurred which forced on foreign intervention.

Salnave was a bold, unscrupulous man, who had been put forward by some discontented deputies and others to do their work; but his main reliance was on the mob. Those of Geffrard's friends who could not escape from the town took refuge with the Consuls, and the English and American naval officers had constantly to interfere, even by landing men, to prevent the violation of the Consulates. Captain Heneage, of H.M.S. "Lily," conspicuously distinguished himself. At last Geffrard left the capital to command the army, but he found he could do little among his intriguing officers: he, however, certainly showed want of dash on this occasion.

Then came the "Bulldog" incident. Captain Wake had excited the ire of the insurgents by protecting a British vessel; and to show their anger, under the direction of Delorme, Salnave's principal adviser, they rushed down to our Consulate, and took by force certain persons who were under the protection of our flag. The "Bulldog" steamed into harbour to obtain redress, and ran aground. A combat ensued, and finding he could not get his vessel off, Captain Wake blew her up, and retired with the crew in his boats.

All the persons taken from our Consulate had in the meantime been murdered. On hearing of these transactions, I went up in H.M.S. "Galatea" with the "Lily," and being unable to obtain any adequate satisfaction, the outer forts were bombarded. Geffrard's army rushed in, and the insurrection was at an end. Salnave and followers escaped in the United States ship "Desoto," after leaving orders to burn down the town, which his men only partly effected.

I may notice that the right of asylum under foreign flags is considered so sacred in Hayti, that it was once introduced as an article of the constitution. All parties are equally interested in its observance, as only thus can they hope to escape the first fury of their adversaries, and give time for passions to cool.

If 1865 was a disastrous year for Hayti, 1866 was worse. A great fire broke out in Port-au-Prince, and eight hundred houses are said to have been destroyed. I again noticed the apathy of the negroes, whether official or otherwise. They came and looked on, but did nothing either to check the flames or arrest the incendiaries. Whilst we were working to save our Legation from the fire, which was already scorching its walls, my servant called my attention to some negroes that had entered with torches ill concealed under their coats. I had to seize a revolver and hold it to a man's head before I could force them to retire. Had our brick house taken fire, they knew the rest of the town must go. Few except the Europeans cared to exert themselves, and when they brought out a fire-engine the mob instantly cut the hose and gave themselves up to pillage. The French *chargé d'affaires* asked a man why he did not assist in putting out a fire burning before him? His answer was, "My house is already burned: why should I aid others?"

Geffrard could not but notice, in his opening speech to the Chambers, that the northern insurrection had created so great an expenditure that all progress was checked; but it had no effect. Another effort at revolution was made at Gonaives, where the mob plundered and burnt about fifty houses, to be followed by further troubles and incendiary fires at Cap Haïtien, Port-au-Prince, and St. Marc. The arsenal in the capital was blown up in September; two hundred houses were overthrown, and the guard killed, besides many of the inhabitants. One little boy whom I knew had his ear taken off by a piece of shell without further injury. During these occurrences, bands of negroes were wandering through the south burning and pillaging, unchecked by the local authorities. It was asked, how could a people exist under such circumstances? But people must eat; the majority do not join in these disorders, and all the women and children work. The following years showed to what a country can submit from the perverse conduct of interested politicians.

It was now evident that Geffrard must give up power, as, rightly or wrongly, people were dissatisfied with him, find wanted a change. In

February 1867 there was a hostile movement on the part of some companies of Geffrard's favourite troops, the tirailleurs, the only disciplined battalions that I ever saw in Hayti; and though this was suppressed by their companions, the Government was irretrievably shaken. The comparatively bad crops of 1865 and 1866 were said to be the fault of the authorities, and no amnesties or changes in the Ministry could satisfy the discontented. Geffrard determined therefore to abdicate, and on March 13, 1867, he embarked for Jamaica. He had convoked the Senate for the 16th in order to give over the reins of power to them, but his timid friends persuaded him to go at once, as the north was in insurrection. The Spanish *chargé d'affaires* was with him throughout these scenes, and Geffrard's last words were, "Poor country! what a state of anarchy will follow my departure!"

In my chapter on the Mulattoes, I have given a sketch of Geffrard, and I need not repeat it here. I was not blind to his faults, but of all the rulers of Hayti he was certainly the most enlightened, and the most thoroughly devoted to his country. Had he been as perfect a ruler as the world could produce, he would never have satisfied his countrymen. The blacks wanted a black, the mulattoes wanted any one else, so that there was a change. And yet I believe the mass of the people cared little except for tranquillity.

A committee was formed to revise the constitution, but Salnave had landed in Cap Haïtien, assumed power, and proceeded to exercise it. He arrested some chiefs of the negroes dwelling in the Black Mountains, and instantly shot them; their friends took up arms, and, under the name of the "Cacos," were a thorn in the side of the new *régime*. He then marched on Port-au-Prince, seized the Government, and arrested General Montas, who commanded in the north under Geffrard. Tired of the delays of a Constituent Assembly, he sent a mob to frighten them. They took the hint, voted the constitution the next day, and, *l'epée à la gorge*, elected Salnave President of Hayti, June 16, 1867. In July a treaty was signed between Hayti and Santo Domingo, thus ending the long war.

The Chambers met in the autumn, and Madame Montas presented a petition on the subject of the imprisonment of her husband. On some deputies insisting on an explanation, Delorme, the Chief Minister of Salnave, sprang on the table and denounced these deputies as enemies of Government. Pistol-shots were fired; Salnave advanced at the head of his guards, and the Assembly dispersed. Riots followed. The Government attempted to arrest five prominent members of the Opposition, but they escaped and returned home to their constituents, and constitutional government ceased to exist.

The movement of the Cacos in the Black Mountains now began to alarm the Government, and Salnave started for the north to put himself at the head of the army operating against the insurgents. There were many skirmishes, that at Mombin Crochu being the most important, where Salnave lost heavily.

I do not think it necessary to do more than briefly notice the events of Salnave's Presidency of thirty months. It was one long civil war. Disgusted at the treatment of their deputies, the towns began to declare against the Government. The uprising was accelerated by the meeting of the Chambers being postponed and Salnave being declared Dictator. In April 1868, Nissage-Saget took up arms in St. Marc; the south was in movement and the insurgents marching towards the capital, where a crowd of young men armed with swordsticks and pocket-pistols made a feeble attempt at insurrection, but dispersed at the first fire. In the midst of this commotion Salnave came into the harbour with five hundred men, to whom he gave permission to plunder the Rue de Frentfort, where the principal retail dealers live. The phrase of their colonel on this occasion has become a proverb: "Mes enfans, pillez en bon ordre." Only the vigorous remonstrances of the diplomatic corps prevented further outrages. Delorme, accused by Salnave of having shown weakness whilst in charge of the Government during his absence, retired from office and left the country.

The insurgent armies closed in round Port-au-Prince, but as the town did not capitulate at their martial aspect, they did nothing, whilst the garrison was only waiting for the excuse of an attack in order to disperse. This delay was fatal; the chiefs, instead of confronting the common enemy, were quarrelling as to the choice of the future President, each thinking himself the most worthy, when the negroes of the mountains, encouraged by the Government, rose in arms to attack the towns, and forced the besieging army to retire to protect their own families and property. These bands of negroes, under the name of "Piquets," were only formidable from their numbers, but the injuries they did in the south have not been repaired to this day. The insurgents raised the siege of the capital in August; and in September, to prevent further dissensions, Nissage-Saget was chosen President for the north at St. Marc, and Domingue at Les Cayes for the south.

The year 1869 was the most disastrous I have known in Haytian history. Fighting was going on in every district. In the north the insurgents were besieging Cap Haïtien; in the south the Government was vainly attacking Jacmel, Jérémie, and Les Cayes. In the beginning of the year President Salnave had the advantage of commanding the seas with his steamers, and surrounding Les Cayes on every side, he vigorously pressed the siege. When it was about to fall, General Monplaisir-Pierre assembled a small army around him, cut his way through the besieging forces, and arrived just in time to save Domingue and his Government, who were preparing to embark for Jamaica. This was one of the few gallant actions of the war.

Another was General Brice's splendid defence of Jérémie when attacked by superior forces and bombarded by vessels purchased by Salnave in America.

In July 1869 the insurgents obtained a couple of steamers, and the aspect of the war changed. They were enabled thus to relieve the south by capturing the vessels that blockaded Les Cayes; and then, returning north, excited the fears of the Government partisans. Gonaives surrendered to the insurgents under conditions, and General Chevalier arrived with the garrison to increase the confusion at the capital. The Ministry resigned under his threats, and only the sudden arrival of Salnave from the south prevented Chevalier from usurping his place.

From this time forward the fortunes of Salnave paled. Cap Haïtien surrendered to the insurgents; the President's army under Chevalier besieging Jacmel went over to the enemy; and suddenly, on the 18th December 1870, the insurgents made the most gallant dash of the whole war. Before daylight, two vessels laden with troops steamed quietly into the harbour, surprised a new gunboat belonging to the Government, and then immediately landed about a thousand men. The leaders of this expedition were Generals Brice and Boisrond-Canal. It was a splendid *coup*, as Salnave's garrison consisted of over three thousand men. Some sharp fighting occurred, and the insurgents could just hold their own, when General Turenne-Carrié arrived by land with strong reinforcements, and rendered the combat more equal.

Whilst the fighting was going on, a strong appeal was made by chiefs of both parties to the diplomatic corps to interfere and try to save the town, which was menaced with destruction. The representatives of France, England, and the United States therefore went to the palace, but could do no more than effect a truce till the next morning.

Salnave, however, hoping to surprise his enemies during this truce, made a sudden onslaught on them; but after about two hours' fighting, his men were repulsed with heavy loss. Early in the morning, the gunboat that had been surprised in harbour opened fire upon the palace under the direction of the insurgents, and its heavy shell falling in the courtyard began to disperse the garrison, when another pitched on the palace ignited a small powder-magazine, and a severe explosion took place. As great stores of powder existed there, every one near fled. Salnave and his troops retired to the mountains *viâ* La Coupe, and soon after another terrific explosion took place that shook the town, followed by one still more severe. Fortunately the fire did not reach the great magazine, or few houses would have resisted the concussion.

Before leaving, Salnave ordered fire to be set to the town to retard pursuit. Our men were disembarked from H.M.S. "Defence" under the present admiral, Noel Salmon, and greatly contributed to prevent the spread of the flames; but it was calculated that at least a thousand houses and huts were destroyed.

I have passed rapidly over the events of this year, but it was certainly the most trying I have ever known. The diplomatic corps was continually forced to interfere to check the arbitrary conduct of the authorities, who seized our ships, arrested our subjects, insulted us in the streets, and to awe the disaffected employed bands of villanous negroes and negresses to parade the town, who murdered those selected by their enemies, wantonly killing a young Frenchman and many others.

Nothing was saved from them, neither our mail-bags nor our property. Fortunately we were well supported by our naval officers, and we were thoroughly well backed by the French marine. Admiral Mequet and Captain De Varannes of the "D'Estrés" were conspicuous by their friendly feeling; and as Admiral Phillimore was at that time commodore in Jamaica, the English were sure of receiving all the support that it was in his power to give. I think we owed our lives to the aid we received from the presence of our ships, commanded by Captains Kelly, M'Crea, Glynn, Murray Aynesley, Carnegie, Lowther, Allington, and many others.

I may conclude my account of Salnave by saying that he attempted to reach Santo Domingo city, but was stopped on the frontiers by the Dominican insurgent Cabral, who took him and his followers prisoners, and sent them to Port-au-Prince. Six chiefs were shot as insurgents taken with arms in their hands, whilst Salnave was brought into the capital, tried by a military commission under General Lorquet, condemned to death for incendiarism and murder, and shot that same evening at sunset. He behaved with considerable coolness and calmness, and when he heard the sentence pronounced, asked for a quarter of an hour's respite, and then wrote his wishes as to the disposition of his property, and a few words to his family.

Salnave was in every respect unfitted to be a ruler; he was ignorant, debauched, and cruel; loved to be surrounded by the lowest of the low, who turned the palace into a rendezvous where the scum of the negresses assembled to dance and drink, so that no respectable person ever willingly entered it. He attended the meetings of the Vaudoux, and is accused of joining in their greatest excesses. He first brought himself prominently forward by attempting to murder General Philippeaux, and during his Presidency shot his enemies without mercy. I do not think that he had a redeeming quality, except a certain amount of determination, and perhaps bravery, though he was never known to expose himself to personal danger.

General Nissage-Saget was elected President of Hayti on the 19th March 1870, and four years of peace followed. The country was so exhausted by the long civil war, that although there was some discontent among the followers of Salnave and the extreme black party, no movement had a chance of success. The Chambers occasionally quarrelled with the executive, but their title to esteem rests on their efforts to restore the currency. They decided to withdraw the depreciated paper notes and introduce silver dollars, and in this they completely succeeded. It caused some suffering at first, but on the whole it was a sound measure, wisely carried out.

Nissage-Saget, though incapable in many respects, generally adhered to the constitution. However, in 1872 he created some commotion by pardoning all political prisoners at the demand of the army, though legally such a measure required the previous assent of the Chambers. But Haytians like their Presidents to show authority.

In 1873 there was a formal quarrel in the Chambers which led to all the subsequent disasters. A question arose as to the validity of the election of Boyer-Bazelais, deputy for Port-au-Prince. It was decided in his favour by forty-four to twenty-one, upon which the minority retired, and left the House without a quorum. As the Government sided with the minority, no steps were taken to fill vacancies, but a session was called for the month of July.

The real question at issue was a serious one. The Opposition wished to elect as the next President General Monplaisir-Pierre, a respectable black, whilst the Government favoured General Domingue, an ignorant and ferocious negro born in Africa, whose party had rendered itself notorious by the massacre of all the prisoners confined in the jail in Les Cayes in 1869.

The Senate and Chambers met in July, and it was evident that a great majority were hostile to the Government. Boyer-Bazelais, rendered imprudent by the strong party he led, passed a vote of want of confidence in two Ministers, and refused to receive their budgets, upon which the President adjourned the session to April 1874. He did this to prevent the public discussion of the scandalous jobbery of his Ministers and to aid Domingue in his candidature.

When the Congress met in April 1874, there was no doubt as to the feeling of the people being hostile to Domingue and his nephew, Septimus Rameau, the most grasping and unpopular jobber that the country had ever seen. The Government had used all its influence and had employed the military to support Domingue candidates, but in spite of this pressure his opponents had been returned. But the Government persevered, and Nissage retired May 15, handing over power to a Council of Ministers that named Domingue commander-in-chief. A Constituent Assembly was called for June 10, which was quite unconstitutional, and under violent military pressure Government nominees were chosen, who unanimously elected General Domingue President of Hayti.

As soon as this Government was in power, it was clearly seen that all the constitutional leaders had better go into exile, as their death was certain if they remained. Many prudently retired to the neighbouring colonies, but the three gallant leaders of the war against Salnave, Monplaisir-Pierre, Brice, and Boisrond-Canal, remained, and turned their attention to industrial pursuits. I could not but warn Brice that I knew for certain that if they remained they would fall victims, but they had a better opinion of their rulers than I had.

Naturally a new constitution was voted, by which the President was chosen for eight years; the Senate was to be selected from a list sent in to Government; the executive had power to dissolve the Chambers and to establish a Council of State to aid the Government. Power was also given for one year to change the judges and magistrates, thus to fill the bench with their own creatures.

The Government was not slow to show its intentions. The first was to render the residence of foreigners impossible by passing a law of license to trade which would have been prohibitive; but through the interference of the diplomatic corps the application of this law was postponed. At the head of the Ministry was Domingue's nephew, Septimus Rameau, who considered that "the whites had no rights which the blacks were bound to respect." His own friends had foretold an age of peace and enlightenment when Septimus came to power, but of all the narrow-minded negroes with vast pretensions to superiority, none equalled this man. As a rule, the abler a negro is, the more wicked and corrupt he appears. But we could never discover this much-vaunted ability, though the wickedness and corruption were manifest to all.

The only wise act by which Domingue's Government will be known was the signing of a treaty of peace, friendship, and commerce with Santo

Domingo; and this was brought about by foreign aid, which smoothed down the difficulties raised by the intolerable pretensions of the Haytian Ministers.

As usual, when there was political discontent, the year 1875 was ushered in by a great fire in Port-au-Prince. On May 1, taking advantage of an assembly of troops to celebrate the *"Fête de l'Agriculture,"* Rameau ordered an attack to be made on the three rivals he most feared. General Brice was sitting writing in his office when the soldiers sent to murder him appeared; his bravery, however, was so well known, that they dreaded to approach him, but firing at a distance, gave him time to seize his arms and defend himself. But having only revolvers, he thought it prudent to endeavour to take refuge in the English Legation. He was wounded fatally in doing so, and died, notwithstanding the care bestowed upon him by the Spanish Consul Lopez and his wife, who were then residing there.

Monplaisir-Pierre was also attacked in his own house, but being better armed, he made a long defence; he killed seventeen soldiers, wounded thirty-two, mostly mortally, and could only be subdued by the employment of artillery. Then finding he could do no more, as, severely wounded, he could not escape, he put an end to his existence. General Lorquet commanded this attack of the garrison of Port-au-Prince on two veritable heroes.

The third destined to death by the Government was Boisrond-Canal. Whilst defending himself Brice had thought of his friend, and had sent his clerk to warn him of his danger. On the approach of the soldiers he and his friends readily put them to flight, but then were forced to disperse, Canal taking refuge with the American Minister, who, after five months of tedious correspondence, was enabled to embark him in safety.

Decrees followed banishing forty-three eminent citizens, and later on seventeen were condemned to death for a pretended conspiracy. Thus Rameau thought to clear the country of his enemies or rivals.

The Government finding that the amount received in taxes would not satisfy their cupidity, decided to raise a loan in Paris of about £2,500,000. The history of this scandalous transaction is about the worst of its kind. A portion of the money was raised and divided among the friends of the Government; but the details are not worth recording.

The murder of Brice and Monplaisir-Pierre made a profound impression on the country, as it justified all previous apprehensions; and the conduct of the Government was such, that it appeared as if it were guided by a madman. Decrees against the trade carried on by foreigners, hatred of the whites shown by Domingue, Rameau, and Boco, then insults in the official journal, in which even foreign agents were not spared, followed by the illegal expulsion of Cuban refugees, at length roused the country, and a general movement commenced.

Domingue and Rameau were furious: an order was given to murder all the political prisoners confined in the jail, but the chief jailer escaped with them to a Legation, and leaving the gates open, three hundred and fifty malefactors got away at the same time. Then the Government tried to rouse the masses, and issued orders to fire the town and pillage it, and murder the whites and coloured; but even the lowest negroes felt that these were the decrees of a madman. Finding that the Government could not hold its own in Port-au-Prince, Rameau determined to retire to Les Cayes; but being unwilling to leave behind him the money destined to form the capital of a National Bank, he sent it down to the wharf to be embarked. This at length roused the population, and a tumult ensued. Abandoned by all, Domingue abdicated, and the French Minister De Vorges and the Spanish Consul Lopez went to the palace to try and save the President and his Chief Minister. The crowd was large and threatening, but the two brave diplomats took these despicable chiefs under their protection and endeavoured to escort them to the French Legation; but the crowd was so excited against these murderers, that Rameau was killed in the streets and Domingue was seriously wounded.

General Lorquet had been sent at the head of a force to check the advance of the northern insurgents; but, as might be expected, he joined them and marched at their head to take possession of the Government. But no sooner had he entered the town than a murmur arose. The friends of those he had murdered, as Monplaisir-Pierre, Brice, and Chevalier, began to collect. Lorquet fled to his house, but was pursued and attacked, and killed whilst trying to hide in a cupboard.

Thus fell the very worst Government that even Hayti had ever seen. Cruel and dishonest, it had not a redeeming quality. Domingue, brutal and ignorant, was entirely dominated by his nephew, Septimus Rameau, whose conduct has been only excused by his friends on the ground of insanity. There was too much method in his madness for that plea to be accepted. His hatred of foreigners may be partly accounted for by his being a member of the Vaudoux; it is even asserted that he was a Papaloi or priest of the sect.

When Domingue fell there was a struggle for the succession between Boisrond-Canal and Boyer-Bazelais, but the former was preferred on account of his energy and courage. He had a difficult task, as the dilapidations of the late Government had ruined the finances, and France insisted that the Domingue loan should be recognised before she would acknowledge the new President.

Boyer-Bazelais, although, like Boisrond-Canal, a man of colour, bitterly resented his rival being chosen President, and created every difficulty possible for the new Government. These events, however, are too recent for me to dwell on them. I may, however, notice that the principal attention of both Government and Opposition was directed to the finances, and that in 1879 the French Government forced Hayti to acknowledge the Domingue loan.

In July 1879 a disturbance took place in the House of Representatives, and it was adjourned amidst much tumult. Boyer-Bazelais and his party retired to his house and took up arms, they said, to defend themselves. Their opponents attacked them, and a desperate fight ensued. Fire was put to the adjoining houses, and amidst this fierce conflict our acting Consul-General Byron and the French Chancellor Hullinot intervened, and at the greatest personal risk rescued the ladies from the burning houses and took them to a place of safety. A *sauve qui peut* soon followed, and Boyer-Bazelais' party was dispersed with heavy loss, two of his brothers being killed in the fight.

The insane ambition of what was called the Liberal party thus ruined the most honest Government that Hayti had seen since the days of Boyer. These disorders in the capital were followed by others in the provinces; and Boisrond-Canal, disgusted with the treatment he had received from those who should have supported him, resigned, and left the country with his chief Ministers, July 17, 1879. Great sympathy was shown him by the people, who cheered him as he left the wharf. As usual, he was embarked by a foreign officer, Commander Allington of H.M.S. "Boxer." What would these exiled Presidents do without the foreign element?

Boisrond-Canal, though not a brilliant ruler, was thoroughly honest, and if he had been supported instead of being opposed by the Liberal party, his four years' Presidency would have been a happy one. His coloured opponents used to call him a *putate* or sweet potato—in fact, a King Log. They soon had a chance of comparing his Government with that of a King Stork.

Boyer-Bazelais' party now thought that they would have all their own way, but they soon found that the country would have none of them. The blacks were again in the ascendant, and after some feeble attempts at revolution, the Liberal chiefs had to take the path of exile, and be thankful that it was no worse.

The mob of Port-au-Prince, wearied by the long debates, forced the Assembly to close its discussions, and General Salomon was elected President of Hayti, October 23, 1879, and in December of the same year a twelfth constitution was promulgated, by which the chief of the state was chosen for seven years.

Illegal military executions, murder, and pillage, encouraged by the authorities, have been the principal episodes of the history of the last four years.

CHAPTER IV
THE POPULATION OF HAYTI

The amount of the population in Hayti is not accurately known, as no census has been taken since the country became independent. At the close of the last century the population was found to consist of—

Whites	46,000
Freed men, black and coloured	56,666
Slaves of both colours	509,642
	602,308

In giving these figures, Mr. Madion adds ("Histoire d'Haïti," vol. i. p. 29) that the planters, in order not to have to pay the full capitation-tax, omitted from their return of slaves all the children, as well as those over forty-five years of age, so that at least 200,000 should be added to those in servitude, among whom were 15,000 coloured of both sexes. Up to 1847 Mr. Madion considered that the population had neither increased nor decreased. Deducting the whites, there would remain about 750,000.

Mr. Mackenzie, in his "Notes on Hayti," vol. ii., discusses the question of population, but the tables he inserts in his work vary so greatly that no reliance can be placed on them. In one, the population in 1824 of the French portion of the island is stated to be 351,716; in another, given in full detail as to each district, it is put at 873,867, whilst he adds that Placide Justin had previously estimated the population at 700,000, and General Borgella, a good authority, stated it at a million. It is evident that no one had very precise data on which to found an estimate.

During the struggle between the French and the coloured races, the whole of the whites were either driven out of the country or killed, and some slaves were exported to Cuba and the United States. What remained, therefore, of the two other sections constituted the population of the empire of Dessalines.

During the Presidency of General Geffrard (1863), I heard him remark, that from the best official information he could get, the population had increased to over 900,000. This estimate must be largely founded on conjecture. The negro race is undoubtedly prolific, and in a hundred years ought to have more than doubled—nay, in so fertile a country, with unlimited supplies of food, more than quadrupled its population. The losses during the war of independence were considerable, as there was no mercy shown by either side, and the sanguinary strife lasted many years. The long civil war between Pétion and Christophe was kept up during the whole reign of the latter, but probably did not cost the country so many lives as the building of the great mountain-fortress of La Ferrière and the handsome palace of Sans Souci. During the Presidency of Boyer, lasting twenty-five years, there was peace, and ample time was given, for the population to make up for all previous losses; but after his departure came the wars with Santo Domingo and civil strife.

All these causes, however, would only have slightly checked population. If you ask a Haytian how it is that his country remains comparatively so thinly peopled, he will answer that the negresses take but little care of their children, and that at least two-thirds die in infancy. After reading the chapter on Vaudoux worship and cannibalism, I fear some of my readers may come to another conclusion. I cannot, however, think that these fearful excesses can be carried to the extent of greatly checking the increase of population. That the negresses are careless mothers is highly possible, and in the interior there are few, if any, medical men to whom they can apply in case of need.

After carefully examining every document on the subject which came before me, and noting the state of those portions of the country through which I have passed, and comparing all the information I received during my twelve years' stay, I have come to the conclusion that the population has greatly increased, probably doubled, since 1825. All the old residents appear to be of the opinion that the Haytian is lazier than ever, and many intelligent natives decidedly hold that view; and yet we find that the exports and imports have doubled in quantity during this period, which can only be accounted for by a very great increase in the population. It is possible, however, that the augmentation is much less than it should have been.

Either on account of losses from warlike operations, or more probably by diseases produced from the greater excesses of the men, the female population is much larger than that of the male. Some go so far as to say there are three women to one man; others, two-thirds females. I am myself inclined to fix it at about three-fifths. The great disproportion in the amount of the women has often been observed among the negro tribes on the coast of Guinea. In Hayti there is no emigration to account for the disproportion; in fact, the movement of population has been the other way, and many recruits arrive from the United States and the European colonies in the West Indies.

The population is generally supposed to consist of at least nine-tenths black to one-tenth coloured, and that the coloured is decidedly more and more approaching the black type. It is natural that, continually breeding in and in, they should gradually assimilate to the more numerous race. As a rule, the coloured population may be said to reside chiefly in the towns and villages.

Mackenzie speaks of some Maroon negroes who lived in the mountains near La Selle in the north-eastern district of Hayti, and held no intercourse with the other inhabitants, but fled at their approach. They were doubtless the descendants of fugitive slaves. When we paid a visit to the mountain above referred to, we heard the peasantry speaking of these people, but it appeared more of a tradition than an ascertained fact. They call them the *Vien-viennent*, from their cry on seeing strangers. From what is told of their being seen in the deep woods at midnight dancing and going through certain ceremonies, it is probable that these strange people were only sectaries of the Vaudoux worship practising their African rites.

The vexed question as to the position held by the negroes in the great scheme of nature was continually brought before us whilst I lived in Hayti, and I could not but regret to find that the greater my experience the less I thought of the capacity of the negro to hold an independent position. As long as he is influenced by contact with the white man, as in the southern portion of the United States, he gets on very well. But place him free from all such influence, as in Hayti, and he shows no signs of improvement; on the contrary, he is gradually retrograding to the African tribal customs, and without exterior pressure will fall into the state of the inhabitants on the Congo. If this were only my own opinion, I should hesitate to express it so positively, but I have found no dissident voice amongst experienced residents since I first went to Hayti in January 1863.

I now agree with those who deny that the negro could ever originate a civilisation, and that with the best of educations he remains an inferior type of man. He has as yet shown himself totally unfitted for self-government, and incapable as a people to make any progress whatever. To judge the negroes fairly, one must live a considerable time in their midst, and not be led away by the theory that all races are capable of equal advance in civilisation.

The mulattoes have no doubt far superior intelligence, and show greater capacity for government, but as yet they have had no marked success. It is pitiable to read their history, and see how they are almost ever swayed by the meanest impulses of personal interest and ambition, and how seldom they act from patriotic motives. During the twenty years which have elapsed since I first became acquainted with the country, what a dreary succession of meaningless conspiracies, from the abortive attempt of General Legros in 1863, to the disastrous civil strife between two sections of the mulatto party, led by Boisrond-Canal and Boyer-Bazelais, when the latter completed the ruin of those of his own colour, and let in their worst enemies, the blacks, who had dreamed for twenty years of their extermination (1879).

Scarcely one of these plots and insurrections, by which the country has been bathed in blood, but was founded on the hope of office and the consequent spoils. The thoughts of the conspirators are concentrated on the treasury and the division of its contents. "Prendre l'argent de l'état ce n'est pas volé," is the motto of all parties, of every shade of colour.

Politically speaking, the Haytians are a hopeless people, and the most intelligent and best educated among them are more and more inclined to despair of the future of their country when they see the wreck that follows each wave of barbarism which every few years passes over their republic. President Geffrard, on going into exile in 1867, remarked to my Spanish colleague, that, putting aside all personal feelings and regrets, he could only foresee for his country a disastrous series of convulsions. He spoke prophetically; for Hayti has never recovered from the effects of the civil war which followed his expulsion, and he must have observed, from his secure retreat in Jamaica, how the leaders of every section of his enemies were, one by one, executed, killed in battle, or sent into exile.

I will now attempt to examine some characteristic traits of the Haytian negro and mulatto.

The Negro

A French admiral once asked me, "Est-ce que vous prenez ces gens au sérieux?" And at first sight it is impossible to do so in Hayti; but after the eye becomes used to the grotesque, the study of the people is both interesting and instructive. To a foreigner accustomed to regard the negro as he is depicted by our latest travellers, a half-naked savage, brutal and brute-like, it is not possible to contemplate as otherwise than incongruous a black general with heavy gold epaulettes and gorgeous uniform galloping on a bedizened steed, surrounded by a staff as richly apparelled, and followed by an escort of as ragged a soldiery as ever Falstaff was ashamed to march with. The awkward figure, the heavy face, the bullet head, the uncouth features, the cunning bloodshot eyes, seen under the shade of a French officer's cocked hat, raise the hilarity of the newcomer, which is not lessened when he discovers that this wretched imitation of a soldier declares himself the most warlike of a warlike race. But putting aside the absurdities which appear inherent to the blacks, you soon discover that there is something sympathetic in that stolid being.

In treating of the Haytians, one must carefully separate the lower-class negro as he appears in a large commercial town from the black who lives in the plains or mountains. The former, brought into constant contact with the roughest of the white race, as represented by an inferior class of merchant seamen, is too often insolent and dishonest, whilst the countryman, who only sees a select few of the whites, appears to have an innate idea of their superiority, and almost always treats them with respect and deference, and with a hospitality and kindness which is not found in the cities.

Whilst the civilised Haytian is essentially inhospitable towards foreigners, the contrary is the case among the country population. They have the virtues as well as the vices of wild races; and although their long intercourse with their more civilised compatriots has given them a species of French varnish, yet they are essentially an African people removed from their parent country.

Circumstances, however, have naturally modified their character. After the departure of the French, their estates ultimately fell into the hands of the coloured freedmen and enfranchised slaves. Many of the latter squatted among the coffee plantations, regardless of the nominal proprietor, and there gathered and sold the crops without paying much attention to the rights of the owner. With the thirst, however, to be the real possessor of land, so characteristic of all peasantry, as soon as the negro acquired a little capital from savings, his first thought was turned to secure the tenure of his household, and in many parts the land has been morselled out among them. President Pétion encouraged this system by the action of Government.

The popular stories current in Hayti of the difference between the races that inhabit it are rather characteristic. It is said that a white man, a mulatto, and a negro were once admitted into the presence of the Giver of all good gifts, and were asked what they wished to possess. The first-named desired to acquire a knowledge of the arts and sciences; the second limited his pretensions to fine horses and beautiful women; the third, on being asked, shuffled about and said that he had been brought there by the mulatto, but being pressed to answer, replied he should like a bit of gold lace.

They say again, Mark the difference of the three when arrested and thrown into prison: the white man demands paper and ink in order to draw up a protest; the second looks about for the means of escape; whilst the third lies down and sleeps twenty-four hours at a stretch; then waking up, he grumbles a little, but soon turns on the other side and sleeps a second twenty-four hours.

Another curious saying among them is:—

"Nègue riche li mulatte,

Mulatte pauvre li nègue."

These trifles indicate the opinion the different sections of the people have of each other, and there is much truth in the estimation.

The politeness of the country negro is very remarkable, and you hear one ragged fellow addressing another as monsieur, frère, or confrère; and this civility is very pleasing, as it gives promise of better things whenever education shall be extended to the country population.

The town negro rarely, however, equals the peasant in manners, though among each other there is not much left to be desired. Both classes, at the same time, are infinitely superior to our colonial negroes, who are in Port-au-Prince proverbial for their insolence.

Every one who mixes in Haytian society is struck by the paucity of black gentlemen to be met with at balls, concerts, or the theatre, and the almost total absence of black ladies. At some of the largest parties given by the late President Geffrard, I have counted but three black ladies to perhaps a hundred coloured; and although the gentlemen were more numerous, it was evident that their presence arose from their official positions, and not from a desire to mix with the society.

There is a marked line drawn between the black and the mulatto, which is probably the most disastrous circumstance for the future prosperity of the country. A faithful historian, after carefully studying past events, can come to no other conclusion than that the low state of civilisation which still obtains in the island arises principally from this unmeaning quarrel. The black hates the mulatto, the mulatto despises the black; proscriptions, judicial murders, massacres have arisen, and will continue to arise as long as this deplorable feeling prevails. There is no sign of its abatement; on the contrary, never was it so marked as at the present day. A black Minister once said to me, "We blacks and whites like and respect each other, because we are of pure race, but as for those mulattoes" — —

I remember, on my arrival in Port-au-Prince in 1863, having a conversation with a young mulatto lady, no longer in the freshness of youth, on the subject of intermarriage; and having faintly indicated that I thought she had been unwise in refusing the hand of one of the best-mannered, best-educated, and richest blacks in the country, I received a reply which completely surprised me, "Sir, you insult me to imagine I would marry a black. No, I will never marry any one but a white." I soothed her as well as I could, but on looking at her faded charms, her unhealthy-looking skin, and her heavy under-jaw, I thought with reason that she might wait long; and, poor girl, she waited in vain till death released her.

This contempt of the black is felt by nearly every coloured girl, and is bitterly resented. I have seen young mulatto women refusing to dance with blacks at a ball, and the latter, in fury, threatening to call out the father or brother of the offending beauty. Yet what can be more absurd than such a pretension or prejudice, when, but two generations removed, their mothers were African slaves! I have heard coloured women talking about their families and their aristocratic connections, when I have known that in a back-room, slowly fading away, was some black "mamselle," the grandmother of the proud beauties.

The blacks naturally feel and resent this childish insolence, and when they get the upper hand, as in the time of Soulouque and since, they unfortunately quench in blood their outraged feelings.

Towards the white man, whatever jealousy he may feel on account of former political questions, the black is usually both respectful and cordial, and in return is liked by them. I heard a black magistrate say, "My father came from Africa. He was apparently a respectable man in the kingdom of Congo, because he was not only treated with distinction by his countrymen on board the slaver, but on landing was taken into confidence by a white planter, who ultimately made him his partner. That is the history of my family." Certainly as respectable as any other in Hayti.

Notwithstanding all the interested denials of the mulattoes, there is no doubt but that the lower-class negro, in particular, respects the white man as a superior being, and therefore respects his religion as superior to his own; but, as I shall show in my chapter on the Vaudoux, although he follows the white man's religion to a certain extent, he does not in consequence forsake his serpent-worship, which appeals to his traditions, to the Africa of his nursery tales, and, above all, to his pleasures and his passions. The Vaudoux priest encourages lascivious dancing, copious drinking, and the indiscriminate intercourse of the sexes, but he at the same time inculcates the burning of candles in the Roman Catholic churches. He keeps a serpent in a box in his temple, whilst the walls are covered with the pictures of the Virgin Mary and the saints. No other brain but that of a negro could accept such a juxtaposition of opposing beliefs.

Occasionally a negro will say to a white in an insolent manner, "Nous sommes tous égaux içi;" but he does not believe it, and shows he does not believe it by soon sneaking away with his invariable oath, "F— —." The crowd may grunt acquiescence, and though they may appear amused by the fellow's insolence, they are still more amused by his slinking off. Burton, speaking of the people on the coast of Africa, says that a negro will obey a white man more readily than a mulatto, and a mulatto more so than one of his own colour.

Among the black gentlemen you find some of polished manners and cultivated minds, as my friend Alexander Delva and the late M. Paul, or a genial companion like Lubin, the son-in-law of the late Emperor Soulouque. Yet, notwithstanding these exceptions, and the more remarkable ones I have noticed in my historical chapter, there can be no doubt that the blacks have not yet arrived at that state of civilisation which would enable one to compare them favourably with any other civilised race, or to say that they are competent to govern a country.

During the reign of Soulouque, Chancellor Delva and General Salomon were considered great statesmen, but between them they managed to exhaust the country, and no monument remains of their rule. But when an example is required of a man who applies his official position to his own benefit, it is said, "He will become as rich as Chancellor Delva."

Another negro who was expected by his own party to show himself a great statesman was Septimus Rameau, of Les Cayes. When, however, he obtained unlimited power under his doting uncle, President Domingue, he proved himself a mere visionary, incapable of a single sensible measure, and turning every project into a fresh means of plundering the State. Whilst the people were sinking daily into greater poverty, and the public service was starved for want of funds, he ordered an expensive Pantheon to be constructed, in which should be erected statues to Hayti's famous men; and for fear posterity should be oblivious of his own merits, he ordered a statue of himself, which, however, was never erected, as before it arrived he had, by a violent death, paid the penalty of his crimes.

During my twelve years' residence in Hayti, no black statesman appeared who was capable of managing with credit any important official position, with the exception of General Lamothe, a talented and agreeable man; but I fear that the charity which begins at home so predominated in him, that the interests of his country were sometimes forgotten.

Though very unwilling to meet death on the field of battle when a loophole to escape is at hand, yet no one faces it more courageously than the Haytian, both black and coloured, when on the place of execution. He stands dauntless before the trembling soldiers, who, shutting their eyes or turning away their heads, fire at random, and who too often only wound, and have to charge and recharge their muskets before their prisoner dies. The soldiers have a superstitious dread of shooting any particular man in cold blood, and fancy that his spirit will haunt that individual whose bullet has sent him into the other world.

The black in his family relations is in general kindly, though few of the lower orders go through any civil or religious marriage ceremony; in fact, it was at one time the custom of all classes to be *"placé,"* and only since the priests have regained some of their ancient influence have those who are considered respectable consented to go to church. The first daring innovators were almost stoned by the people, and even such men as Presidents Pétion and Boyer were only "placed," the latter succeeding to the authority and *"placée"* of the former. Yet the children of these unions are by Haytian law legitimate, as the agreement to live together, as in our old common law, was considered equivalent to marriage.

In the interior a well-to-do black lives openly with several women as wives, and I have seen the patriarch sitting at the door of the central house, with huts all around in which his younger wives lived, as they could not be made to dwell under the same roof. On Friday evenings he descends to market on a horse or mule, perhaps holding in his arms the latest born, while following in his train are a dozen women and sturdy children either carrying loads or driving beasts of burden. No one is mounted but himself. The French priests attempted to alter this state of things, but they did not succeed, as the wives, surrounding the intruder, asked him what was to be their position if the husband selected one among them and abandoned the rest. The priests have for the most part wisely decided not to meddle with the present, but rather endeavour to act upon the minds of the younger generation. They can hardly expect success as long as the numbers of women greatly exceed those of the men.

The blacks, though in general kind to their children, neglect them, and the mortality is said to be great. They are, however, very passionate, and in their anger they use in correction the first thing that comes to hand. A Spanish friend with a tender heart was riding one day in the country when his attention was drawn by the piercing shrieks of a child. He turned his head, and saw a black woman holding a little boy by the arm and beating him with the handle of a broom. He rode up, and catching the next blow on the handle of his whip, said, "Don't beat the child in that manner." The woman looked up surprised at the interference, and coolly replied in their patois, "Consite, li nègue; li pas fait li mal." — "Consul, it is a negro; it will do him no harm."

Another day he saw a gigantic black beating with his club an interesting-looking young negress, giving blows that only a black could stand without being maimed. Again he interfered, but both set upon him, first with foul words, and then with such menacing gestures, that he was too glad to put spurs to his horse and gallop away. He found he had been interfering in a domestic quarrel.

The brutal use of the cocomacaque or club is universal, as I shall have to notice when describing the police. Under Toussaint's regulations the use of the whip, as an unpleasant memento of slavery, was abolished, but the club was introduced. Dessalines, as Inspector-General of Agriculture, brought it into vogue. At Les Cayes he one day ordered a woman to be beaten for neglecting some agricultural work; she was far advanced in pregnancy, and her child was prematurely born whilst the punishment was being inflicted. Whenever Dessalines' name is mentioned, it is associated with some act of fiendish cruelty.

As might be expected, few marriages take place between the whites and blacks; the only instance of which I heard was a German clerk who married the daughter of a Minister in the hope of making his fortune through the contracts he expected to obtain from his unscrupulous father-in-law; but within a fortnight of the marriage the Minister was expelled from office. Contrary to general expectation, the German boldly faced his altered prospects, and the marriage appeared to have turned out more happily than could have been anticipated from so ill-assorted a union.

Whilst travelling in Hayti one is often surprised at the extraordinary difference in the appearance of the population, many being tall, fine men with open countenances, whilst others are the meanest-looking gorillas imaginable. Then their colour: some have shiny skins, that look as if blacking and the blacking-brush had been conscientiously applied, whilst others have the skin completely without lustre, looking almost as if disease were there. Again, others are of the deepest black, whilst their next neighbours may be of a reddish tinge.

During my residence in Hayti I only saw one handsome negress, and she was a peasant girl of La Coupe near Port-au-Prince: her features were almost perfect, and she might well have said—

"Mislike me not for my complexion,
The shadowed livery of the burnished sun,
To whom I am a neighbour and nigh bred."

She was not misliked, but she apparently stood the test of every temptation that her white admirers could offer. She had soft pleasant ways and a sweet voice, and talked her jargon of a language in so pretty a manner as almost to make one inclined to admit the Creole into the list of things civilised. But such a girl must be rare indeed, for I saw no other. In general they are very ugly, having no point of beauty. The marked difference in the appearance of the negroes in Hayti doubtless arises from their origin, as they were brought from every tribe in Africa, not only from those frequenting the coast, but also as prisoners from the interior. From all I have read of the African negro, the Haytian must be far advanced from that low type.

It is a curious trait that the negro has a shy dislike of monkeys; he has an uneasy feeling that the whites imagine that there is no great difference between a very ugly negro (and there are ugly ones) and a handsome gorilla. The first evening I went to the theatre in Port-au-Prince, I was started by the exclamation of my companion, "Qui est ce monstre africain?" I turned, and saw in the President's box a perfect horror; but use reconciled me even to this man. An Italian once came to the capital with a dancing-monkey. Crowds followed him everywhere. One day he stopped before a German merchant's, and a fair little girl came out. The monkey would not dance, whereon the disappointed child said to her father in Creole, "Faut-il batte petit nègue là." The mob were furious at the mistake, and the father was too glad to hurry in with his child to escape a shower of stones.

There are still many negroes in Hayti who were born in Africa, being principally the remains of certain cargoes of slaves which the English cruisers captured and landed among their free brethren. One whom I knew had been taken, then freed by an English officer, sent to England, and educated at the expense of Government. When of age he was asked what he would desire to do. He replied, "I should wish to go to Hayti." When I knew him he was an old man, and had risen to occupy the position of Minister of Justice.

The principal trouble to the female negro mind is her unfortunate wool. How she envies her more favoured sisters their long tresses! how she tries to draw out each fibre, and endeavours to make something of it by carefully platting it with false hair! Even the smallest negro servant will spend hours in oiling, brushing, and tending this poor crop, whose greatest length will only compass three or four inches. It is only when women are more than half white that the wool turns into hair, and even then it has sometimes a suspicious crispy wave, which, however, looks well. Of late years chignons have been a regular importation from France, and the little negresses are delighted with them.

The negroes have a very curious habit of talking aloud to themselves. You will hear them in the streets or in the country roads carrying on apparently a long conversation, repeating all they have said or intended to say on a certain occasion, and in a very loud voice; every other sentence is varied by a grunt or guttural ejaculation. Sometimes they are evidently excited, and are enacting a violent quarrel. They are apparently oblivious that all their remarks are heard, or may be; they are delighted to take so many people into their confidence. It is a general observation that in nine cases out of ten the subject of which they are treating is money.

It has often been remarked what curious names are affixed to negroes, as Cæsar, Lord Byron, Je-crois-en-Dieu. This doubtless arose from a rule which existed during the French occupation, that no slave could be given a name which was used by their masters, so that the latter were driven to very curious expedients to find appellations for their bondsmen; this rule applied in a lesser degree to the freedmen.

Blanc pas trompé nègue is the name given by the Haytians to common blue shirting.

I may notice another peculiarity of the negresses. They object to carrying anything in their hands—they will invariably poise it on their heads. I have often seen them carrying a bottle thus, talking, laughing, running, without having the slightest fear of its falling.

The negroes have very singular words of insult, and I remember seeing a man roused to fury by a little black servant of mine, who, after exhausting every offensive word in her vocabulary, suddenly said in Creole-negro, "Mangé chien." The black fellow darted at her, and had she not made a precipitate retreat into the house, she would have felt his club on her shoulders.

It is an offensive custom among people of all classes in Hayti to repeat, as a sort of ejaculatory oath, a rather dirty Creole word. Men educated in a former generation cannot get rid of the habit, and many of the lower orders appear to use it at the close of every sentence. When Soulouque was Emperor he often consulted our Acting Consul-General, the present Sir Charles Wyke, now our Minister in Lisbon, as to the usages of the Courts of St. James's and Hanover, and it is said that our agent gave him a hint that habitual swearing was certainly contrary to courtly usages. Soulouque took this hint in good part, and thought that he would try his hand on an old general notorious for this habit. So the Emperor watched his opportunity, and the first time his victim swore, he called him up and said, "General, I have decided that no one who comes to court can be permitted to use that offensive word with which you interlard your conversation." The general looked surprised, and answered, "Emperor, f——, of course I will obey, f——, your commands, f——." "There, you see," replied his "Altesse," "you have used the forbidden word three times." The poor general now completely lost his head, and answered, "F— —, Emperor, f— —, if, f— —, I am not allowed, f— —, to use the word f— —, I will cease, f— —, from coming to court, f— —." The Emperor could not but laugh, and troubled the general no more, for the habit was too engrained. I should have treated this story as an exaggeration had not I myself heard an old officer equally profuse in his ejaculations.

The Emperor Soulouque was a very ignorant man, and a good story is told in illustration. The French Consul-General, Raybaud, I believe, went once to plead some cause before his Majesty, and wound up by saying that if he did what was required, he would be considered "plus grand qu'Annibal." "Comment, Consite," replied the startled Emperor, "moué cannibal!" And it required all the Frenchman's tact to explain his reference. As Soulouque was known to be affiliated to the Vaudoux sect, the illustration was not happy in its sound.

The negroes and mulattoes are very fond of queer expressions, and their odd noises in conversation quite disconcert a stranger. Assent, dissent, anger, playful acquiescence, are all expressed by the variety in which 'ng-'ng are sounded, though a modified or even a musical grunt can scarcely be expressed on paper. The untravelled ladies in Hayti are very proud of thus being able to express their sentiments without having recourse to words.

The negroes of the lower orders are, like all other inhabitants of hot countries, very fond of bathing, but they are careless as to the cleanliness of their clothes. This I also noticed among the Malays and Dyaks of Borneo; they would bathe several times a day, and then return to their dirty garments. The dress of the peasantry in Hayti is often but an imitation of their European neighbours, though the females generally keep to a long white chemise, covered over with a blue cotton dress that reaches to their bare feet, and is drawn in round the waist. They wear a coloured handkerchief on their heads. On feast days and other gala occasions the young negresses dress in white, which makes a pleasant contrast of colour.

Markets used formerly to be held on Sundays. When this custom was abolished the female peasantry began to frequent the churches, and the comparison between their blue cotton gowns and the silk dresses of the ladies created envy. But when, in 1863, the price of cotton trebled, the peasantry had the means placed at their disposal to vie with the rich in Gonaives and St. Marc, and many availed themselves of it to go to church richly dressed. This fashion, however, lasted but a short time, and certainly did not survive the great fall in prices which followed the conclusion of the civil war in the United States.

The upper classes dress exactly like European ladies, but they never look well in fashionable Parisian hats, while their tignon, or handkerchief, tied gracefully round the head, is most becoming. A white tignon is a sign of mourning. There is nothing of which a Haytian lady is more proud than the amount of her personal and household linen. Her *armoires* are generally full of every kind, and the finer they are in quality the more they are esteemed; and the blacks are, if anything, more particular than the coloured in securing the most expensive underclothing. How they plume themselves on the condition of their best bedroom! It is fitted up expensively, in order that people may see it, but it is very seldom used, except to receive their lady friends in. Then they bring out with great pride the treasures of their *armoires*, and show how well supplied they are with what they do not make a general use of.

There is one thing for which all Haytians are equally remarkable—their love of "*remèdes*." For everything, from a toothache to yellow fever, they have a variety of prescriptions, which are probably well suited to the country, but which a foreigner should be wary in taking. I have not yet forgotten a *remède*, consisting partly of the juice of the sour orange, which a good old lady gave me on my first arrival in the country. It was my first and my last experience. The natives like being physicked, and apothecary shops appear to thrive in every town and village. I remember a Haytian doctor, educated in Paris, telling me how he lost his patients when he first commenced practice by not dosing them enough.

The lower orders in Hayti have been accused of great incontinence, and the higher classes have not escaped the same accusation; but in no tropical country are the lower orders continent. People affect to say that it is the effect of climate, but I have never thought so. You have but to put your hand on the skin of a negro or of any tropical race, to find it as cold as that of a fish, and their blood is but little warmer. Their food of vegetables would alone prevent their having the fiery blood of a well-fed people.

The fact is, that continence is not considered a virtue by the lower orders in the tropics, and love-stories are told by mothers before their young daughters in all their crudest details, and no effort whatever is made to keep the minds or bodies of the young girls chaste. The consequence is that in early life, particularly among relatives, intercourse is almost promiscuous. As amusements are very scarce, young and old give themselves up to gallantry; but it is constant opportunity and the want of occupation and amusement which are the causes of incontinence, not their warm blood.

There are two things on which both negroes and mulattoes pride themselves: their fine ear for music, and their proficiency in dancing. A talented French bandmaster told me, that, if taken young, he thought he could train his Haytian pupils to be excellent musicians; and as they are fond of the study and practice, he had no difficulty whatever in keeping them to their classes; and many of the military band in Port-au-Prince played fairly well, though, from inefficient and irregular instruction under native teachers, much was still to be desired. The drum, however, was a very favourite instrument, and the noise produced was sometimes startling. The travelled wife of a President used to say that she thought no music in Paris equal to the Haytian, *especially the drums.*

The dancing of the upper classes is much the same in all countries, though in Hayti the favourite dance is a special one, called "Carabinier." Among the people, however, are still to be observed the old dances they brought from Africa.

Moreau St. Mèry, in his admirable work on Santo Domingo during the French colonial days (new edition, p. 52), has described the dances of the slaves as he saw them previous to 1790, and his words might be used to depict what occurs at the present day.

With the negroes dancing is a passion, and no fatigue stands in the way of their indulging in it. The announcement that a dance will take place brings people from surprising distances, and the sound of the drums acts like a charm, and all fatigue is forgotten. Young and old, although they may have walked twenty miles, with heavy burdens for the next day's market, join in it with enthusiasm.

But the most interesting dances are those performed by the professionals. Generally they consist of a couple of men to beat the drums, a very fat woman as treasurer, and three or four younger woman famous for their skill. Soon after President Salnave came into power I was a guest at a picnic at a place where some famous dancers had invited the young men of the district to come and meet them.

Our hosts had heard of this affair, and invited us to go down to the spot, where a large space was covered in with the leaves of the palm tree, as even there seasoned performers could not stand the burning mid-day sun. The two men with the drums were there, coarse instruments made out of a hollowed piece of wood, one end open, the other closed with the skin of a goat or sheep, on which the men play with their knuckles, one slowly and the other faster; calabashes with pebbles or Indian corn in them are shaken or stricken against the hand, and the spectators intone a chant. Then the master of the ceremonies and the chief of the band calls out a name, and one of the professionals stands forth and begins to perform. Any man from the crowd may come and dance with her, holding his hand raised over his head with a small sum in paper money, worth perhaps a penny. When she wishes a change she takes this money in her hand, and one of the impatient lookers-on cuts in and supplies the place of the first; other performers arise, until the whole shed is full. As the excitement grows, some of the young girls of the neighbourhood also join in. I noticed that every note collected was religiously handed to the treasurer, to be employed in supporting the band and paying for the dresses, which, however, did not appear expensive, as the women were clothed in white gowns, coloured headdresses, and handkerchiefs always carried in their right hands. I noticed, however, that what could be seen of their under-linen was remarkably fine.

The dance itself is not striking or interesting, but they keep time very exactly. To show how African it is, I may mention that an officer from our West Coast squadron was one day passing near these performers, when he was suddenly seized with a desire to dance, and struck in before the prettiest negress of the band. His dancing was so good that gradually all the blacks sat down, and left these two performers in the midst of an interested crowd, who by shouting, clapping their hands, and singing urged on the pair to renewed exertions; and I have heard several who were present say that never had they seen anything equal to this dancing in Hayti. Our friend had learnt the art on the coast of Africa, and was as strong as a lion and as active as a gazelle; he was called "the pocket Hercules."

To return to our party. After some very insignificant dancing, a new tune was struck up, and the performers began to go through something more attractive to the crowd. This dance was called *chica*, but popularly I have heard it named *bamboula*, from the drum, which often consists of a hollow bamboo: so it is said. This lascivious dance is difficult to describe. I think I will let Moreau St. Méry do it for me:—

"Cette danse a un air qui lui est spécialement consacré et où la mesure est fortement marquée. Le talent pour la danseuse est dans la perfection avec laquelle elle peut faire mouvoir ses hanches et la partie inférieure de ses reins, en conservant tout le reste du corps dans une espèce d'immobilité, que ne lui font même pas perdre les faibles agitations de ses bras qui balancent les deux extrémités d'un mouchoir ou de son jupon. Un danseur s'approche d'elle, s'élance tout-à-coup, et tombe en mesure presque à la toucher. Il recule, il s'élance encore, et la provoque à la lutte la plus séduisante. La danse s'anime, et bientôt elle offre un tableau dont tous les traits d'abord voluptueux, deviennent ensuite lascifs. Il serait impossible de peindre le chica avec son véritable caractère, et je me bornerai à dire que l'impression qu'il cause est si puissante que l'Africain ou le Créole de n'importe quelle nuance, qui le verrait danser sans émotion, passerait pour avoir perdu jusqu'aux dernières étin celles de la sensibilité."

I watched its effect on the bystanders of all colours, and St. Méry has not exaggerated: the flushed faces, the excited eyes, the eager expression, the looks of ill-concealed passion, were fully shared by all. No modest woman would be present at such a scene; but the young females of the neighbourhood were delighted. Drink was flying freely about, and all the performers appeared half-intoxicated: the dance grew fast and furious; as night came on a few candles were lit, and then all are said to give themselves up to the most unreserved debauchery. I ought to add that few respectable girls of the peasant class would care to be seen at one of these dances, where the professionals, without shame, perform regardless of appearances. The *bamboula*, as practised among the peasantry, is more quiet, but sufficiently lascivious.

I was once witness of a rather curious scene. A French opera company arrived at Port-au-Prince with a couple of ballet-girls. On the opening night of the theatre they commenced dancing; the pit, crowded with negroes, was at first quiet. The untravelled Haytian could not at first understand it; but shortly the applause became uproarious; shouts filled the house; the unaccustomed sight of two *white* girls thus exhibiting themselves provoked the sensuality of the negro nature to such a degree that it was almost impossible to keep them quiet, and their admiration was so warmly expressed as even to frighten the girls, who turned pale with astonishment mingled with fear. This kind of applause made the foreigners feel uncomfortable, and we were not sorry when the ballet ceased.

I have not noticed any particular ceremonies at the birth of children, nor at marriages. In the latter some are striving to imitate the upper classes, and marry in church, but the mass of the people are still not regularly married. I have noticed, however, their great fondness for a display of jewellery on these occasions, and if they do not possess enough themselves, they borrow among their friends, and every one who lends is sure to attend the wedding, as much to keep an eye on their cherished property as to join in the amusements inherent to these occasions.

Though I have attended many funerals of the upper classes, I have had no occasion to be present at one of the peasantry, though I have seen the body being carried at night from the town to the house of the deceased in the hills. One evening, at about ten, we heard a roar of voices in the distance; presently we saw torches flashing in the road, and soon after a crowd, perhaps of a hundred people, swept by at a running pace, all screaming, yelling, or shrieking at the top of their voices. Those who led this awful din were hired mourners, who pass the night near the corpse, making it hideous with their professional lamentations. There are regular wakes, at which eating and drinking are permitted, and drunkenness not prohibited. All classes in Hayti, like their brethren on the Guinea coast, love pompous funerals, and it is quite a passion among the female portion of the community to attend them, as it is only at funerals and at church that the ladies can see and be seen in their most careful toilettes.

The most curious wake I ever saw was at Santo Domingo city. I was walking about after dark, when my attention was drawn to a house where music and dancing were going on. I approached, and looking through a window, saw a most singular sight. In a high chair was placed in a sitting position the corpse of a child, dressed up in its very best clothes, as if a spectator of the scene. The music was playing briskly, and a regular ball appeared to be going on, in which the mother of the child took the principal part. I inquired of my companion what this meant, and he said that the people explained it thus:—The priests had taught them not to weep, but rather rejoice, at the death of a child, as it passed directly to heaven. They took this teaching literally, and danced and made merry.

"Whom the gods love, die young."

The negroes, as a rule, live to a good old age, and bear their age well; they also keep their magnificent white teeth to the last, which they ascribe to diligent cleanliness and the crushing of the sugar-cane under their strong grinders: their hair also preserves its colour much later than that of the white. In fact, it is difficult to guess the age of a negro.

The negro is rarely seriously ill, though he often fancies himself so; he suffers most from his indulgences and the indifferent skill of those who undertake his cure. He bears pain exceedingly well, which may partly arise from his nerves not being highly strung. The negro is distinguished for his (for want of a better word I may call) *insouciance*. It is a most provoking characteristic, and one of the causes of his want of progress.

The general impression is that serious crime is rare in Hayti, except that which is connected with the Vaudoux worship. This, however, is a mistake; crime is treated with too much indifference, and the professional poisoners are well known to the police. Before the civil war of 1868 and 1869 crimes of violence were more rare; that civil strife, however, demoralised the population. Pilfering is their great failing, and it is said a negro never leaves a room without looking round to see that he has not forgotten something.

They have much superstition with regard to *zombis, revenants*, or ghosts, and many will not leave the house after dark; yet the love of pleasure often overcomes this, and the negro will pass half the night hieing to his lusting-place.

Of their pleasures, smoking is one equally enjoyed by every class, and quietly by most women after a certain age. The cheapness of tafia or white rum has an evil effect on the male population, who as a rule drink to excess.

The black Haytians resent being spoken of by foreigners as negroes, though they use the word freely among themselves. They prefer being called *gens de couleur*, as both the expressions *nègres* and *mulâtres* are considered as implying contempt. During the tiresome quarter of an hour before dinner, my friend Villevalein (coloured) turned round to a Minister of State (black) and said, "What do you think the French *chargé d'affaires* remarked when he first saw you?—'Quel beau nègre!'" The blood rushed to the face of the Haytian, and his cheeks became of a deeper black; and we were all thankful that at the moment dinner was announced. I doubt whether the Minister ever forgave the author or the repeater of the remark.

The negro has the greatest, in fact, an almost superstitious, reverence for the flags of foreign nations. A well-known partisan chief, Acaau, came once to the English Consulate at Les Cayes, and demanded that all the refugees there should be given up to him to be shot. Our Acting Vice-Consul, Charles Smith, refused, and as Acaau insisted, the Vice-Consul took up the Union Jack, and placing it on the staircase, said to the chief, "If any of you dare to tread on that flag, he may go upstairs and seize the refugees." Acaau looked at the flag a moment, and then said, "Not I," and walked away, followed by his men. This was not from fear of material consequences, although there were two English ships of war in harbour, as, when one of the captains threatened to bombard the town if foreigners were troubled, Acaau answered, "Tell me which end you will begin with, and I will commence to burn the other end." He was a mountaineer, who would have been delighted to burn and destroy the whole place. Many years afterwards, to avoid being shot by the Government, he perished by his own hand.

I must add an anecdote to mark the respect shown by the negro to the white. In April 1866, on account of a quarrel between an officer on board a steamer and some blacks, the mob determined to revenge themselves. Watching their opportunity, they seized an English sailor belonging to the ship and bound him to a log. Hundreds of excited negroes surrounded him with drawn razors and knives, threatening to cut him to pieces; when Mr. Savage, an English merchant, happening to be passing by, inquired the cause of the disturbance, and hearing what had happened to his countryman, forced his way through the mob, and when he reached the sailor, drew a penknife from his pocket, and, despising the yells and threats of the crowd, cut the cords, freed the man, and walked him down to the steamer's boat. The cool courage shown by Mr. Savage perfectly awed the mob. As the

Haytian police who were present had not interfered to prevent this outrage on the sailor, a hundred pounds indemnity was demanded of the Haytian Government, which was paid, and subsequently transmitted to the sailor.

I will conclude with noticing that the apathy and listlessness of the Haytians, mentioned by Mackenzie in 1826, might apply to the present day, as well as his reference to the lean dogs and leaner pigs which infest the capital. He heard an Englishman say one day, "D—— these Haytians; they can't even fatten a pig."

The Mulattoes

"They hate their fathers and despise their mothers," is a saying which is a key to the character of the mulatto. They hate the whites and despise the blacks, hence their false position. That they are looked down upon by the whites and hated by the blacks is the converse truth, which produces an unfortunate effect upon their character. They have many of the defects of the two races, and few of their good qualities. Those who have never left their country are too often conceited, and presumptuous to a degree which is scarcely credible; whilst many who have travelled appear but little influenced by bright examples of civilisation, or by their intercourse with civilised nations, retaining but the outward polish of a superficial French education. Foreigners who casually meet Haytians are often only struck by their agreeable manners, but to understand their real character one must live among them, hear their talk among themselves, or read the newspapers published for local circulation.

Travel, indeed, has little outward effect on the majority; and they return to their own country more presumptuous than ever. It has struck many attentive observers that this outward parade of conceit is but a species of protest against the inferior position they occupy in the world's estimation, and that with their advance in civilisation and education they will rise in the opinion of others, and thus lose the necessity for so much self-assertion. I believe this to be highly probable, but until the mulattoes are convinced of their present inferiority, the improvement must be slow indeed.

It may be remarked, however, that those who have been educated in Europe from their earliest years show few or none of those defects which are implanted in them by their early associations. I have known coloured men whose first real knowledge of their own country was acquired in manhood, who were in every respect equal to their white companions, as manly and as free from absurd pretensions, and naturally without that dislike of foreigners which is instilled into home-educated mulattoes. These men, knowing the consideration in which they were held by all, had no necessity for any self-assertion.

The early training in Hayti is much at fault; their mothers, generally uninstructed, have themselves but few principles of delicacy to instil into their children's minds. I will mention a case in illustration. A lady was asked to procure some article for a foreign visitor. She readily undertook the commission, and sent her son, a boy of ten, to seek the article. He returned shortly afterwards and said to his mother, "Our neighbour has what you want, but asks twenty-seven paper dollars for it." "Go and tell our friend that you have found it for forty, and we will divide the difference between us." A mutual acquaintance heard of this transaction, and subsequently reproached the lady for the lesson of deceit and swindling she had taught her child; she only laughed, and appeared to think she had done a very clever thing. The subsequent career of that boy was indeed a thorn in her side.

Their financial morality is very low indeed. A friend of mine expressing his surprise to one of the prettiest and most respectable girls in Port-au-Prince that such open robbery of the receipts of the custom-house was permitted, received for answer, "Prendre l'argent de l'état, ce n'est pas volé." — "To take Government money is not robbery." With such ideas instilled into the minds of all from their earliest youth, it is scarcely to be wondered at that the Haytians grow up to be completely without financial honour. Truth is another virtue which appears to be rarely inculcated by parents, and this perhaps may be accounted for by their origin. Slaves are notoriously given to falsehood, and this defect has been inherited by succeeding generations, and can scarcely be eradicated until a higher moral teaching prevails.

I was struck by an anecdote told me by a French gentleman at Port-au-Prince: it is a trifle, but it shows the spirit of the Haytian youth. A trader, in very moderate circumstances, sent a half-grown son to be educated in Paris, and as the father had no friends there, he said to my informant, "Will you ask your family to pay my son a little attention?" In consequence, a lady called at the school and took the youth for a walk in the Luxembourg Gardens. Approaching the basins, she said, "I suppose you have none like these in Hayti?" "Oh," was his reply, "my father has finer ones in his private grounds;" the fact being, that he had nothing there but a bath a few feet square. This miserable pretence is one of the causes of the slow improvement in Hayti; they cannot or they will not see the superiority of foreign countries.

A late Secretary of State was present at a review in Paris, when ten thousand splendid cavalry charged up towards the Emperors of France and Russia. "It is very fine," he said; "but how much better our Haytian soldiers ride!" Another gentleman, long employed as a representative at a foreign court, returning home, could find nothing better to say to President Geffrard than, "Ah! President, you should send some of our officers to Paris, that their superiority of *tenue* may be known in Europe." I wish I could present some photographic illustrations of a Haytian regiment in support of this assertion.

I am, in fact, doubtful whether travel as yet has done much good to the general public, as they see their young men returning from Europe and America, after having witnessed the best of our modern civilisation, who assure them that things are much better managed in Hayti.

Their self-importance may be illustrated by the following anecdote of another ex-Secretary of State. He went with a friend to see the races at Longchamps. They had their cabriolet drawn up at a good spot, when presently an acquaintance of the driver got up on the box-seat to have a better view. "I must tell that man to get down," said the ex-Minister. "Leave him alone," answered his French friend. "It is all very well for you, a private individual, to say that; but I, a former Secretary of State, what will the people say to my permitting such familiarity?" and he looked uneasily around, thinking that the eyes of the whole Parisian world were bent on their distinguished visitor. I once saw some boxes addressed thus:—"Les demoiselles — —, enfants de M. — —, ex-Secrétaire d'Etat."

Of the profound dislike of the genuine coloured Haytian for the whites I will give an instance. We were invited to a school examination given by the Sisters of Cluny, and naturally the official guests were put in the front rank, with the officers of a French gunboat, from which position we assisted at a distribution of prizes, and some little scenes acted by the pupils. The next day a Haytian gentleman, one who was an ornament to his country for his extensive knowledge and legal erudition, made this remark—"When I saw those whites put into the front row, it reminded me of the time when the ancient colonists sat arms akimbo watching the dances of their slaves." As he said this before a party of white gentlemen, we may imagine what were his utterances before his own countrymen.

Moreau de St. Méry gives a table of the different combinations of colour among the mixed race, amounting to one hundred and twenty, which produce thirteen distinct shades between the pure white and the pure black. Each has a name, the most common of which are: Quateron, white and mulatto; mulatto, white and black; griffe, black and mulatto. These were the original combinations, but constant intermarriages have produced a great variety of colour, even in the same families, some breeding back to their white, others to their black forefathers. It appears as if the lighter shades of mulatto would die out, as many of this class marry Europeans, and leave the country with their children, and the others marry Haytians more or less dark, and the tendency is to breeding back to their black ancestors. There are too few whites settled in the country to arrest this backward movement. In Santo Domingo, however, the stay for a few years (1859-64) of a large Spanish army had a very appreciable effect on the population.

The personal appearance of the coloured Haytians is not striking. Being in general a mixture of rather a plain race in Europe with the plainest in Africa, it is not surprising that the men should be ugly and the women far from handsome. Of course there is a marked distinction between the men who have more dark blood in their veins and those who approach the white; in fact, those who are less than half-European have in general the hair frizzled like a negro's, the forehead low, the eyes dark in a yellow setting, the nose flat, the mouth large, the teeth perfect, the jaw heavy; whilst as they approach the white type they greatly improve in appearance, until they can scarcely be distinguished from the foreigner, except by the dead colour of the skin and some trifling peculiarities.

Of the women it is more difficult to speak; they are rarely good-looking, never beautiful. As they approach the white type, they have long, rather coarse hair, beautiful teeth, small fleshless hands and feet, delicate forms, and sometimes graceful movements, due apparently to the length of the lower limbs. Their principal defects are their voices, their noses, their skins, and sometimes the inordinate size of the lower jaw. Their voices are harsh, their skins blotchy or of a dirty brown, their noses flat or too fleshy, and the jaw, as I have said, heavy. Occasionally you see a girl decidedly pretty, who would pass in any society, but these are rare. In general they are very plain, particularly when you approach the black type, when the frizzled hair begins to appear.

There is one subject necessary to mention, though it is a delicate one. Like the negroes, the mulattoes have often a decided odour, and this is particularly observable after dancing or any violent exercise which provokes perspiration, and then no amount of *eau de cologne* or other scents will completely conceal the native perfume. The griffes, however, are decidedly the most subject to this inconvenience, and I met one well-dressed woman who positively tainted the air.

With the exception of those who have been sent abroad, the Haïtiennes have had until lately but few chances of education, and are therefore little to be blamed for their ignorance. This want of instruction, however, has an ill effect, as the time necessarily hangs heavy on their hands, and they can neither give those first teachings to their children which are never forgotten, nor amuse themselves with literature or good music.

It is the fashion in Hayti to vaunt the goodness and tenderness of their women in sickness; but what women are not good and tender under similar circumstances? I have received as much kindness in suffering from the Malays when wandering in Borneo as any one has perhaps ever received elsewhere. The fact is, that these qualities are inherent to women in general. Perhaps the greatest praise that can be given to the Haytian ladies is, that they do not appear inferior to others who reside in the tropics in the care of their children, or in the management of their households, or in their conduct towards their husbands.

They have their ways in public and their ways in private, but their greatest defect is their want of cleanliness, which is observable in their houses, their children, and their own clothes. Without going so far as to say, with the naval officer, that "their customs are dirty, and manners they have none," I may say that they have habits which are simply indescribable; and when not dressed to receive company they are veritable slatterns, sauntering about their houses all day in dirty dressing-gowns, and too often in unchanged linen. Their bedrooms have a close, stuffy smell, the consequence of the above referred to indescribable habits, which is highly displeasing to a stranger, and induced an American gentleman to remark that their rooms had the smell of a stable. They are also very careless in another way, and will go into their kitchens even in their silks, and aid in preparing sweetmeats; and the stains on their clothes from this cause reminded me of a young Malay lady cooking a greasy curry whilst dressed in a rich gold brocade, and upsetting half of it over her dress in an endeavour to conceal herself or her work.

The conduct of the Haytian ladies who are married to foreigners is much to their credit, as rarely a case occurs to draw the attention of the public to their private life; and almost the same may be said of their married life in general, and this in defiance of the debauchery of their Haytian husbands. This virtue was, perhaps, unfairly ascribed by a French diplomatist to their sluggish temperaments and their want of imagination. But, whatever may be the cause, it appears to exist to a considerable extent.

The habit of having no fixed hours for meals appears to prevail in most tropical countries; and in Hayti, though there are fixed times for the husband and the other males of a family, who can only return from business at certain hours, yet the ladies of the family prefer cakes, sweetmeats, and dreadful messes at all hours, and only sit down to the family meal *pro formâ*. No wonder they are ever complaining of indigestion, and taking their wonderful *remèdes*.

From my own observation, and that of many of my friends, I may assert with confidence as a general proposition, that the Haytian black or mulatto is more given to drink, and to a forgetfulness of his duty to his family, than any other people with whom we were acquainted. With some marked, and I should add numerous exceptions, after his early coffee the Haytian begins the day with a grog or cocktail, and these grogs and cocktails continue until at mid-day many of the young men are slightly intoxicated, and by night a large minority at least are either in an excited, a sullen, or a maudlin state.

It appears also to be a rule among them, that, whether married or not, a Haytian must have as many mistresses as his purse will permit him; these are principally drawn from the lower classes. This practice is not confined to any particular rank; from the Presidents downwards all are tainted with the same evil. The mistresses of the first-named are always known, as they are visited publicly, often accompanied by a staff or a few select officers. I have met them even at dinner in respectable houses, and have been asked to trace a resemblance between their children and the reputed father. No one seeks to conceal it, and the conversation of married ladies continually turns on this subject. One excuse for it is that many of the ladies whom you meet in society were only married after the birth of their first children. However, according to French law, that ceremony renders them all legitimate.

Some of those admitted into society are not married at all, but their daughters' being married prevents notice being taken of the false position of the mother.

An excuse has been made for the debauchery of the Haytians. It is said that there are three women to every two men, which is probably true, and that therefore the latter are exposed to every kind of temptation, which is also true.

I have already referred to the want of financial honour observable in Hayti; but what is equally pernicious is their utter forgetfulness of what is due to their military oath. As I shall have to notice in my remarks on the army, scarcely a single name can be cited of a superior officer who under President Geffrard did not forget his duty, and either conspire against him or betray him to the enemy. This was particularly observable during the siege of Cap Haïtien in 1865. And yet were these officers who were false to their military honour looked down upon by their countrymen? On the contrary, their only title to consideration was their treachery to their former superior, who in turn is said to have betrayed every Government he had served.

A Frenchman once wittily said, that when Geffrard was made President, being no longer able to conspire against the Government, he conspired against his own Ministers. It is the whole truth in a few words. No encouragement is given to those who hold firmly to their duty; and an officer who did not desert a tottering Government would be sure to be neglected, perhaps even punished, by those who succeeded to power.

One reason for the dislike entertained by the mulatto for the white man is the evident partiality of their fair countrywomen for the latter. It is well known that the first dream or *beau ideal* of the young Haïtienne is a rich, and if possible a good-looking European, who can place her in a respectable position, give her the prospect of occasional visits to Europe, with the ultimate expectation of entirely residing there. Few young girls lose the hope of securing this desirable husband, particularly among those who have received their education in Europe, until their charms begin slightly to fade, when they content themselves with the least dark among their countrymen. It is unfortunate that this should be the case, as those who are most enlightened among the Haytian ladies are thus withdrawn from the civilising influence they would otherwise naturally exert. This preference for the white to the coloured man was also very conspicuous during the French occupation; and all things considered, it is not to be wondered at, as the whites make much better husbands.

The young mulatto, seeing this evident partiality for the foreigner, naturally resents it, but instead of trying to put himself on an equality of position with his rival by the exercise of industry and by good conduct, expends his energies in furious tirades in the *cafés* or by low debauchery.

The Haytians are distinguished for what the French call *jactance*, a better word than boasting. Mackenzie tells the story of a mulatto colonel saying to him, "Je vous assure, monsieur, que je suis le plus brave de tous les mulâtres de ce pays-ci." He was lost in admiration of his own noble qualities. At the fortress of La Ferrière, during Mackenzie's visit, a Captain Elliot said about some trifle, "N'ayez pas peur?" Immediately the officers of the garrison clapped their hands to their swords and talked five minutes of inflated nonsense.

I remember a Haytian general once calling upon me, and asking me to get inserted in the daily London papers a long account of the battles in which he had been engaged, and of his personal exploits. He was anxious that the English people should know what a hero they had among them. As he was really a brave fellow, and a man whom I liked, I was anxious that he should not make himself ridiculous by publishing a pompous account of battles which were but skirmishes among the peasantry. I therefore gave him a letter of introduction to an editor, who, I was sure, would explain to him that the English public would not be interested in the affair. I heard no more of it, but my friend was persuaded that since Napoleon no greater general than he had arisen.

As an ideal type of the better class of mulatto, I would take the late President Geffrard; he had all the qualities and defects of the race, and was one whom I had the best opportunity of studying. In a report which for some reason I never forwarded, I find myself thus sketching his portrait when almost in daily intercourse with him (1866):—"I am loth to analyse the character of President Geffrard, but as he is the Government itself, it is necessary to know him. In manner he is polished and gentle, almost feminine in his gentleness, with a most agreeable expression, a winning smile, and much fluency in conversation. But the impression soon gains possession of the listener that, with all his amiable qualities, the President is vain and presumptuous, absorbed in himself and in his own superiority to the rest of mankind. He imagines himself a proficient in every science, although he is as ignorant as he is untravelled. There is not a subject on which he does not pretend to know more even than those whose studies have been special, as lawyers, doctors, architects, and engineers. He seriously assures you that he discovered the use of steam by independent inquiries, and that he is prepared to construct a machine which shall solve the problem of perpetual motion; and he who has not ridden anything larger than a middle-sized pony imagines he could give hints in riding to our Newmarket jockeys."

Geffrard, like many other coloured men, was much distressed by the crispness of his hair and his dark colour, and having a half-brother very fair, he persisted in assuring us that he had been born nearly white, with straight hair, but that having unfortunately bathed in the streams of Sal Tron during many months, the water, being deeply impregnated with iron, had curled his hair and darkened his skin. In any other man I should have suspected a jest.

One of the things which contributed to the unpopularity of the Emperor Soulouque was the waste of the public finances and the extravagance of his court. General Geffrard, who lived in penury before becoming President, promised to reform this; but instead of doing so, he gradually raised his own allowance to £10,000 a year; he also had the sole control of £4000 a year for secret service, and another £4000 a year for the encouragement of the arts and sciences. The grateful country had also presented him with two large estates, the expenses of which were largely borne by the State, whilst the profits were Geffrard's.

As nearly every one of his countrymen would have acted in the same manner if he had had the opportunity, Geffrard's conduct excited envy rather than blame. Even in the smallest details of the household there was a mean spirit; the expenses of the meat of the family were put down to the *tirailleurs*, whilst some exquisite champagne purchased of a colleague was charged to the hospital. Geffrard was certainly one of the most distinguished of his race, yet he sullied his good name by all these petty meannesses. I once asked a Haytian friend why she and others were always running down Geffrard and his family. She answered, "Because when I knew them intimately, they were as poor as myself, but now Madame Geffrard insults me by calling on me in a carriage. What right has she to a carriage more than I?"

Geffrard was personally brave, which quality is not too common among his countrymen, who are rather wanting in martial qualities. He had no idea of true liberty, nor of freedom of discussion. A son of a black Minister wrote a pamphlet in favour of strict protection for the manufactures of Hayti, in order to encourage native industry. A young mulatto replied, demolishing with ease the absurd idea that manufactures could be readily established in a tropical country, which could only be made to prosper by encouraging agriculture. The father was offended by this liberty, and, to soothe his wounded feelings, Geffrard had the young mulatto arrested, put as a common soldier into a regiment, and set to work to carry on his head barrels of powder to a village five miles in the mountains. The argument was unanswerable, and it is no wonder that the pamphleteer became a protectionist, though I believe that subsequently, when he was made a senator, he was inclined to return to his primitive views.

If I wished to describe a mulatto of the most unscrupulous type, I should have selected the late General Lorquet, but I have already referred to him.

There are among the mulattoes men eminently agreeable, and perhaps the one who best pleased me was Auguste Elie, at one time Minister for Foreign Affairs. He had been brought up in France, was highly educated, and had an astonishing memory. My Spanish colleague and myself used to visit him almost every evening, and pass a pleasant hour in varied conversation. One day my friend remarked, "I am often surprised at the knowledge shown by Auguste Elie, and the elegance of the language in which it is expressed." I replied, "This evening turn the conversation on agriculture in the South of France." He did so, and he was again struck by the minute knowledge shown and the manner in which it was conveyed. On our return home, I opened the last number of "La Revue des Deux Mondes," and showed him paragraph after paragraph which Auguste Elie had repeated almost word for word. I knew that he read the review regularly, and was persuaded he had not missed reading the article on the agriculture of that part of France which interested him most, and his memory was so exact that he had forgotten nothing. I had often remarked his quotations, but he could digest what he read as well as remember. A few men like Auguste Elie would have given a better tone to Haytian society.

A strong desire to appear what they are not is a defect from which the best-known Haytians are not free. A French colleague once called upon a Secretary of State, whose *writings have been compared to those of Plato*, and found him, book in hand, walking up and down his verandah. "Ah! my friend, you see how I employ my leisure hours. I am reading Demosthenes in the original." But the sharp Frenchman kept his eye on the volume, and soon found that it was an interlinear translation.

Every Haytian appears fully persuaded that his countrymen never seek office except for the purpose of improving their private fortunes, and the most precise stories of official robbery were falsely made against Auguste Elie and M. Bauce, both Secretaries of State. At Auguste Elie's death there was little left for the family, and Madame Bauce declined the succession to her husband's effects, as the debts were not covered by the inheritance. Liaulaud Ethéart and M. Darius Denis, though long Secretaries of State, afterwards honourably supported their families, the one in retail trade, the other by keeping a school.

Perhaps, as a rule, the accusation is well founded, and nearly all, black and coloured, believe in the saying, "Prendre l'argent de l'état, ce n'est pas volé."

When I first arrived in Port-au-Prince a small club was formed among the foreigners, and one of the first rules was, "No Haytian to be admitted." I asked why, and was answered, that they introduced politics into every place they entered. I soon found, however, that the real reason was that their society was disliked; and one day, after listening for an hour or two to the criticism on the people—and be it remembered that half those present were married to Haytian ladies—I could not help remarking, "If I had such an opinion of this race, I would not have sought my wife among them." The married men looked foolish, the bachelors laughed, and one of the former observed, "The women are so superior to the men."

The following story shows some delicacy of feeling; it is told by Mackenzie, and I have heard it repeated. When the decree was issued by Dessalines that mulatto children should inherit the estates of their white fathers, two young men met, and one said to the other, "You kill my father and I will kill yours;" which they accordingly did, and took possession of their estates. On another occasion, the Emperor Dessalines said to a young man who claimed to be a mulatto, "I don't believe it, but you can prove it by going and poniarding your French friend." The man did not hesitate, and was accepted as a Haytian citizen. A negro general, grandfather of a lady I knew in Hayti, went to Dessalines after the appearance of the decree to murder all the white French left in the island and said, "Emperor, I have obeyed your decree: I have put my white wife to death." "Excellent Haytian," answered he, "but an infernal scoundrel. If ever again you present yourself before me I will have you shot,"—the only saying of his that I have seen recorded showing any humane feeling.

CHAPTER V
VAUDOUX WORSHIP AND CANNIBALISM

When the news reached Paris of the massacres in Port-au-Prince of the mulattoes by orders of the black President Soulouque in April 1849, it is said that Louis Napoleon took the opportunity of saying at a public reception, in presence of the sable representative of Hayti, "Haïti, Haïti! pays de barbares." Had he known all the particulars relating to Vaudoux worship and cannibalism, he would have been still more justified in so expressing himself.

There is no subject of which it is more difficult to treat than Vaudoux worship and the cannibalism that too often accompanies its rites. Few living out of the Black Republic are aware of the extent to which it is carried, and if I insist at length upon the subject, it is in order to endeavour to fix attention on this frightful blot, and thus induce enlightened Haytians to take measures for its extirpation, if that be possible.[8]

It is certain that no people are more sensitive to foreign public opinion than the Haytians, and they therefore endeavour to conceal by every means this evidence of the barbarism of their fellow-countrymen. It is, however, but the story of the foolish ostrich over again; every foreigner in Hayti knows that cannibalism exists, and that the educated classes endeavour to ignore it instead of devising means to eradicate it.

The only Governments that endeavoured to grapple with the evil were those of President Geffrard and President Boisrond-Canal, and probably they in some measure owe their fall to this action on their part.

The first question naturally asked is, "Who is tainted by the Vaudoux worship?" I fear the answer must be, "Who is not?" This does not necessarily imply that they are tainted with cannibalism, as I shall hereafter explain. It is notorious that the Emperor Soulouque was a firm believer, and that the mulatto general Therlonge was one of its high priests, and in his younger days used to appear in a scarlet robe performing antics in the trees. A late Prime Minister, whose bloody deeds will be an everlasting reproach to his memory, was said to be a chief priest of the sect, and many others whom I will not at present indicate.

If persons so high placed can be counted among its votaries, it may be readily believed that the masses are given up to this brutalising worship. During the reign of Soulouque, a priestess was arrested for having performed a sacrifice too openly; when about to be conducted to prison, a foreign bystander remarked aloud that probably she would be shot. She laughed and said, "If I were to beat the sacred drum, and march through the city, not one, from the Emperor downwards, but would humbly follow me." She was sent to jail, but no one ever heard that she was punished.

President Salnave (1867), inclined at first to court the support of the educated classes, kept clear of the Vaudoux. But when he found his advances repulsed, for the gross debauchery at the palace prevented any respectable person from ever willingly entering it, and when the fortunes of the civil war that then raged began to turn against him (1869), he, from some motive or other, whether superstition or the desire to conciliate the mass of his ignorant troops, went to consult a well-known priest living near Marquissant, in the neighbourhood of Port-au-Prince, and there went through all the ceremonies that were required. He bathed in the blood of goats, made considerable presents to the priests and priestesses, and then feasted with the assembly, who all gave themselves up to the lowest debauchery, and kept up these festivities so long that even the iron frame of the President gave way, and he was confined to his bed for many days after.

The fortunes of war still continuing adverse, he again consulted the Papaloi or priest, who insisted that he must now go through the highest ceremony; that the "goat without horns" must be slain, and that he must be anointed with its blood. If he agreed to this, then the priest assured him of certain victory over his enemies.

Whether Salnave gave in or not I cannot say positively. His enemies of all classes declared he did; his friends among the lower orders confirmed the story; but the few respectable people who adhered to his cause naturally denied the truth of the accusation. I think the weight of evidence was more against him than for him.

To explain the phrase of "the goat without horns," I must notice that there are two sects which follow the Vaudoux worship—those who only delight in the blood and flesh of white cocks and spotless white goats at their ceremonies, and those who are not only devoted to these, but on great occasions call for the flesh and blood of the "goat without horns," or human victims.

When Hayti was still a French colony Vaudoux worship flourished, but there is no distinct mention of human sacrifices in the accounts transmitted to us. In Moreau de St. Méry's excellent description of the colony, from whose truthful pages it is a pleasure to seek for information, he gives a very graphic account of fetishism as it existed in his day, that is, towards the close of the last century.

After describing certain dances, he remarks that the Calinda and the Chica are not the only ones brought from Africa to the colony. There is another which has been known for a long time, principally in the western part of the island (Hayti), and which has the name of Vaudoux.[9] But it is not merely as a dance that the Vaudoux merits consideration; at least it is accompanied by circumstances that give it a rank among those institutions in which superstition and ridiculous practices have a principal part.

According to the Arada negroes, who are the true sectaries of the Vaudoux in the colony, who maintain its principles and its rules, Vaudoux signifies an all-powerful and supernatural being, on whom depend all the events which take place in the world. This being is the non-venomous serpent, and it is under its auspices that all those assemble who profess this doctrine. Acquaintance with the past, knowledge of the present, prescience of the future, all appertain to this serpent, that only consents, however, to communicate his power and prescribe his will through the organ of a grand priest, whom the sectaries select, and still more by that of the negress whom the love of the latter has raised to the rank of high priestess.

These two delegates, who declare themselves inspired by their god, or in whom the gift of inspiration is really manifested in the opinion of their followers, bear the pompous names of King and Queen, or the despotic ones of Master and Mistress, or the touching titles of Papa and Mama. They are during their whole life the chiefs of the great family of the Vaudoux, and they have a right to the unlimited respect of those that compose it. It is they who decide if the serpent agrees to admit a candidate into the society, who prescribe the obligations and the duties he is to fulfil; it is they who receive the gifts and presents which the god expects as a just homage to him. To disobey them, to resist them, is to disobey God himself, and to expose oneself to the greatest misfortunes.

This system of domination on the one hand, and of blind obedience on the other, being well established, they at fixed dates meet together, and the King and Queen of the Vaudoux preside, following the forms which they probably brought from Africa, and to which Creole customs have added many variations, and some traits which betray European ideas; as, for instance, the scarf, or rich belt, which the Queen wears at these assemblies, and which she occasionally varies.

The reunion for the true Vaudoux worship, for that which has least lost its primitive purity, never takes place except secretly, in the dead of night, and in a secure place safe from any profane eye. There each initiated puts on a pair of sandals and fastens around his body a number, more or less considerable, of red handkerchiefs, or of handkerchiefs in which that colour predominates. The King of the Vaudoux has finer handkerchiefs and in greater number, and one that is entirely red, with which he binds his forehead as a diadem. A girdle, generally blue, gives the finishing-stroke to the tokens of his resplendent dignity.

The Queen, dressed with simple luxury, also shows her predilection for the red colour,[10] which is generally that of her sash or belt.

The King and Queen place themselves at one end of the room, near a kind of altar, on which is a box where the serpent is kept, and where each adept can see it through the bars of its cage.

When they have verified that no curious stranger has penetrated into the place, they commence the ceremony by the adoration of the serpent, by protestations of being faithful to its worship and entirely submissive to its commands. They renew, holding the hands of the King and Queen, the oath of secrecy, which is the foundation of the association, and it is accompanied by everything horrible which delirium could imagine to render it more imposing.

When the followers of the Vaudoux are thus prepared to receive the impressions which the King and Queen desire them to feel, they take the affectionate tone of a tender father or mother; vaunt the happiness which is the appanage of those who are devoted to the Vaudoux; they exhort them to have confidence in him, and to give him the proofs of it by taking his counsel in all the most important circumstances of their lives.

Then the crowd separates, and each one who may desire it, and according to his seniority in the sect, approaches to implore the aid of the Vaudoux. Most of them ask for the talent to be able to direct the conduct of their masters. But this is not enough: one wants more money; another the gift of being able to please an unfeeling one; another desires to reattach an unfaithful lover; this one wishes for a prompt cure or long life; an elderly female comes to conjure the god to end the disdain with which she is treated by the youth whose love she would captivate; a young one solicits eternal love, or she repeats the maledictions that hate dictates to her against a preferred rival. There is not a passion which does not give vent to its vow, and crime itself does not always disguise those which have for object its success. At each of these invocations the King of the Vaudoux appears absorbed in thought. The spirit seizes him; suddenly he takes hold of the box in which the serpent is confined, places it on the ground, and commands the Queen to get on it. As soon as the sacred ark is beneath her feet, the new Pythoness is filled by the spirit of their god; she trembles, all her body is in a state of convulsion, and the oracle speaks by her mouth. Now she flatters and promises happiness, now she bursts into reproaches; and according to her wishes, her interest, or her caprice, she dictates as decrees without appeal everything which she is pleased to prescribe, in the name of the serpent, to this imbecile crowd, that never expresses the slightest doubt of the most monstrous absurdity, and that only knows how to obey what is despotically dictated to it.

After all these questions have received some kind of an answer from the oracle, many of which are not without ambiguity, they form a circle, and the serpent is again placed on the altar. Then his followers bring as tribute the objects they think most worthy, and that no jealous curiosity shall raise a blush, the offerings are placed in a covered hat. The King and Queen then promise that the offerings shall be accepted by their god. It is from this collection that the expenses of the meetings are paid, that aid is afforded to absent members, or to those present who may be in want, or to others from whom the society may expect something in favour of its glory or renown. They now propose and settle their future plans, they consider what is to be done, and all this is declared by the Queen the will of the god; often enough these plans have not for object either good order or public tranquillity. A fresh oath, as execrable as the first, engages each one to be silent as to what has passed, to aid in what has been settled; and sometimes a vase, in which there is the blood of a goat, still warm, seals on the lips of those present the promise to suffer death rather than reveal anything, and even to inflict it on any one who may forget that he is thus so solemnly bound to secrecy.

After these ceremonies commences the dance of the Vaudoux.

If there should be a new candidate, it is by his admission that the *fête* commences. The King of the Vaudoux, with some black substance, traces a large circle, and in this the novice is placed; and in his hand he puts a packet of herbs, horsehair, pieces of horn, and other trifling objects. Then lightly touching him on the head with a slight wooden wand, he thunders forth an African song, which is repeated in chorus by those who stand around the circle; then the new member begins to tremble and to dance, which is called to practise Vaudoux. If, unhappily, excess of excitement makes him leave the circle, the song immediately ceases, the King and Queen turn their backs to avert the evil omen. The dancer recollects himself, re-enters the circle, again trembles, drinks, and arrives at length at so convulsive a state, that the King orders him to stop, by striking him lightly on the head with his wand, or, should he think it necessary, with a heavy *kurbash*. He is taken to the altar to swear, and from that moment he belongs to the sect.

This ceremony over, the King places his hand or his foot on the box in which the serpent is confined, and soon becomes agitated. This impression he communicates to the Queen, and from her it gains the whole circle, and every one commences certain movements, in which the upper part of the body, the head and shoulders, appear to be dislocated. The Queen above all is a prey to the most violent agitation. From time to time she approaches the serpent in order to add to her frenzy; she shakes the box, and the hawkbells attached to it sound like a fool's bauble, and the excitement goes on increasing. This is augmented by the use of spirituous liquors, which the adepts do not spare. With some, fainting fits follow, with others a species of fury; but a nervous trembling seizes them all, which they appear unable to master. They go on spinning round, and in their excitement some tear their clothes, others bite their own flesh; then again many fall to the ground utterly deprived of sense, and are dragged into a neighbouring dark apartment. Here in the obscurity is too often a scene of the most disgusting prostitution.

At length lassitude puts an end to these demoralising scenes, to be renewed again at a date which is carefully settled beforehand.

In reading this account, freely given from Moreau de St. Méry, I have been struck how little change, except for the worse, has taken place during the last century. Though the sect continues to meet in secret, they do not appear to object to the presence of their countrymen who are not yet initiated. In fact, the necessity of so much mystery is not recognised, when there are no longer any French magistrates to send these assassins to the stake.

Notwithstanding their efforts to keep strangers far from their sacrifices, two Frenchmen succeeded in being present on different occasions.

At a dinner at which I was present, I heard the Archbishop of Port-au-Prince give the following account of what had occurred the preceding week (in 1869). A French priest who had charge of the district of Arcahaye, had the curiosity to witness the Vaudoux ceremonies, and he persuaded some of his parishioners to take him to the forest, where a meeting of the sect was to be held. They were very unwilling, saying that, if discovered, he and they would be killed; but he promised faithfully that, whatever happened, he would not speak a word. They blacked his hands and face, and disguising him as a peasant, took him with them. In Salnave's time the Vaudoux priests were so seldom interrupted, that few precautions were taken against surprise, and the neighbouring villagers flocked to the ceremony. With these the Catholic priest mixed, and saw all that went on. As in the previous description, the people came to ask that their wishes should be gratified, and the priestess stood on the box containing the serpent. At first she went into a violent paroxysm, then, in a sort of half-trance, she promised all that they could desire. A white cock and then a white goat were killed, and those present were marked with their blood. Up to this point, it appeared as if Monseigneur were repeating some pages from Moreau de St. Méry, but it soon changed. He continued:—Presently an athletic young negro came and knelt before the priestess and said, "O Maman, I have a favour to ask." "What is it, my son?" "Give us, to complete the sacrifice, the goat without horns." She gave a sign of assent; the crowd in the shed separated, and there was a child sitting with its feet bound. In an instant a rope already passed through a block was tightened, the child's feet flew up towards the roof, and the priest approached it with a knife. The loud shriek given by the victim aroused the Frenchman to the truth of what was really going on. He shouted, "Oh, spare the child!" and would have darted forward, but he was seized by his friends around him, and literally carried from the spot. There was a short pursuit, but the priest got safely back to the town. He tried to rouse the police to hasten to the spot, but they would do nothing. In the morning they accompanied him to the scene of the sacrifice. They found the remains of the feast, and near the shed the boiled skull of the child.

The authorities at Arcahaye were exceedingly incensed with the priest for his interference, and, under pretence that they could not answer for his safety, shipped him off to Port-au-Prince, where he made his report to the Archbishop.

Another Frenchman, who resided in a village in the southern department, witnessed the whole ceremony, and, as he remained silent, was undiscovered; but on its being rumoured that he had been present, his wife's Haytian family insisted on his leaving the district, as his life was in danger.

I have frequently heard similar details from educated Haytians, and a proof will presently be given.

I may notice that the Haytians have corrupted the compounds Papa Roi and Maman Roi into Papaloi and Mamanloi.

The temples of the Vaudoux, called Humfort, are to be found in every district of the country. They are in general small, though one I visited in the interior was spacious, and was papered with engravings from the *Illustrated London News*, and the walls were hung with the pictures of the Virgin Mary and of various saints. I may notice that in every one I entered I found similar pictures. In the largest one, a Catholic priest had often said mass during his inland tours. Though he could not prove it, he shrewdly suspected that the Vaudoux worship was carried on there during his frequent absences. He showed me some very curious polished stones of various forms, which he had induced some of his disciples to give up. One was a stone axe in shape of a crescent; and the negroes said that they had been brought from Africa, and formed part of the relics they worshipped. I believe my informant obtained these stones from a young negress during the absence of her husband, who was very indignant on discovering their loss. The French priest destroyed them, to prevent their falling again into the hands of his congregation.

Beside various Christian emblems, I found in one of the temples a flag of red silk, on which was worked the following inscription:—"Société des Fleurs za Dahomïan," whatever that may refer to. This flag was said to have been the gift of the Empress, the consort of the Emperor Soulouque.

Once whilst strolling with a friend in the mountains at the back of La Coupé, about six miles from Port-au-Prince, I was shown another small temple. As the guardian was a sort of dependant of the Haytian gentleman who was with me, we were allowed to enter, and were shown a box under a kind of altar, in which we were told the serpent was confined, but we could not induce the man to let us see it, as he feared the anger of the Papaloi.

I have remarked that the temples are generally small. To accommodate the crowd, however, permanent or temporary sheds are erected near, and there is generally the guardian's house besides, in which to take shelter or carry on their debauch.

The Papalois may generally be distinguished by the peculiar knotting of their curly wool, which must be a work of considerable labour, and by their profusion of ornaments. We noticed the former peculiarity at the trial of some sorcerers, whilst the jailers probably had relieved them of the latter. I have frequently remarked these knotted-headed negroes, and the attention they received from their sable countrymen.

In general, when incidents are spoken of in society in Hayti relating to the Vaudoux worship, Haytian gentlemen endeavour to turn the conversation, or they say you have been imposed upon, or the events have been exaggerated. But the incidents I am about to relate formed the subject of a trial before a criminal court, and are to be found detailed in the official journal of the period, and I was present during the two days that the inquiry lasted.

It occurred during the Presidency of General Geffrard, the most enlightened ruler that that unfortunate country possessed since the time of President Boyer; it too plainly proved that the fetish worship of the negroes of Africa had not been forgotten by their descendants, nor to be denied by any one, and the attention of the whole country was drawn to the subject of cannibalism. As the case greatly interested me, I made the most careful inquiries and followed it in its most minute particulars. It is worth while relating the whole story in its disgusting details, as it is one of the truth of which there is not a shadow of a doubt.

A couple of miles to the west of Port-au-Prince lies the village of Bizoton, in which there lived a man named Congo Pellé. He had been a labourer, a gentleman's servant, an idler, who was anxious to improve his position without any exertion on his own part. In this dilemma he addressed himself to his sister Jeanne, who had long been connected with the Vaudoux—was, in fact, the daughter of a priestess, and herself a well-known Mamanloi— and it was settled between them that about the new year some sacrifice should be offered to propitiate the serpent. A more modest man would have been satisfied with a white cock or a white goat, but on this solemn occasion it was thought better to offer a more important sacrifice. A consultation was held with two Papalois, Julien Nicolas and Floréal Apollon, and it was decided that a female child should be offered as a sacrifice, and the choice fell on Claircine, the niece of Jeanne and Congo.

This was the account given in court; but it appears also to be an undoubted fact that human sacrifices are offered at Easter, Christmas Eve, New Year's Eve, and more particularly on Twelfth Night, or *Les Fêtes des Rois*.

On the 27th December 1863, Jeanne invited her sister, the mother of Claircine, to accompany her to Port-au-Prince, and the child, a girl of about twelve years of age, was left at home with Congo. Immediate advantage was taken of the mother's absence, and Claircine was conducted to the house of Julien, and from thence to that of Floréal, where she was bound, and hidden under the altar in a neighbouring temple. In the evening, the mother, returning home, asked for her child, when her brother Congo told her it had strayed away; a pretended search was made by those in the plot, and another Papaloi was consulted. This man told the mother not to be uneasy, as the Maître d'Eau, or the spirit of the water, had taken her daughter, but that in a short time her child would be restored to her. The woman believed, or pretended to believe, this story, and, by the papa's recommendation, burnt candles before the altar of the Virgin Mary for the prompt return of her offspring,—another proof of the strange mingling of Catholicism and Vaudoux worship.

On the evening of the 31st of December a large party assembled at the house of Jeanne to await the arrival of the child, who had remained for four days bound under the altar. When the chief members of the plot came to the temple to bring her out, she, guessing the fate reserved for her, gave two or three piercing shrieks, which were soon stifled, and, gagged and bound, she was carried to Jeanne's house, where preparations were made for the human sacrifice. She was thrown on the ground, her aunt holding her by the waist, whilst the Papaloi pressed her throat, and the others held her legs and arms; her struggles soon ceased, as Floréal had succeeded in strangling her. Then Jeanne handed him a large knife, with which he cut off Claircine's head, the assistants catching the blood in a jar; then Floréal is said to have inserted an instrument under the child's skin, and detached it from the body. Having succeeded in flaying their victim, the flesh was cut from the bones, and placed in large wooden dishes; the entrails and skin being buried near to the cottage. The whole party then started for Floréal's house, carrying the remains of their victim with them. On their arrival Jeanne rang a little bell, and a procession was formed, the head borne aloft, and a sacred song sung. Then preparations were made for a feast.

Roused by the noise caused by the arrival, a woman and girl sleeping in another chamber looked through some chinks in the wall and saw all that passed,—Jeanne cooking the flesh with Congo beans, small and rather bitter (*pois congo*), whilst Floréal put the head into a pot with yams to make some soup. Whilst the others were engaged in the kitchen, one of the women present, Roséide Sumera, urged by the fearful appetite of a cannibal, cut from the child's palm a piece of flesh and ate it raw (this I heard her avow in open court).

The cooking over, portions of the prepared dish were handed round, of which all present partook; and the soup being ready, it was divided among the assistants, who deliberately drank it. The night was passed in dancing, drinking, and debauchery. In the morning the remains of the flesh were warmed up, and the two witnesses who had watched the proceedings were invited to join in the repast: the young woman confessed that she had accepted the invitation, but the girl did not.

Not satisfied with this taste of human flesh, the priests now put the young girl, who had watched their proceedings from a neighbouring room, in the place of Claircine, and she was bound in the temple, to be sacrificed on Twelfth Night. It came out in evidence that she had been decoyed to the house for that purpose, and that the young woman who was sleeping in the same room was in reality in charge of her.

Fortunately for her, the inquiries which Claircine's mother had made on her first arrival home and the disappearance of the second girl had roused the attention of an officer of police, and a search being made, the freshly-boiled skull of the murdered girl was found among the bushes near Floréal's house, where careless impunity had induced the assassins to throw it. A further search led to the discovery of the girl bound under the altar and the other remains of Claircine.

Fourteen persons were arrested, against eight of whom sufficient evidence could be obtained, and these were sent to prison to answer for their crime before a criminal court. The trial commenced on the 4th of February 1864, and lasted two days. Incidents were related in the course of the evidence which showed how the lower classes are sunk in ignorance and barbarity, and renewed the proofs, if any fresh proofs were required, that the Vaudoux worship is associated by them with the ceremonies of the Catholic religion, even the Papalois recommending the burning of tapers in the Christian churches, and the having crosses and pictures of the Virgin Mary strangely mingled on their altars with the objects of their superstition.

In the dock we saw the eight prisoners, four men and four women, with faces of the ordinary Haytian type, neither better nor worse. Their names were: men—Julian Nicholas, a Papaloi; Floréal Apollon, another Papaloi; Guerrier François and Congo Pellé: the women—Jeanne Pellé, a Mamanloi, Roséide Sumera, Neréide François, and Beyard Prosper. Some had been servants to foreigners, others had been gardeners and washerwomen. The French procedure is observed in all trials in Hayti, and to an Englishman the procedure, as practised in that republic, is contrary to the first principles of justice. The prisoners were bullied, cajoled, cross-questioned, in order to force avowals, in fact, to make them state in open court what they were said to have confessed in their preliminary examinations. I can never forget the manner in which the youngest female prisoner turned to the public prosecutor and said, "Yes, I did confess what you assert, but remember how cruelly I was beaten before I said a word;" and it was well known that all the prisoners had at first refused to speak, thinking that the Vaudoux would protect them, and it required the frequent application of the club to drive this belief out of their heads. That prisoners are tortured to make them confess is known to be a common practice in Hayti.

However this may have been in the present case, there, on a table before the judge, was the skull of the murdered girl, and in a jar the remains of the soup and the calcined bones; and the avowals of the prisoners in court and the testimony of the witnesses were too clear and circumstantial to leave a doubt as to their criminality.

As I have remarked, I was in court during the two days' trial, and I never was present at one where the judge conducted himself with greater dignity. His name was Lallemand, and he was one of the few magistrates who had the courage to do justice, even when political passion would have condemned victims unheard.

Among those who gave their evidence was the young girl who witnessed the ceremonies, and for whom was reserved the fate of Claircine. The judge called her up to his side, and gently asked her to tell the court what she had seen; but, with a frightened look, she started and burst into tears, and the judge, looking up sharply, saw the prisoners making the most diabolical grimaces at the poor child. He then turned round to the jury and said, in view of the intimidation attempted, he would do what was not strictly regular; the child should whisper the story to him, and he would repeat it to the court. He placed her with her back to the prisoners, and putting his arm round her, drew her gently to him, and said in a soft voice, "Tell me, chère, what occurred." The girl, in a very low tone, began her testimony, but the silence in court was so profound, that not a word she uttered was lost, and, almost without faltering, she told her story in all its horrible details; but her nerves then gave way so completely, that she had to be taken out of court, and could not be again produced to answer some questions the jury wished to ask.

Then the young woman, her companion of that night, was called, and she confirmed the account, and confessed that in the morning she had joined in the feast; the mother's testimony followed, and that of numerous other witnesses. The guilt of the prisoners was thus fully established, when one of the female prisoners, Roséide, in the hopes perhaps of pardon, entered into every particular of the whole affair, to the evident annoyance of the others, who tried in vain to keep her silent. Her testimony was the most complete, and left not a doubt of the culpability of the whole of the prisoners. I did in consequence suggest that her life should be spared, but President Geffrard reminded me that it was she who had confessed, in open court, that she had eaten the palms of the victim's hands as a favourite morsel.

Jeanne, the old woman, though she showed the utmost coolness during the trial, did at length appeal for mercy, saying she had only been practising what had been taught her by her mother as the religion of her ancestors. "Why should I be put to death for observing our ancient customs?"

They were all found guilty of sorcery, torture, and murder, and condemned to death.

I asked the public prosecutor if he thought that the mother had been really ignorant of the fate reserved for her child. He replied, "We have not thought proper to press the inquiry too closely, for fear that we should discover that she partook of the feast; we required her testimony at the trial." After a pause, he added, "If full justice were done, there would be fifty on those benches instead of eight."

The execution took place on Saturday, February 13, 1864, the authorities wisely selecting a market-day, in order that the example might have the greater effect. The following particulars relating to it I received from the

American Commissioner, Mr. Whiddon, who was present at this last scene. The prisoners, men and women, were all clothed in white robes and white headdresses, the garments reserved for parricides, and were drawn in carts to the place of execution, and all but one had a sullen look of resignation, and neither uttered a word nor a complaint, whilst the eighth, the young woman Roséide, kept up a continued conversation with the crowd around her.

Every effort was made by the Government to give solemnity to the occasion; the troops and National Guard were summoned, for even the word "rescue" had been pronounced; the principal authorities attended; and thousands of spectators gathered round the spot. The prisoners, tied in pairs, were placed in a line, and faced by five soldiers to each pair; they fired with such inaccuracy, that only six fell wounded on the first discharge. It took these untrained men fully half an hour to complete their work, and the incidents were so painful, that the horror at the prisoners' crimes was almost turned into pity at witnessing their unnecessary sufferings. As usual, the prisoners behaved with great courage, even the women standing up unflinchingly before their executioners, and receiving their fire without quailing, and when at last they fell wounded, no cry was heard, but they were seen beckoning the soldiers to approach, and Roséide held the muzzle of a musket to her bosom and called on the man to fire.

The Vaudoux priests gave out, that although the deity would permit the execution, he would only do it to prove to his votaries his power by raising them all again from the dead. To prevent their bodies being carried away during the night (they had been buried near the place of execution), picquets of troops were placed round the spot; but in the morning three of the graves were found empty, and the bodies of the two priests and the priestess had disappeared. Superstitious fear had probably prevented the soldiers from staying where they had been posted, and as most of the troops belonged to the sect of the Vaudoux, they probably connived at, rather than prevented, the exhumation.

Among those who attended the trial were the Spanish *chargé d'affaires*, Don Mariano Alvarez, and the Admiral, Mendez Nuñez, but they were so horrified by the sight of the child's remains on the judge's table and the disgusting evidence, that they had precipitately to leave the court. For years Congo beans were forbidden at our table.

Mr. Alvarez had a great liking for Haytian society, and lived much with certain families, and was very familiar with what was occurring in the country. I therefore asked him if he had any objection to give me some extracts from his official reports on the subject of the Vaudoux; he freely consented, and authorised me to publish the same in any way I pleased. I propose to insert some extracts in this chapter, as they confirm my own inquiries.

I have elsewhere remarked, but I may repeat it, that all prisoners condemned to death in Hayti, whether their crimes be political or otherwise, are shot, and as but two or three soldiers are told off to each prisoner, the consequence is that almost every execution that takes place resembles, instead of a solemn warning, a frightful and pitiable butchery.

President Geffrard behaved with great courage on this occasion, for though continued appeals were made for pardon, he remained firm. He was warned that such an execution would sap the attachment of the masses, but he insisted that the condemned should be put to death. The example probably deterred others from openly committing such crimes, or from committing them near civilised centres; but when Geffrard quitted power, the sect again raised its head, and human sacrifices became common. We, however, heard little of these dreadful rites after the fall of Salnave. It can scarcely be said that civilisation is making progress; it is more probable that the authorities, absorbed in their petty intrigues to maintain power, did not care to inquire too closely into the disappearance of children.

I believe that the latter is the true explanation, and that instead of there having been any amelioration, the subject is only ignored, as one likely to give trouble. Instead of the country advancing in civilisation since the fall of Geffrard, it has retrograded. Civil wars and the imbecile Government of Nissage-Saget followed, and then again insurrections and civil war. It cannot be supposed that under the Government of General Domingue (1874 and 1875) the Vaudoux worship was discouraged, when it was openly stated and believed that one of his Ministers was a Papaloi, and head of the sect in the southern province. His brutal character and love of bloodshed would add to the suspicion. Under the next President (1876-78), Boisrond-Canal, a decree was issued forbidding any Vaudoux dances, as, under cover of these, other rites were carried on; but that decree has, I hear, been since repealed. Who is to think of the improvement of the masses whilst struggling to maintain a precarious tenure of power?

Mr. Alvarez's account of the Claircine incident differs only in a few trifles from mine, but he had not the opportunities I had fully to investigate it. He says:—"I have previously reported on the subject of the fetish sect of Vaudoux, imported into Hayti by the slaves coming from the tribes on the western coast of Africa, and mentioning the crimes of these cannibals. To-day I enclose an extract from the official *Moniteur*, in which they have commenced to publish the process against four men and four women, who were shot near this capital on the 13th instant, convicted on their own confession of having eaten, in Bizoton, near Port-au-Prince, on the night of the 10th of December last, a young child of six years old, called Claircine, whose own aunt delivered her to these anthropophagi, and for having another child that they were feeding up to sacrifice and eat on the first days of January, in commemoration of the feast of the King of Africa. I assisted at the trial, and there appeared to have been no doubt that if the public prosecutor had desired to verify the case minutely, not only the witnesses, but even the mother of the victim, merited the same fate as the cannibals who were proved to have eaten her."

"President Geffrard, who is not afraid of the Vaudoux, although all the mountains and plains of the republic are full of these anthropophagi, with an energy which does him honour has caused the authorities to throw down the altars, collect the drums, timbrels, and other ridiculous instruments which the Papalois use in their diabolical ceremonies, and in the district of Port-au-Prince has imprisoned many individuals of both sexes, who, on being interrogated, confessed what had been the fate of other children who had disappeared from their homes, and whose whereabouts were unknown."

As an instance of what occurred in the time of the Emperor Soulouque, I may again seek the testimony of Mr. Alvarez. In 1852, in consequence of a denunciation, Vil Lubin, governor of Port-au-Prince, arrested in the neighbourhood of that city about fifty individuals of both sexes. On examining the house in which human sacrifices were offered, packages of salted human flesh were found rolled up in leaves. These were thrown into the sea. During the examination of the prisoners, they declared that among the members of the best families of the city were many associates of the society of the Vaudoux, and that if the authorities desired to be satisfied of this assertion, let them be permitted to beat the little drum. They would present themselves even to the Emperor Soulouque himself, for among the Vaudoux worshippers no one under peril of his life would be wanting to his engagements. This case was allowed to drop.

In part proof of the above statement, Mr. Alvarez tells the following story:—One of the principal ladies of Port-au-Prince, rich, and of good family, was found late at night by General Vil Lubin stretched out at the door of the Catholic cathedral, wearing only the blue dress of the country negresses, without shoes, and going through certain incantations called *wanga*. The governor accompanied this lady to her house. I knew the person to whom Mr. Alvarez alludes, and certainly she was one of the last women whom I should have suspected to have belonged to the Vaudoux.

I add some further observations of Mr. Alvarez, as they give the view held by a Catholic who represented a Catholic power:—"1862.—The delegate of his Holiness, Monseigneur Testard du Cocquer, has left, much disgusted with this country on account of the corruption of its customs, the dearth of religion among the sectaries of the Vaudoux, and the opposition and want of confidence with which he met in what is called in Hayti civilised society. In order that you may appreciate the accuracy of the incidents which pass here, a simple narration of some of a very recent epoch will be sufficient to show the powerful influence exercised on the inhabitants by the sect or the society of the Vaudoux, so spread throughout the country; this, with other causes inherent in the race, to which it would be tiresome to refer, prove that Hayti is, of all the republics in America, the most backward and the most pernicious in every point of view. From the same motive, I will not stop to speak of the origin of the fetish religion of the Vaudoux, or the worship of the serpent, imported from the tribes of the west coast of Africa by the slaves coming from that country, and I now pass to facts.

"In the month of August past (1862) there died, in the section called Belair, a negro, and his body was taken to the Catholic church. The defunct belonged to the society of the Vaudoux. The men and women who accompanied the corpse began in the temple to scream like those possessed, and they commenced a scene such as might occur in Mid-Africa. The Abbé Pascal tried to re-establish order; his requests that they should respect the sacred precincts were useless; and the Abbé having refused, on account of this scandalous conduct, to accompany the body to the cemetery, the mourners fell upon him, seized him by the collar, and he had to fly to the sacristy, the interference of a foreigner alone saving him from further ill-treatment; but the tumult was so great that even the cross which is used at funerals was broken to pieces. Two women were taken out fainting, and the rabble marched off to the cemetery to bury the body; some arrests were made, but it is not known what punishment was inflicted, as the tribunals always leave unpunished the misdemeanours of the sectaries of the Vaudoux, as I am going to prove."

Mr. Alvarez then tells a horrible story, to which I shall refer farther on, as it belongs to a different section of this chapter.

"In February 1862 a negro was taken prisoner at Ouanaminthe for having assassinated his father. He was condemned to death by the tribunals; but he defended himself by saying that he had done no more than follow the orders of the serpent. In a few months he was set at liberty.

"It is not long since that in one of the streets of Port-au-Prince was found at early morn the body of an unknown youth, of about twenty years of age, who had a weapon piercing his heart, and attached to that a thin hollow cane. It was supposed that he was assassinated in order to suck his blood. I might cite many other facts of which I have taken note, but what I have related appear sufficient for the object I have proposed to myself. The disappearance of children is frequent at certain epochs or seasons, and it is supposed that they are eaten by the cannibals of this society.

"In the secret ceremonies of the Vaudoux the drink in use is the blood of animals mixed with white rum, and the Papaloi, either from the immoderate use they make of alcohol mixed with blood, or from the handling of the poisons they use in their devil craft, die in general, although at an advanced age, covered with leprosy and incurable sores." I myself heard this stated whilst in Hayti, but I fear that a few exceptions have in this case made the rule.

"The people endure every possible oppression from the Papaloi, and if you ask them why they permit these vexations and the abuses which are committed against one another, they answer, 'We are indeed obliged, unhappy that we are: if we denounced our neighbours, certainly we should quickly die.' From which it may be inferred that they tolerate this conduct because they fear, and they fear because they know each other." This fear of one another is noticed by all foreign residents in Hayti: it extends to the higher classes.

"The society of the Vaudoux, although now (1862, time of Geffrard) not so preponderant as in the time of Soulouque, who was one of its most believing followers, is very extended in all the republic, but there are few initiated into the secrets; they have their signs and symbols, and the society meddles in the politics of every Government which has existed in Hayti; they sometimes sustain them, as in certain cases they will act as a secret police, and the Vaudoux is looked on as one of the firmest props of the independence of the country."

I may notice that the Papaloi lead the most depraved lives. They are feared by all, and the fear inspired is so great, that few women among the lower orders would resist their advances. It may probably be looked upon as an honour. Unlimited drink is the next idea of happiness to a negro, and in this the offerings of their followers enable the priests to indulge to their hearts' content.

After studying the history of Hayti, one is not astonished that the fetish worship continues to flourish. The negroes imported from the west coast of Africa naturally brought their religion with them, and the worship of the serpent was one of its most distinguishing features. St. Méry speaks of the slaves arriving with a strange mixture of Mohammedanism and idolatry, to which they soon added a little Catholicism. Of Mohammedanism I have not myself observed a trace. When they found the large, almost harmless, serpent in Hayti, they welcomed it as their god, and their fetish priests soon collected their followers around them. The French authorities tried to put down all meetings of the Vaudoux, partly because they looked upon them as political, but they did not succeed in their object. Many of the tribes in Africa are to this day cannibals, and their ancestors imported probably this taste into the French colony. It was difficult at that epoch to indulge in it, as all the children of the slaves were carefully registered, and their disappearance would have been immediately remarked; they may, however, have made use of the expedients for producing apparent death, to which I will presently refer.

Many persons appear to think that cannibalism is a later importation, and came with the Africans freed by our cruisers. If it were so, the seed fell on good ground, as the practice has spread to every district of the island. This opinion, however, can scarcely be correct, as Moreau de St. Méry, in naming the different tribes imported into Hayti, says:—"Never had any a disposition more hideous than the last (the Mondongues), whose depravity has reached the most execrable of excesses, that of eating their fellow-creatures. They bring also to Santo Domingo those butchers of human flesh (for in their country there are butcheries where they sell slaves as they would calves), and they are here, as in Africa, the horror of the other negroes."

This is a fitting introduction to the second part of this chapter, in which I must refer to the great knowledge of herbs as poisons and antidotes shown by the Papaloi—which, though possibly exaggerated by some inquirers, is no doubt very great—and to cannibalism as not connected with religious rites.

In the following passages from Mr. Alvarez's notes, the first impression will be that there must be gross exaggeration. I thought so when I first read them, but the more my inquiries extended, the less I was inclined to doubt them. If not exactly true, it is the firm belief of all classes of society that they are so. During thirteen years, I had the best opportunities of hearing the opinion of Presidents, intelligent Secretaries of State, the principal members of the medical profession, lawyers, merchants, both foreign and native, as well as other residents, who had passed a lifetime in the republic, and the testimony was more or less unanimous as to the profound knowledge of the use of herbs possessed by the Papaloi.

"The human imagination cannot conceive anything more absurd, more barbarous, or more ridiculous than the acts committed by these ferocious sectaries, who are called Papaloi, Papa Boco, or other names as stupid as they are ill-sounding. They produce death—apparent, slow, or instantaneous—madness, paralysis, impotence, idiocy, *riches or poverty*, according to their will.

"It has happened on occasions that persons have retired to bed in the possession of their senses to awaken idiots, and remain in that state in spite of the aid of science, and in a few days to be completely cured, when the causes which have produced the alienation have ceased. One individual struck another; the latter threatened him with impotency. At the end of fifteen days he was paralytic in all his members.[11] Following the counsels of a friend, he consulted a Papaloi, who had the coolness to confess that he had himself sold to his enemy the philter that had reduced him to that state, but for the sum of about £20 he would cure him. In fact, in a few days, by means of the remedies of the Papa, he was completely restored to health. And if it be doubted that these individuals, without even common sense, can understand so thoroughly the properties of herbs and their combinations, so as to be able to apply them to the injury of their fellow-creatures, I can only say that tradition is a great book, and that they receive these instructions as a sacred deposit from one generation to another, with the further advantage that in the hills and mountains of this island grow in abundance similar herbs to those which in Africa they employ in their incantations."

One case occurred in 1860, which was really so remarkable, and drew so much attention at the time, that there was no possibility of doubting it. It was supported by ample testimony. It was first told me by one of the most eminent medical men in Port-au-Prince, and confirmed by another, who had been an eyewitness of some of the details, and pledged his word as to its truth. I one day mentioned the story in the French Legation, as I was still somewhat sceptical, when, to my surprise, I found that it had been made the subject of an official report. Count Mégan, at that time *chargé d'affaires* (1867), offered to give me an extract relating to that crime, with permission to publish it in any book I might write.

The following are the particulars:—"The police having been informed that some shrieks had been heard at night in the cemetery of Port-au-Prince, went there in the morning, and found a grave disturbed, and near it an open coffin, and lying at the side the body of a lady that had been buried on the previous day. A dagger had been thrust into her bosom, and as blood covered her burial clothes, it was evident that she had been buried alive. Many arrests took place, but the affair was hushed up. It was currently reported, however, that the husband had a mistress, whom he neglected after marriage, and that this woman applied to a Mamanloi for aid. She received a sleeping potion which she contrived to give to the lady during her first confinement, and she was hurriedly buried, to be restored to consciousness in the graveyard at dead of night, with her rival armed with a dagger before her. Her shrieks drew the attention of some Jamaica negroes, who ran towards the spot shouting, but whom superstition prevented from entering the cemetery. Their shouts, however, caused the murderers to fly, and leave the corpse where it was found next morning." This is the story as told me by my medical friends, and it was universally believed to be true, and in fact was true, and was never denied by those in authority with whom I conversed on the subject.

The accounts given by my French and Spanish colleagues were more complete, and probably more exact, as they were both in Port-au-Prince when this tragedy occurred. My previous French colleague (the Marquis de Forbin Janson) wrote, 2d August 1860:—

"Deux jours après mon arrivé à Port-au-Prince, une femme endormie au moyen d'un narcotique et enterrée le soir au cimetière de la ville, fut exhumée dans la nuit; elle respirait encore, on la tua, puis on enleva la cervelle, le cœur et la foi de la victime, dont on retrouva de débris près de la tombe: le lendemain matin une enquête fut ordonnée, on fit plusieurs arrestations, entre autres celle d'une prêtresse du Vaudoux (Mamanloi). Cette femme fit des révélations y, offrit même de livrer à la justice les auteurs du meurtre et de la profanation en les attirant à la prison par une puissance irrésistible ou ballant de son tambour d'une manière particulière. La justice et la police, déjà effrayées du nombre et de l'importance des personnes compromises, reculèrent devant cette nouvelle épreuve. On ordonna aux journaux de se taire et l'affaire fut étouffée. On croit que la principale mobile du crime fut un sentiment de vengeance, mais on tient pour certain que les parties mutilées ont été destinées à la célébration de quelque mystère Vaudoux du fétichisme africain encore pratiqué, quoiqu'on dise, par la grande majorité des Haïtiens."

I think this case of so much importance, that, at the risk of repetition, I will give the report made by Mr. Alvarez:—

"In July of 1860 there was committed in Port-au-Prince a horrible, almost an incredible crime. A young woman died suddenly, and was buried on the following day. At night several individuals of both sexes went to the cemetery, dug up the coffin, and opened it. What they actually did is not known, but what is positive is that the unburied began to shriek and shout for help. The guard near the cemetery, composed of Jamaicans, Louisianians, and Creoles, approached, and saw the woman sitting in the coffin, and various persons—a torch in one hand and a dagger in the other—vociferating words they could not understand. The Creole soldiers of the country fled dismayed, but the Louisianians, as soon as they had overcome the first feeling of terror, ran to the succour of the unburied; already it was too late, they found her dead from the stroke of a dagger, and her heart and lungs torn from her bosom. The assassins escaped, but subsequently some prisoners were made. In a few days the prisoners were at liberty; and it is related that the lungs and the heart had been cooked and eaten in one of the country-houses in Bizoton."

My friend, Auguste Elie, Secretary of State for Foreign Affairs, deplored but could not deny the truth of this story; and having no Vaudoux prejudices himself, having been born and bred in France, conversed freely on the subject, and told us many particulars that had come to his knowledge.

Of the truth of the following story I had the testimony of ocular witnesses. A lady hearing that a child near her house was ill, went down to see it. She found it lying stupefied in the mother's lap. Her suspicions were aroused, and she sharply questioned the mother as to what had been done to the child. Her answers were so unsatisfactory, yet mournful, that the lady determined to keep a watch on the case. She called in the evening, and was told the child was dead. She insisted on seeing the corpse, and found that though the heart was still and the pulse had ceased to beat, yet that the child did not look dead, and made the remark to the bystanders, but they answered, "Yes, it is dead." She told the mother she was not satisfied, and that she would return in the morning with her husband, and that in the meantime the body must not be buried. Next day she and her husband walked down to the house, and asked to see the body. The mother replied that the neighbours having insisted, she had allowed them to bury her child, and pointed out the grave. The French gentleman called to some of his labourers, and had the grave opened. There they found the coffin, but the child's body was absent. Arrests were made, but nothing came of it. It is supposed that it was by this means that the Papalois were enabled to obtain victims during the French colonial period.

It is useless to multiply instances of these horrors; but that they are practised all over the island more or less under every government that has existed in Hayti is certain.

You often hear the expression used in Hayti, "Li gagné chagrin," which, though, referring occasionally to a known cause, often applies to a sort of anæmia of the mind, when a person appears to care for nothing, or for what becomes of him. I have inquired as to what had been done to the man, and the answer, if in company, was, "We don't know;" if you asked a person privately, he would probably reply that somebody had given him *wanga*, a generic word for poisons, philters, and charms.

The remark I made when I first began to inquire into this subject may naturally be repeated by others. If the majority of Haytians be tainted by the Vaudoux, who is it that denounces these horrible crimes, and how could a remedy be found? The answer is, that there are in Hayti, as I have before noticed, two sects of Vaudoux worshippers; one, perhaps the least numerous, that indulges in human sacrifices, the other that holds such practices in horror, and is content with the blood of the white goat and the white cock. At one time the police took no notice of the latter, and permitted them to carry on their ceremonies in Port-au-Prince in a large courtyard adjoining a house in which a friend of mine lived. To preserve as much secrecy as possible, the courtyard was hung round with cloth hangings, and watchmen placed to keep prying eyes at a distance; but my friend, though not curious, occasionally got a glimpse of the proceedings. They were much as those described by Moreau de St. Méry. In the country districts the Catholic priests say this sect calls themselves, "Les Mystères," and that they mingle Christian and Vaudoux ceremonies in a singular manner. The name probably refers to the rites they practise. I have been assured by many gentlemen connected with the Haytian police, that if the followers of this sect did not secretly denounce to them the crimes committed by the others, it would be almost impossible for them to keep the assassin sect in check. It is probable that, acting with these comparatively harmless savages, the Haytian Government might be able to do much, if ever it seriously desires to put an end to the shedding of human blood.

I have been told that, besides the goat and cock, the Vaudoux occasionally sacrifice a lamb; this idea they have probably taken from the Catholic Church—the paschal lamb; it is carefully washed, combed, and ornamented before being sacrificed.

All that I have hitherto related refers more or less to human sacrifices as connected with religion; but there is another phase—cannibalism as practised for the sake of the food which the slaughtering of human beings affords to a vile section of the community.

In Mr. Consul Hutchinson's paper on the traits of African tribes, published in the "Transactions of the Ethnological Society," New Series, vol. i. p. 338, he states: "I have during the last year seen it stated in a Sierra Leone newspaper, on the authority of Mr. Priddy, a missionary of the Countess of Huntingdon's Connection in that colony, not that *he had heard of*, but *that he had seen* hampers of dried human flesh carried about on men's backs, to be sold for eating purposes, in the progress of a recent civil war between the Soosoo and Tisnney tribes."[12] This is very similar to what was seen by a lady of my acquaintance in Hayti.

A lady, the widow of a missionary, was forced to stay in the interior of Hayti (north-east of Gonaives), after the death of her husband, on account of the civil war in the surrounding districts in the years 1868 and 1869, and she related some horrible incidents which were of her own knowledge. She declared that human sacrifices were constant, that human flesh was openly sold in the market. One would willingly have believed in exaggeration; but similar incidents, which occurred during the reign of Soulouque, related to me by one so intelligent and truthful as Auguste Elie, compelled me to accept as veritable the horrible stories she told in full detail.

Monsieur Desjardins, an eminent French merchant in Port-au-Prince, remarked to me that, walking near Cap Haïtien, he met a party of soldiers beating a man with their clubs; he inquired the reason, and they told their prisoner to open his basket, and there he saw the body of a child cut up into regular joints.

Auguste Elie told me he knew the following incident as a fact, which occurred during the reign of Soulouque. A man with whom he was acquainted was visiting in the plains with his wife, when she complained of feeling unwell, and they mounted their horses to return to town. At sunset, a violent storm coming on, they determined to halt at a cottage they saw near. They entered, and found two men and a woman there; his wife becoming worse, he determined to seek help, but was a long time before he could find any one to accompany him. On his return to the house, he inquired for his wife, and the people said that, becoming uneasy at his long absence, she had followed him. He rode away without saying a word, and calling at the next police station, induced the men to follow him; they surrounded the cottage, arrested the three inmates, and on searching the premises, found the body of the woman, already dismembered, in a cask in an outhouse. A thick layer of salt had been thrown over the remains. The only punishment these assassins received was that administered by the clubs of the police whilst conducting them to prison.

The Haytians occasionally publish accounts of these crimes. I read the following in one of their local papers. At Jacmel, on the southern coast, an old woman, a midwife, was lying on her death-bed surrounded by her neighbours, and they were somewhat surprised at her long struggles and loud groaning. At last she said, "I cannot die in peace; put aside the bed and dig underneath;" and on doing so, great was their astonishment to come on numerous small skeletons, which the old fiend acknowledged were the remains of children she had eaten. After this confession they say she died quietly. One cannot but be reminded of the horrible picture in the Wiertz Gallery in Brussels of the woman cutting up and cooking the infant. It must have been painted under the influence of nightmare.

That the practice of midwives slaying children for the purpose of eating them is an old one in Hayti is proved by the following story, related by Moreau de St. Méry:—

"On a eu à Saint Domingue (Haïti) des preuves que les Mondongues y avait gardé leur odieuse inclination, notamment en 1786, dans une negresse accoucheuse et hospitalière sur une habitation aux environs de Jérémie. Le propriétaire ayant remarqué que la plupart des negrillons périssait dans les huit premiers jours de leur naissance, fit épier la matrone; on l'a surpris mangeant un de ces enfans récemment inhumé, et elle avoua qu'elle les faisait périr dans ce dessin."

As late as 1878, the last year of which I propose to treat, two women were arrested in a hut near Port-au-Prince. They were caught in the act of eating the flesh of a child raw. On further examination it was found that all the blood had been sucked from the body, and that part of the flesh had been salted for later use. In 1869 the police arrested, in that beautiful valley to which I have referred in my first chapter, about a dozen cannibals, and brought them bound to La Coupe. They had been denounced by the opposing sectaries of the Vaudoux. From the time they were taken from their houses they were beaten in the most unmerciful manner, and when thrown into prison they were tortured by the thumbscrew and by tightened cords round their foreheads, and under the influence of these they made some fearful avowals, in which, however, little confidence could be placed. A French priest, with whom I was on intimate terms, hearing of their arrest, had the curiosity to go and see them. At first they would not converse with him, but when they found him protesting against the inhumanity with which they had been treated, and threatening the jailer that he would officially report him should such conduct continue, they placed more confidence in him. He visited them nearly every day, and had many conversations with them in private. They confessed to him that their avowals under torture were true; and when the priest, horrified by the details, said to a mother, "How could you eat the flesh of your own children?" she answered coolly, "And who had a better right,—est-ce que ce n'est pas moi qui les ai fait?"[13]

One of these prisoners died under the torture of the cord tightened round his forehead.

Though the Haytians believe in the mythical *"loup garou,"* they have also the fullest faith in his counterpart among their fellow-countrymen. It is the *loup garou* who is employed by the Papaloi to secure a child for sacrifice in case the neighbourhood does not furnish a suitable subject; and they are supposed to hang about lonely houses at night to carry off the children. I have often heard my young Haytian servants rush into my country-house laughingly saying that they had seen a *loup garou*—their laugh, however, tinged with a sort of dread. They have often said that these human monsters prowl about the house at night, and that nothing but the presence of my dogs kept them in respect. I have occasionally seen the object of their fear in an ill-looking negro hanging about the gate, but the sight of my dogs was enough to induce him to move on. The negroes have fortunately an almost superstitious terror of dogs.

There is no doubt that these *loup garous* do carry off many children, not only for the priests, but for cannibals. They generally look only for native children, and I have only heard of one instance in which they attempted to carry off a white girl. She was snatched from the arms of her nurse, whilst walking on the Champs de Mars, by a huge negro, who ran off with her towards the woods, but being pursued by two mounted gentlemen who accidentally witnessed the occurrence, he dropped the child to save himself.

One of my Haytian friends who had studied botany informed me that the number of poisonous plants to be found on the island is very great, and that it was absolutely certain that the Papalois made use of them in their practices. I believe in some French botanical works lists of these plants have been published, and their medical value would appear to merit further study. It is not more remarkable that the Papalois should know the properties of the plants in Hayti than that the Indians of Peru and Bolivia should have discovered the properties of the cinchona bark and the coca-leaf.

If it be remembered that the republic of Hayti is not a God-forsaken region in Central Africa, but an island surrounded by civilised communities; that it possesses a Government modelled on that of France, with President, Senate, and House of Representatives; with Secretaries of State, prefects, judges, and all the paraphernalia of courts of justice and of police; with a press more or less free; and, let me add, an archbishop, bishops, and clergy, nearly all Frenchmen,—it appears incredible that sorcery, poisonings for a fee by recognised poisoners, and cannibalism, should continue to pervade the island. The truth is, that except during one year of Geffrard's Presidency, no Government has ever cared resolutely to grapple with the evil. If they have not encouraged it, they have ignored it, in order not to lose the favour of the masses.

CHAPTER VI
THE GOVERNMENT

The government of Hayti[14] is in form republican, but is in fact a military despotism, all power being concentrated in the hands of the President, who carries out or ignores the laws according to his pleasure. There are Secretaries of State, a Senate, and House of Representatives; but in General Geffrard's time the Ministers had no power in their respective departments, but were simply clerks to register the will of the chief of the state. The Senate was very humble, whilst the House of Representatives, when it showed any signs of independence, as in the memorable session of 1863, was summarily dismissed, and a packed Chamber substituted.

During the time of the next President, General Salnave, the civil war prevented the Congress meeting regularly. The Chambers met once; but drawn swords, pistol-shots, and yelling mobs caused the deputies to understand that with Salnave as chief of the State constitutional government had disappeared. "In revolutionary times, revolutionary measures," said Salnave's Chief Minister; "we must return to the immortal principles of 1793." He talked much of cutting off heads, but, to his credit be it said, whilst Minister he never shed a drop of blood. Enough had been done of that during the revolution of 1865.

The presidency of Nissage-Saget followed. Though the shooting of General Chevalier showed that he could act as illegally as any of his predecessors, yet he was a quiet man, who would have worked with the House of Representatives if they had connived at some of his peccadilloes, and been blind to those of his Ministers, who were often most unhappily chosen. But they were of more than Roman sternness with their friends in power. However, both the Senate and the Chamber of Deputies certainly influenced the Government; but as the majority was generally in opposition, quarrels with the executive followed, and Nissage-Saget, in revenge, connived at the illegal appointment of General Domingue to the presidentship in the spring of 1874. From this time forward Hayti has been going from bad to worse, until revolution after revolution has brought the old Finance Minister of Soulouque into the Government, and General Salomon is now President of Hayti.

It may be seen from the above sketch that constitutional government is not likely to be favourably developed in such a soil as that of Hayti. The mass of the population, being ignorant Africans, wish to be governed by a despotic chief, and not by what they irreverently call a "tas de voleurs." No constitutional checks are sufficiently strong to overcome the popular will, and as yet few Presidents have been able to resist the desire of the people for personal government. They themselves seldom show any disposition to thwart this national predilection.

I have known Hayti for upwards of twenty years, and I must confess that one by one my illusions have passed away, and my opinions are very changed indeed from what they were during my first year's residence in that country. I then knew a number of enthusiastic young lawyers and others, deputies and government employés, who talked admirably of their projects of reform, and of their desire to see the country advance in civilisation. I believed in this party, and was eager to see it arrive at power; but when it did have a chance of having a Government united with the Legislature in carrying out judicious reforms, it proved a most lamentable failure. Boisrond-Canal was President, a man full of good intentions, honest, who had fought gallantly against the savage tyranny of Salnave, and whose conduct then had merited the eulogium passed on him of a man "sans peur et sans reproche." No sooner was this chief in power, than his former friends, jealous of his advancement, fell away from him, raised opposition in the Chambers, thwarted every project of Government, and at last, by their plots and an appeal to arms, brought on a revolution, which ultimately swept Boisrond-Canal and all his mean plotting and scheming opponents out of the country, and brought in General Salomon. The question of "What will he do with it?" is anxiously watched; and there are many who believe that a paternal despotism is the best solution, and may give the country some years of comparative peace.

The Government of General Salomon has had its baptism of blood, and dozens of those whom I well knew have been shot since its advent. The Government accuse these gentlemen of having conspired. Their friends declare that General Salomon wished to revenge private wrongs of old standing, and imitate General Soulouque in terrifying the coloured population by wholesale massacres. Septimus Rameau, under President Domingue, followed this policy. He selected three of his most formidable adversaries to murder; succeeded with two, and drove many of the coloured population into exile. This is what is termed energetic action. It appears the starting-point for black Presidents, who know that no sooner are they installed in power than the coloured population begin to conspire. How far there is any truth in the charge of conspiracy against those gentlemen who were then residing in Hayti, I will not at this distance of time attempt to determine; but it is probable that their deaths may be somewhat laid at the door of those who, from their secure retreat in Jamaica, launched their pamphlets against the new Government.

Constitution-making is almost the necessary result of any change of government in Hayti. In 1805 Dessalines issued the first constitution, which was revised next year by President Pétion. In the northern province Christophe had his own constitution as President, which he also had to revise in 1811 when he became King. In the western and northern provinces under Pétion, the constitution was also changed in 1816, and had a long life, as it lasted till the expulsion of President Boyer in 1843, when the successful insurgents determined to have a fresh constitution, which, however, did not last long, as President Riché returned in 1846 to that of Pétion of 1816, only somewhat revised. In 1849 Soulouque, becoming Emperor, had a new constitution to suit the occasion, which lasted till his expulsion. Geffrard did not attempt to construct a new social pact; but the revolution under Salnave voted one in 1867, which was set aside in 1874 by Domingue. The last constitution is that which was voted in 1879 under General Salomon, and is the one now in force in Hayti.

On the 23d October 1879, General Salomon was elected President for seven years, and the constitution is dated 18th December 1879. It consists of 205 Articles.

Article 1. "The republic of Hayti is one and indivisible; its territory and the dependent islands are inviolable, and cannot be alienated by any treaty or convention." This is a very favourite formula in America, and was the pretext for continuing a useless war on the Pacific coast, as both Peru and Bolivia declared that their constitutions forbid a cession of territory. That its territory should remain inviolable depends on its own conduct and the will of others, and is therefore rather superfluous.

The articles relating to Haytians and their rights have been somewhat modified, and are more liberal than in former constitutions. Article 4 declares that every African or Indian and their descendants are capable of becoming Haytians; and a concession is added, that, on the proposition of the President of Hayti, any foreigner fulfilling certain conditions may became a citizen.

Article 6 declares that only a Haytian can become the possessor of real property. This is less offensive than the form of the old article:—"Aucun blanc quelque soit sa nation ne pourra mettre le pied sur ce territoire à titre de maître ou de propriétaire." It would be better for their prosperity to allow every one to acquire property in their country, but one is not surprised that their fear of the interference of foreign Governments should make them exclusive.

Articles 8 to 13 contain the civil and political rights of the citizens. Article 8 in the constitution of 1874 is omitted. It declared the right of asylum (in legations and consulates) to be sacred and inviolable, a curious subject to mention in a constitution.

Articles 14 to 40 are devoted to public right.

Article 14. Haytians are equal before the law, but a naturalised foreigner is not admissible to legislative and executive functions.

Article 16. "Individual liberty is guaranteed." This article has never been attended to by any Government. Every petty official thinks he has a right to "flanqué en prison" any one he pleases; and the next article, Art. 17, that he must be sent before the judge named by the constitution is also forgotten, and people have been kept years in prison without redress. Art. 18. Every house in Hayti is an inviolable asylum.

Article 24 declares "en matière politique elle (la peine de mort) est abolie, et remplacée par la détention perpétuelle dans une prison." Nothing could better illustrate the absurdity of Haytian laws and Haytian constitutions. The pen was scarcely dry that signed this constitution than political proscriptions commenced, and there is scarcely a city in Hayti that is not red with the blood of men accused or suspected of conspiring against the Government of General Salomon.

Article 25. "Every one has the right to express his opinions on every subject, and to write, print, and publish his thoughts," &c. &c., — full liberty of the press. This is on a par with Article 24.

Article 26. Liberty of worship. This is carried to its full extent, and every religion, African and Christian, is free.

Article 30. "Instruction is free. Public instruction is free and gratuitous. Primary instruction is obligatory and gratuitous." This is for the future. In Hayti to decree the establishment of anything is supposed to be sufficient for its fulfilment.

Article 31. Trial by jury is established in all criminal and political cases.

Article 35. "The secrecy of letters is inviolable." In President Salnave's time, the letters were taken to the Prefect of Police, opened and read, and then delivered without any attempt to close them; the letters addressed to foreigners were not respected.

Article 40. "Public debts are guaranteed and placed under the safeguard of the loyalty of the nation." When General — — went to a famous banker in Paris to contract a debt for Hayti, the capitalist asked him what security he proposed to offer. The Minister replied, "La constitution place les dettes publiques sous la sauvegarde de la loyauté de la nation." The banker looked fixedly at him for a moment and then coolly said, "I have *business* to attend to, — good morning."

Articles 41 to 49 are on the sovereignty and the exercise of the powers therefrom derived. Art. 41. The national sovereignty resides in the universality of the citizens. Art. 42. The exercise of that sovereignty is delegated to three powers. The three powers are the legislative, the executive, and the judicial. They form the government of the republic, which is essentially democratic and representative. Art. 44. The legislative power is exercised by two representative chambers, — a chamber of deputies and a senate. Art. 45. These two can be united in a National Assembly according to the constitution.

Article 46. The executive power is delegated to a citizen, who takes the title of President of the republic.

Article 47. Affairs which exclusively relate to the communes are regulated by the communal councils, under the control of the executive power.

Article 48. The judicial power is exercised by a court of cassation, civil courts, courts of appeal, of commerce and of police.

Article 49. Individual responsibility is distinctly attached to every public function.

Articles 50 to 56. Representatives are elected by the primary assemblies of each commune. Representatives must be twenty-five years of age, and are elected for five years, and are paid £60 a month, during the duration of the session.

Articles 57 to 66 treat of the Senate: it consists of thirty members elected for six years. The senators are elected by the Chamber of Deputies from two lists of candidates, one presented by the electoral assemblies, and the other by the executive power. A senator must be thirty years of age; the Senate is renewed by thirds every two years. The Senate can only meet during the legislative session, save in exceptional cases: on adjournment it leaves a standing committee composed of five members. The salary of each senator is £360 a year.

Articles 67 to 69 refer to the National Assembly, or union of the Senate and House of Representatives in one chamber. The National Assembly meets at the opening of every session. The prerogatives of the National Assembly are:—To elect a president, to declare war, to approve treaties, which will have no effect until so approved, to authorise the contraction of loans, the establishment of a national bank, to change the capital of the republic, to revise the constitution, to give letters of naturalisation.

Articles 70 to 100 refer to the exercise of the legislative power.

Article 71. The Legislature meets by full right on the first Monday in April of each year.

Article 73. The President, with the consent of two-thirds of the Senate, can dissolve the Chambers.

Article 77. Every member takes an oath to maintain the rights of the people, and to be faithful to the constitution.

Article 79. Money bills must originate in the Commons. The rest of the articles refer to the duties and the rights of the members.

Articles 101 to 123 refer to the President. He is elected for seven years, and not immediately re-eligible—must be forty years of age and proprietor of real estate. The President is called upon to swear the following oath:— "Je jure devant Dieu, devant la nation, d'observer, de faire observer fidèlement la constitution, et les lois du peuple Haïtien, de respecter ses droits, de maintenir nationale et l'intégrité du territoire." I wonder whether any President, when he took that oath, really intended to observe it. For example—

Article 24. On the non-punishment with death of political offences. General Salomon must have suffered greatly on this account.

Articles 110 and 111. The President commands the forces by sea and land, and confers rank in the army according to law, and appoints as well all civil functionaries.

Article 112. He makes treaties.

Article 114. He has the right of amnesty and pardon.

Article 115. Every measure must be submitted to a council of Secretaries of State, and (Art. 116) every act countersigned by one of them.

Article 120. The Chamber can impeach the President before the Senate.

Article 122. Salary of President, £5000 a year.

Articles 124 to 131 treat of the Secretaries of State, who must be thirty years of age; they form a council presided over by the President; they have free entry into both Chambers, to institute measures or to oppose others; they can be called before the Chambers to answer interpellations, which they must answer in public or in secret session; they are responsible for all acts they may sign or countersign; their pay is £1200 a year.

Articles 132 to 135 relate to communal institutions. Each commune has an elective council, of which the paid head, under the title of communal magistrate, is named by the President of the republic.

Articles 136 to 158 refer to the judicial authority.

Article 138 is especially important in Hayti: "No extraordinary tribunals can be created under any denomination whatever, particularly under the name of courts-martial." A court of cassation is established in the capital; five courts of appeal are established, one for each of the departments. Each commune has at least a justice of the peace; civil courts are established for one or more arrondissements. All judges are appointed by the President; they are immovable, and cannot be transferred without their own consent. Tribunals of commerce are also established. No political or press offences can be judged in secret session. The other articles relate to the usual functions of judges.

Articles 159 to 165 treat of primary and electoral assemblies. Every citizen over twenty-one has the right to vote, voting being by ballot. At one election at Port-au-Prince, the Government were very desirous to defeat the popular candidate, and therefore placed soldiers round the polling-booth armed with clubs, who demanded from each elector for whom he was going to vote. Whenever a known supporter of the candidate approached, he was beaten or hustled away by the soldiers; the Government finding that, in spite of these precautions, the election was going against them, occupied the booth and stopped the voting, under the plea of disturbance of the peace.

Articles 166 to 178 refer to the finances. No imports can be levied except according to law; taxes are voted yearly; no emissions of money without legal sanction; no pensions, gratifications, &c., except according to law; no plurality of functions; every minute precaution is taken to ensure the most careful management of the finances, including audit of accounts; no money can be coined abroad or bear any effigy but that of the republic. I understand, however, that all the new dollars were coined abroad.

Articles 179 to 188 relate to the armed forces. The army must not deliberate; no privileged corps; no one but a soldier can be promoted to a military grade. In my time the majority of officers had never been soldiers. The National Guard is composed of those citizens who are not in the active army.

Articles 189 to 205 refer to miscellaneous subjects. The national colours are blue and red, placed horizontally. The white was long ago banished from the flag. The arms of the republic are the palm-tree surmounted by the cap of liberty and adorned by a trophy of arms, with the motto, "L'union fait la force."

Article 192. *"No Haytian or foreigner can claim damages for losses incurred during civil troubles."* A most ridiculous article, to which no foreign Government would pay the slightest attention.

Article 194. The national *fêtes* are those of the independence of Hayti and its heroes, the great hero being Dessalines, who decreed the massacre of every defenceless man, woman, or child of white French parentage to be found in the republic, and who was perhaps, without exception, one of the vilest of men. January 1st is given up to his memory, and the Haytians glory in his bloodthirsty deeds. The second national *fête* is to agriculture—May 1st, which is one of the most ludicrous imaginable in its surroundings. A few cultivators are collected with bunches of bananas and other products, and prizes are distributed by the President, surrounded by hundreds of sneering officers. Even they can but smile at the absurdity called "encouragement to agriculture."

Article 197. No state of siege can be declared except during times of civil trouble, and then the decree must be signed by the President and all the Secretaries of State.

Article 200. The constitution cannot be suspended, in whole or in part, on any excuse whatever. It can, however, be revised under certain conditions.

Article 204. This is a very remarkable article. It suspends those articles for a year which proclaim the immovability of the judges, in order that the President may raise the magistracy to the height of its mission.

Although this constitution appears very elaborate and proclaims great principles, it leaves all details to be settled by special laws, which are seldom passed, and never acted on unless it may suit the pleasure of the chief of the State.

With the habits of the country, the framers of this constitution must have known that, in making the President of Hayti swear to observe it, they were forcing him to commit perjury by anticipation. The President swore to it, but has not kept it, and probably never intended to keep it. Article 24, which abolishes the punishment of death in political cases, has been completely set aside, and dozens of coloured men of mark have been sentenced to death and shot.

As the Russian Government is said to be a despotism tempered by assassination, so the Haytian Government may be called a despotism tempered by revolution and exile, and occasionally by death.

Their first ruler, Dessalines, was shot. Christophe committed suicide to escape a worse fate. Pétion died President after twelve years of power. Boyer was exiled after a Presidency that lasted for twenty-five years. Hérard-Rivière was proclaimed President on December 30, 1843, amid much enthusiasm, but on May 7, 1844, following he was deposed amid greater enthusiasm, and exiled, and General Guerrier was named President. Within less than a year he died, April 15, 1845, and General Pierrot was elected by the Council of State, March 1, 1846. The troops at St. Marc proclaimed Riché President, and Pierrot abdicated. On the 27th February following (1847) Riché died, and on the 2d March Soulouque was elected President. He soon tired of this form of government, and proclaimed himself Emperor in August 1849, and held that position till January 1859, when he was upset by General Geffrard and exiled.

Geffrard restored the republic, and held the Presidency till February 1867, when he also went into exile, to be succeeded by General Salnave in April 1867. In January 1870 the latter was overthrown and shot.

The only President who carried through his term of office, and was neither exiled nor shot, was Nissage-Saget. At the completion of his four years, he retired on a pension to his native city, and I believe still lives. After Saget, General Domingue seized the reins of government, but was expelled in 1876, and sent wounded into exile. Boisrond-Canal followed. In the third year of his Presidency he was overthrown and banished, and in October of the same year (1879) General Salomon was elected for seven years.

It will thus be seen that two only of all these rulers completed their terms of office.

As was natural in an old French colony, the divisions of the country are French. It is divided into departments, arrondissements, and communes, and the governing machinery is most elaborate. There are no lack of candidates for every post. The general of the department and the general of the arrondissement are the officers in whom all power is really delegated, and they are generally absolute in their districts. The Government often, however, trust more to their general of arrondissement than to that of the department, as they fear to render the latter too powerful. They are veritable despots as a rule, and ride roughshod over every law at their pleasure, and are seldom called to account by the supreme authority.

The republic of Hayti is divided as follows:—

Departments.	Chief Cities.	Arrondissements.	Communes.
North	Cap Haïtien	7	18
North-West	Port de Paix	2	5
Artibonite	Gonaives	3	9
West	Port-au-Prince	5	14
South	Les Cayes	6	21
		23	67

The department of the north is generally the most troublesome, from the separatist ideas of the inhabitants. King Christophe carried out that idea, and kept them independent for many years; and in 1865 Salnave tried the same project, but failed. They are, however, always restless, and dislike the other departments of the republic.

The department of the south is, on the whole, the most backward of all, and has been generally neglected, but the present holder of power, being a native of Les Cayes, may aid its progress.

All the other departments are jealous of that of the west, as in it are the capital, the seat of Government, and the Treasury, to which contributions flow from the other departments. Their object is always to divert to local wants as much of the general revenue as possible, and they think that if they could form separate republics, they would have their whole income to spend.

To sum up: At the head of the Government is a President chosen for seven years. He is supported by four or five Secretaries of State, who, when the chief is strong, are but his head clerks. A legislative body exists, consisting of a Senate of thirty paid members, generally very tractable; of a Chamber of Representatives of sixty members, also paid, who, under a chief who has the power of life and death, give him but little trouble. His main reliance, however, as also his main danger, is the army. General Salomon pays particular attention to that institution; has it strongly recruited, and, as long as its chiefs are satisfied, may defy the isolated revolutionary attempts of his enemies. The army is generally composed of blacks, and they look on a black President as their rightful head. They obey a coloured chief, but it is not willingly, and murmur at his punishments, whilst a black general might have a man beaten to death without exciting any dissatisfaction among his comrades.

CHAPTER VII
RELIGION, EDUCATION, AND JUSTICE

Religion

During the long Presidency of General Geffrard, the concordat with Rome was carried out in some of its most essential points. Until then the Roman Catholic clergy in Hayti were a byword and a reproach to every one who respected religion. There were few priests who were not the expelled of other countries, and even adventurers had assumed the clerical garb to obtain an easy and lucrative living. There was one priest in the south, who was considered a *bon enfant* and inclined to luxurious cheer, who turned his attention to money-making, and every week he sallied forth from the town of Les Cayes to forage in the country districts. So that he was paid his fees, it was immaterial to him what he was called upon to bless; he would indifferently sprinkle holy water on a new house or a freshly built temple dedicated to the Vaudoux worship. The simple inhabitants would bring out their stone implements, imported in former days from Africa and used in their fetish rites, and the priest would bless them; then he would return to town in a jovial mood and chuckle over his gains. In comparatively a few years that man remitted to Europe through an English house the sum of twelve thousand pounds sterling.

Another, whom I knew personally, lived in a town not far from the capital, and his amours somewhat scandalised the Archbishop. He tried in vain to have him removed from his parish. The priest was popular, had influence in Government circles, and defied his superior. He might have defied him to the end had he not mixed in politics; but having embraced the losing side, he was ultimately banished.[15]

In the same neighbourhood there lived another priest whom the Archbishop had dismissed for living in the same house with his large family, and for engaging in commerce; and Monseigneur also applied to the Government to have him expelled from the republic. The curé appealed for protection to the French Legation, saying that he should be completely ruined if forced suddenly to abandon the country. The representative of France, thinking he ought to have time granted him to settle his affairs, stated the case to the Haytian Minister of Public Worship, who agreeing with him, remarked, "Il est peut-être mauvais prêtre, mais bon père de famille."

There was a priest who formerly lived at La Coupe, the summer resort of the inhabitants of Port-au-Prince—a dapper Parisian—who was perfectly astonished by the accounts the peasantry gave of one of his predecessors; and I could gather from him that, short of being present at human sacrifices, the man would join in any feast given by the negroes in a district as full of Vaudoux worshippers as any in the island, and his immorality equalled his other qualities.[16]

Several of these ignoble priests were Corsicans who had been driven from their country on account of crime. For fear, however, any one should consider these statements to be exaggerated, I will add to the testimony given by the Archbishop an extract from a speech of M. Valmy Lizaire, Minister of Public Worship (1863):—

"N'éprouve-t-on pas un sentiment pénible et douloureux en contemplant l'état de notre église depuis sa naissance jusqu'à ce jour, en voyant la dignité du saint ministère souvent menacée et compromise par des inconnus sans qualités, par quelque moines la plus part du temps échappés de leur convents et venant offrir jusqu'à chez nous le dangereux spectacle de leurs dérèglements? Je ne ferai point l'horreur à plaisir en essayant de retracer içi tout ce que nos annales religieuses renferment de désordres et d'excès. Il suffit de dire que nulle part, peut-être dans la chrétienté, le clergé n'a profané autant qu'en Haïti le sacerdoce dont il est revêtu."

At length the scandal became so intolerable that the Government of Hayti determined to negotiate a concordat at Rome, and after many difficulties had been overcome, it was signed in 1860, and the Pope sent as his delegate Monseigneur Testard de Cosquer to bring it into practice. He was one of the most pleasing of men, handsome, eloquent, and the romantic but terrible episode related of him as the cause of his leaving the army and entering into holy orders rendered him an object of great interest to the fair sex. He brought with him a body of French clergy, whom he gradually installed in the different parishes of the republic, not, however, without a difficult struggle with those who formerly held possession and disgraced the Church.

The concordat consisted of seventeen articles and two additions, which provided first for the special protection of the Catholic religion; the establishment of an archbishopric at Port-au-Prince, and as soon as possible other dependent bishoprics, paid by the State; nomination by the President of three bishops subject to the approval of the Holy See,—the clergy to take an oath of fidelity to the Government; establishment of seminaries and chapters; nomination of priests by the bishops of persons approved of by the Government, and a few other arrangements of lesser importance.

The Roman Catholic Church, however, although the religion of the State, has never been popular in Hayti. Amongst the upper classes, disbelief, among the lower the influence of the Vaudoux, and the fanatical opposition of the Catholic priesthood to Freemasonry, have combined to prevent the Church from gaining either the confidence or the affection of the nation. Even over the women the priests exercise less influence than in other countries.

Although the Roman Catholic religion is that of the State, all others are tolerated, and many Haytian Ministers have felt inclined to encourage the Protestants, not only to counterbalance any political influence of the priests, but with the object of creating a rivalry in the performance of their missionary duties. These passing fits of enlightenment, however, have been but of short duration, and little has been done to encourage any form of religion.

At present Hayti is divided into five dioceses; but at the time of the last report I have seen, there were only one archbishop and two bishops; these were aided by four vicars-generals.

Port-au-Prince, being the capital, is the seat of the archbishopric, where Monseigneur Guilloux still worthily holds sway, and he is aided in his duties by a vicar and chapter. He has always had a difficult part to play, and during the civil war of 1869 ran many risks, and was nearly expelled the country.

The budget makes allowance for one archbishop at £800 a year; two bishops at £480 a year; the vicar of Port-au-Prince at £160 a year; three other vicars at £120 a year; and sixty-seven parish priests at £48 a year.

Besides this regular pay, the Government is bound to furnish the clergy with suitable residences. The Archbishop has a very comfortable and spacious house, sufficiently furnished for the climate, and situated in the healthiest quarter of the town. The clergy receive also many fees, the amount for baptisms, marriages, and funerals having been fixed by arrangement with the Government. When I was in Port-au-Prince there was a very warm discussion as to whether the fees were to be employed towards the payment of salary, each party accusing the other of wishing to violate the concordat.

After the expulsion of President Geffrard, the revolutionary party desired to upset all his arrangements, even to the concordat. Monseigneur

Guilloux published a strong defence of that treaty, taking very high ground, and claiming a great deal for the Church.

This pamphlet called forth the following epigram from General Alibé Féry:—

Les Deux Enclos.

César ne doit au Christ rien soustraire à la vigne
Dit notre bon prélat plus absolu qu'un czar.
D'accord; mais ce gardien d'un végétal insigne
Doit-il parfois glaner dans le champ de César?

This was a much-admired specimen of Haytian wit.

As I have previously observed, Hayti has never quite reconciled herself to the clergy, and therefore the influence exercised by the priest is less than in other Catholic countries. There are two patent causes: first, the hold that the Vaudoux worship has on the mass of the people, and, second, the pertinacious opposition of the Church to Freemasonry.

It is the fashion to extol the intelligence and far-sightedness of the Church of Rome, but certainly the opposition shown to Freemasonry, that harmless institution in Hayti, has done more to injure the influence of the Catholic clergy among the educated classes than any other cause. All who know what Freemasonry is, know that its objects are to promote good-fellowship, with a modicum of charity and mutual aid. The exercise of ancient rites, which, though a mystery, are as harmless, and perhaps as childish, as the scenes of a pantomime, never deserved the opposition of a serious clergy.

The Haytians are devoted to Freemasonry, and love to surround the funerals of their brethren with all the pomp of the order. I was once invited to a masonic funeral, and we marched through the town with banners displayed, each member wearing the insignia of his rank; but I noticed that as soon as the church was reached, everything pertaining to the order was removed from the coffin, and the members pocketed their insignia. We then entered the sacred building. The funeral was one that greatly touched us all, as it was that of a young officer who had that morning been killed in a duel, under peculiarly unfortunate circumstances. The priests came forward,— suddenly they stopped, and with signs of anger retreated up the church. A gentleman followed to inquire the cause. The abbé answered that until all signs of Freemasonry were removed he would not perform the ceremony. What signs? He replied that all the mourners had little sprigs in their button-holes, which was a masonic sign. We had all to conceal the sprigs until the ceremony was over. It was a trifle, but it excited the utmost anger among the mourners present.

My deceased friend, Seguy-Villevalien, wrote me an account of what occurred on another occasion. A general and high officer in the brotherhood died, and the Freemasons determined to give him a grand funeral, and President Domingue signified his intention to be present. A great procession was organised, and was preparing to start for the cathedral, when a messenger arrived from the vicar to say that he would not allow the funeral to enter the church unless the masonic procession was given up. The President was furious, and being a very violent man, was ready to order a battalion to force a way for the funeral, when a prudent adviser said to Domingue, "The Protestants do not object to Freemasonry; let us send for Bishop Holly, and ask him to perform the service for us."

Bishop Holly willingly consented, and the procession started for the Protestant cathedral, where the funeral service was performed, with banners displayed, and every other masonic sign in full view. Nearly every man present was a Roman Catholic, and probably for the first time in Hayti had a President, his ministers, his aides-de-camp and followers been present in a Protestant church.

The strongest feeling, however, against the Church arises from the prevalence, not only of the Vaudoux worship, but of its influence. There are thousands who would never think of attending one of its ceremonies who yet believe in and fear the priests of this fetish worship. The Papalois, however, as I have stated in Chapter V., do not disdain to direct their followers to mix up with their own the ceremonies of the Christians. They will burn candles before the church doors; will place on the cathedral steps all the rubbish of hair and bone which are religious emblems with them; and will have in their temples pictures of the Virgin Mary and of Jesus Christ. In former times they would gladly pay heavily to the degenerate priests of the ante-concordat days to sprinkle with holy water the altars of the temples under which their slimy god was held confined.

When it is remembered how imbued Haytian society has been with this degrading worship, it is perhaps not a matter of surprise how small is the influence of the clergy among the rural population. The Catholic priests are also comparatively few in number, dislike heartily the life in the interior, and are paid by the State. There is also little enthusiasm awakened by that rivalry which a successful Protestant Church would have brought forth.

There is no doubt but that the conduct of the clergy has been very much criticised in Hayti, and none, from the Archbishop downwards, have escaped the attention of the teller of merry anecdotes; but, as far as I could myself observe, their moral conduct, with very few exceptions indeed, was all that could be desired. At the same time they showed little enthusiasm, cared little for their congregations, were inclined to domineer, and preferred the comfort of their town-houses to missionary toils in the interior, and were persistently opposed to every liberal measure. Whilst I was in Port-au-Prince, a priest slapped a lady's face in church for some error in ceremonial.

The priests of the ante-concordat period no doubt rendered the task of the new clergy as difficult as possible, first by their pernicious example, and then by their opposition; but Archbishop Guilloux has now completely cleared the island of them, and has established a respectable clergy in their place. His friends say that their influence is daily increasing throughout the republic.

The Protestants have not had much success in Hayti. The Episcopalians are represented by a bishop. Mr. Holly, a convert from Romanism and a black, was the first representative of that Church whom I met with in Port-au-Prince. He had many of the qualities which ensure a good reception. He had pleasant manners, was well educated, and was thoroughly in earnest; but the pecuniary support he received was so slight that he never could carry out his views. I believe that those who attend the Anglican services in the whole of Hayti number less than a thousand, and the majority of these are probably American and English coloured immigrants.

The Wesleyans had for their chief pastor Mr. Bird, who was an institution in Hayti. He had a very good school, and was highly respected. There are several chapels in different parts of the island, and I notice, in a recent consular return, that as many as 1400 attend the services. With other denominations combined, the Protestant population may be considered to amount to between 3000 and 4000.

When I first arrived in Hayti, and was curious as to the character of certain individuals, I was often struck by the reply, "Oh! he is an honest man, but then he is a Protestant," — and this from Roman Catholics!

The Protestants are not yet in any way sufficiently numerous or influential to be a counterpoise to the Catholic clergy, and do not, therefore, incite the latter to exertion. I did suggest that the Protestant clergy should all join the Freemasons' lodges, and be ready to perform the religious ceremonies required at funerals. It would have greatly increased their popularity and influence in the country; but I believe my advice was considered too worldly.

Divorce is another bone of contention between the Catholic clergy and the people. By the civil law divorce is recognised, and cases occur every year. The clergy denounce those who re-marry civilly as living in a state of concubinage, and much ill-feeling is the result.

Although, as I have before remarked, the Catholic clergy have greatly improved in conduct since the concordat, yet, in popular estimation, there is still something wanting. I have not forgotten the excitement caused by a song which a young Haytian (black) wrote on the subject. A very good-looking priest had at all events been indiscreet, and the Archbishop decided to banish him from the capital to a rural district. A deputation of females, early one morning, waited on Monseigneur to remonstrate, but he was firm, and then the song declared:—

> "Il fallait voir pleurer les mulâtresses,
> En beaux peignoirs et les cheveux au vent;
> Il fallait voir sangloter les négresses
> Tout ce tableau par un soleil levant.
> Bon voyage,
> Cher petit blanc!
> Tu vas troubler l'église et le ménage.
> Bon voyage,
> Saint petit blanc!
> Que de regrets, O mon sacré galant!"

As there was a certain amount of truth in the scandalous stories afloat, Monseigneur was very irritated with the author, and imprudently applied to Government to have him arrested. He was arrested, but his influential relatives soon procured his release, but under the condition of suppressing the song. Of course he was the hero of the hour, and his verses had a greater success than ever.

Although "the complete ascendancy of the Church of Rome is incompatible with liberty and good government," yet it is a matter of regret that in Hayti the Roman Catholic priests have had so little success. Their task is no doubt difficult, and, under present circumstances, almost a hopeless one. They cannot cope with so vast a mass of brutal ignorance and gross superstition, and one of the best men among them used often to complain of the little assistance they received from what might be considered the enlightened classes. My friend Alvarez, the Spanish *chargé d'affaires*, was very indignant at the idea presented by a French author, Monsieur Bonneau, that Catholicism was incapable of contending with the Vaudoux worship; but there is no doubt that as yet nothing has had much influence in suppressing it.

The Roman Catholic Church, however, has been greatly reinforced since I left Hayti in 1877. It now counts as many as seventy priests, and had above 64,000 Easter communicants in 1863. How many of these were in secret followers of the Vaudoux?

To afford a special supply of priests for Hayti, the Archbishop Testard de Cosquer established in 1864 a Haytian seminary in Paris, to the support of which the Chambers in Port-au-Prince voted 20,000 francs a year. This allowance being irregularly paid, the seminary was closed, but was reopened by Monseigneur Guilloux, who obtained a yearly sum of 10,000 francs from the Haytian Government. It is perhaps needless to say that even this small amount is generally greatly in arrear.

There can be no doubt that Monseigneur Guilloux and his clergy are fighting a good fight in the cause of civilisation, but with such a Government and such a people their progress must be slow.

Education

The following anecdote aptly illustrates the saying, Who shall teach the teachers? It is a custom in Hayti that in all schools, public as well as private, there shall be once a year a solemn examination in the presence of a commission appointed by Government. M. Seguy-Villevalien kept the best private school or college that Port-au-Prince had ever seen, and on the appointed day for the public examination the official commission arrived, and having been duly installed in the seats of honour, teachers and pupils presented themselves, and the work commenced. All went well till the exercises in orthography were nearly over, when unfortunately M. Villevalien turned to the president of the commission, a negro of the deepest dye, but a high Government functionary, and said, "Would you like to try the boys yourself?" "Certainly;" and various words were given, which were written down on the black-board to the satisfaction of all. At last the president gave the word "Pantalon," and a smart boy carefully chalked it up. "Stop!" cried the sable chief, "there is a mistake in that spelling." The master, the teachers, and the boys carefully scanned the word, and could detect no mistake. The black had a smile of conscious superiority on his lips. At length the master said, "I see no mistake, president." "You don't! Do you not know that it is spelt with an *e*—'pentalon'?" After a severe glance at his pupils to prevent an explosion of laughter, my friend, perfectly equal to the occasion, answered, "It used to be spelt so, president, but the Academy has lately changed the mode, and it is now spelt with an *a*." The courtesy and gravity of M. Villevalien's manner was such that the president of the commission was quite satisfied and pleased with himself. He wrote a favourable report on the condition of the school. Had the almost uncontrollable laughter of the boys burst forth, what would have been the report? And yet this man was a leading spirit in his country, and thought fit for the highest offices, though he was as stupid as he was ignorant.

I arrived at the college just too late for this scene, but in time to hear the cheerful laughter of the boys, who, after the departure of the commission, made the playground ring with their merry jokes.

President Geffrard, whose term of office extended from January 1859 to February 1867, did more than any other chief to encourage education, and yet, even in his time, not more than one in ten of the children of school-age attended the educational establishments.

Major Stuart, in his report on Hayti for the year 1876, gives some statistical tables which show the state of these establishments in the year 1875, and little has changed since, so that his figures will sufficiently serve the purpose required. There were—

4 lyceums	with	543	pupils.
6 superior girl schools	"	563	"
5 secondary schools	"	350	"
165 primary schools	"	11,784	"
200 rural schools	"	5,939	"
1 school of medicine	"	25	"
1 school of music	"	46	"
		———	
		19,250	"

To these may be added the pupils in the private schools and in those of the Christian Brothers and the Sisters of Cluny.

It is very difficult to test the results attained at the official schools, but I think, judging from my own experience in Hayti, that they are small indeed. Some of the commissions appointed to examine the scholars report favourably, but, after the example of Monsieur Pentalon, I put but little faith in these judgments.

In the official report for the year 1878 there is much shortcoming confessed, and the feeling after reading it is, that the majority of the teachers are incompetent, as all negligently-paid service must be. Good teachers will not remain in employment with salaries often six months in arrear, and only those who can find nothing else to do will carry on the schools. Negligence is the result, and negligence in the masters acts on the scholars, and their attendance is irregular; and the means of teaching are often wanting, as the money voted for the purchase of books goes in this revolutionary country for arms and powder. Parents, particularly negro parents, rarely appreciate the value of the knowledge to be acquired in schools, and are apt to send their children late and take them away early, in order to aid in the family's support.

The best school in the country is the Petit Séminaire, conducted by priests—Jesuits, it is said, under another name. The head of the college in my time, and, I believe, to the present day, was Père Simonet, a very superior man, quite capable of directing the institution aright; and I have been informed that the favourable results of their system of education have been very marked. In September 1883 this establishment was directed by fifteen priests of the Congregation of the Holy Spirit, and contained as many as 300 pupils.

The Sisters of Cluny have also an establishment near Port-au-Prince, where the daughters of the chief families of the capital receive their education, and their institution is well spoken of. I attended one of their examinations and school exhibitions, when recitals and acting by the young girls were the amusements afforded us. Some of the pupils appeared to be remarkably bright, and they acquitted themselves of their tasks in a very pleasing manner. Since I left Hayti, these establishments for girls have greatly increased in importance. There are now as many as sixty sisters, and twenty others called "Filles de la Sagesse," who have established schools throughout the country, which in 1883 were attended by about 3000 pupils.

The Christian Brothers have also many schools dispersed throughout the country, principally, however, in the larger towns, which are fairly well attended. They are reported to have had also in 1883 as many as 3000 boys under tuition.

It is generally thought that the teaching in all these schools is not such as to develop the intellect of the pupils. As might have been expected, too much time is given to trifling with religious subjects, as teaching the girls an infinity of hymns to Mary, and to the study of the lives of the saints. Such, at least, was the complaint made to me by the relatives of the girls. Nothing appears to be able to avert the evil influence of the immodest surroundings of these schools. A gentleman told me that, entering a room where his nieces were sitting sewing, he heard them singing a most indecent song in Creole, probably quite innocent of the real meaning, and they told him that they had learnt it from the native servants at the school; whilst the pupils at the Petit Séminaire have often suffered from the utter depravity of some of the lower portion of the population.

In one of the official reports on the principal lyceum, the Minister of Public Instruction remarks:—"As regards studies, discipline of pupils and teachers, the national lyceum has fallen into a shameful state. It is to the superior direction that this abasement of the lyceum is in part to be attributed. It so far forgets itself, as to give to professors and pupils scandalous spectacles, which attest the disregard of propriety and of the most ordinary reserve that a teacher ought to observe in presence of early age and youth."

By this account it would appear that the pupils have often but a poor example to imitate. I should have set down to political feeling this strong censure had I not known the lyceum in my time to have fallen very low indeed in public estimation.

Poor, however, as the education is that is given in Hayti, it is nevertheless an advance; and if ever revolutions cease and peace be kept for a few years, the Government may yet turn its attention to founding educational establishments on a solid basis. Of this, however, there is very little hope.

There are several private schools in Hayti. The best, as I have previously observed, was kept by the late M. Seguy-Villevalien. He had a very high opinion of the capacity of Haytian boys to learn, and he turned out some excellent scholars. His school, however, deteriorated in late years from his inability to secure superior teachers, arising first from parents not paying their school-bills, and secondly from the Government omitting to settle their accounts with him for the bursars. I mention this to show what a people the Haytians are. During the civil war in 1868 and 1869, M. Villevalien spent all his capital in supporting some dozens of boarders, whose parents were among the insurgents, and by his energy saved them from being drafted into the army. Yet when the war was over, few, if any, paid him what was due, or did it in depreciated paper, which was almost equivalent to not paying at all.

Education in Hayti is too often sacrificed to political exigencies, and a master of a high school is not chosen for his capacity, but for his political leanings.

We all noticed what has often been remarked in Africa, that negro boys, up to the age of puberty, were often as sharp as their coloured fellow-pupils; and there can be no doubt that the coloured boys of Hayti have proved, at least in the case of one of their number, that they could hold their ground with the best of the whites. Young Fénélon Faubert obtained the "prix d'honneur au grand concours" at Paris in rhetoric, "discours latin," and only missed it the next year by unpardonable carelessness.

Some of the Haytian lads have the most extraordinary memories. M. Villevalien mentioned one to me who came to his school rather over the usual age. My friend took up a book on rhetoric and asked him a few questions, which were answered in the words of the author without an error; curious as to the extent of his proficiency, the schoolmaster kept turning page after page, and found, to his surprise, that the boy knew nearly the whole volume by heart. He then began to converse with him, and found, that although he could repeat his lesson perfectly, he did not really understand the sense of what he was repeating.

Whilst I was at Port-au-Prince the following affecting incident occurred:—Many families who have accumulated a certain amount of wealth by retail trade are desirous of having their children well educated, and therefore send them to France. A Haïtienne of this description placed her daughter at the Convent of the Sacré Cœur in Paris. After seven years' residence there, she passed a few months with a French family, and saw a little society in the capital. She then returned to Port-au-Prince, was received at the wharf by a rather coarse-looking fat woman, whom her affectionate heart told her was her mother, and accompanied her home. Here she found a shop near the market-place, where her mother sold salt pork and rum by retail; the place was full of black men and women of the labouring class, who were, as usual, using the coarsest language, and who pressed round to greet her as an old acquaintance. Traversing the shop, she found herself in a small parlour, and here she was destined to live. Her mother was doing a thriving trade, and was always in the shop, which was a receptacle of every strong-smelling food, whose odours penetrated to the parlour. There the young girl sat within earshot of the coarse language of the customers. What a contrast to the severe simplicity of the convent, the kindness of the nuns, the perfect propriety! and add to this the recollection of the society she had seen in Paris! She was but a tender plant, and could not stand this rude trial, and sickened and died within the first two months. At her funeral many speeches were made, and the doctor who had attended her, whilst declaring that she died of no special malady, counselled parents not to send their children to be educated in Europe, unless, on their return, they could offer them a suitable home. No wonder, under these circumstances, that every educated Haytian girl desires to marry a foreigner and quit the country.

The well-known lawyer, Deslandes, objected to Haytian children being sent to Paris for their education, as likely to introduce into the country French ideas and sympathies, and thus imperil their independence.

At the present time education must be completely neglected, as the whole attention of the country is devoted to mutual destruction.

Justice

My first experience of a court of justice in Hayti was a political trial. Four of the most respectable and respected inhabitants of Port-au-Prince were to be tried for their lives on a charge of conspiracy against the government of President Geffrard. My colleagues and I decided to be present. On approaching the courthouse, we saw a considerable crowd collected and some military precautions taken. Forcing our way through to some reserved seats, we found ourselves in a perfectly plain room,—a dock on the left for the prisoners, opposite to them the jury seats, behind a table for three judges, and a tribune for the public prosecutor.

After a few preliminaries, the trial began with a violent denunciation of the accused by the public prosecutor—a stuggy, fierce-looking negro with bloodshot eyes, named Bazin, who thought he best performed his duty by abuse. As one of the prisoners was a lawyer, all the bar had inscribed their names as his defenders, and they showed considerable courage in the task they had undertaken. On the least sign of independence on their part, one after the other was ordered to prison, and the accused remained without a defender.

The principal judge was Lallemand, of whom I have elsewhere spoken as combining gentleness with firmness; but he could scarcely make his authority respected by Bazin, the military termagant who led the prosecution. He browbeat the witnesses, bullied the jury, thundered at the lawyers, and insulted the prisoners. He looked like a black Judge Jeffreys. At last his language became so violent towards the audience, of whom we formed a part, that the diplomatic and consular corps rose in a body and left the court. I never witnessed a more disgraceful scene.

I may add that the prisoners were condemned to death; but we interfered, and had their sentence commuted to imprisonment, which did not last long; whilst their black persecutor, seized by some insurgents the following year, was summarily shot.[17]

This experience of the working of the trial-by-jury system did not encourage frequent visits to the tribunals, and afterwards I rarely went, except when some British subject was interested.

In the capital are the court of cassation, the civil and commercial courts, and the tribuneaux de paix; and in the chief towns of the departments similar ones, minus the court of cassation. In fact, as far as possible, the French system has been taken as a model. The form is there, but not the spirit.

The statistical tables connected with this subject have been very fully worked out in Major Stuart's very interesting Consular Reports for 1876 and 1877. Here I am more concerned in describing how justice is administered. I may at once say that few have any faith in the decisions of the courts; the judges, with some bright exceptions, are too often influenced by pecuniary or political considerations, and the white foreigner, unless he pay heavily, has but slight chance of justice being done him.

In the police courts they know their fate beforehand. During my stay in Port-au-Prince foreigners avoided them, but sometimes they had unavoidably to appear. An elderly Frenchman was summoned before a *juge de paix* for an assault upon a black. The evidence was so much in favour of the white that even the Haytian magistrate was about to acquit him, when shouts arose in different parts of the court, "What! are you going to take part with the white?" and the Frenchman was condemned. So flagrant an abuse of justice could not be passed over, and the authorities, afraid to have the sentence quashed by a superior tribunal, allowed the affair to drop without demanding the fine.

An American black came one day to Mr. Byron, our Vice-Consul, and said he had been accused of stealing a box of dominoes from his landlady, and asked him to accompany him to court to see justice done him. Mr. Byron, knowing the man to be respectable, did so. The accuser stated that whilst sitting at her door talking to a neighbour, she saw her lodger put the box of dominoes into his pocket and walk off with it. She made no remark at the time, but next day accused him. The man denied having touched the box. The magistrate, however, observed, "She says she saw you; you can't get over that,"—and had not Mr. Byron remarked that the prisoner's word was as good as the accuser's, being at least as respectable a person, he would instantly have been sent to prison.

A remarkable trial was that of two brothers, who were accused of having murdered a Frenchman, their benefactor. The evidence against them appeared overwhelming, and their advocate, a thorough ruffian, was at a loss for arguments to sustain the defence. At last he glanced round the crowded court, and then turned to the jury with a broad grin and said, "Après tout, ce n'est qu'un blanc de moins." The sally produced a roar of laughter, and the prisoners were triumphantly acquitted by the tribunal, but not by public opinion; and the people still sing a ditty of which the refrain is, I think, "Moué pas tué p'tit blanc-là,"—"I did not kill that little white man."

In 1869, among about fifty political refugees that lived for months in the Legation was one of the accused. I was standing watching him play draughts with another refugee, who did not know the name of his opponent, and he kept humming the song about the murder, and every time he made a move he repeated the refrain, "Moué pas tué p'tit blanc-là." I noticed his opponent getting paler and paler. At last he pushed aside the board, started to his feet, and said, "Do you wish to insult me?" We were all surprised, when a friend called me aside and told me the story of the trial.

Though more attention has since been paid to words, the spirit of the old saying remains—that the whites possess no rights in Hayti which the blacks are bound to respect.

In civil cases bribery of the judges is notorious, and the largest or the most liberal purse wins. Most persons carefully avoid a lawsuit, and prefer submitting to injustice.

The judges, curiously enough, are rarely selected from among the lawyers. The Government can appoint any one it pleases, and as these posts are awarded for political services, those selected consider that the appointments are given to enable them to make their fortunes as rapidly as possible. As the pay is small, their wives often make it an excuse to keep shops and carry on a retail trade; but the fact is that the Haïtienne is never so happy as when behind a counter.

The active bar of Port-au-Prince is composed of very inferior men. I often heard my friend Deslandes address the courts. He was at the summit of his profession, and to have him for your advocate was popularly supposed to secure the success of your cause. And yet I heard this eloquent and able advocate, as he was called, whilst defending an Englishman charged with having criminally slain an American negro, drop the legitimate argument of self-defence, and weary his audience for a couple of hours trying to prove that the Englishman was an instrument of Divine Providence to rid the world of a ruffian. Naturally the Englishman was condemned.

Whilst in court the lawyers surround themselves with heaps of books, and continually read long extracts from the laws of the country, or—what they greatly prefer—passages from the speeches of the most celebrated French advocates; whether they explain or not the subject in hand is immaterial. I have often heard my French colleagues say that they have tried in vain to discover what these extracts had to do with the case in point. Few of these lawyers bear a high character, and they are freely accused of collusion, and of other dishonest practices. Unhappy is the widow, the orphan, or the friendless that falls into their hands. Many of my Haytian friends have assured me that, though they had studied for the bar, they found it impossible to practise with any hope of preserving their self-respect. No doubt the bar of Hayti contains some honest men, but the majority have an evil reputation.

The laws of Hayti are not in fault, as they are as minutely elaborate as those of any other country, and the shelves of a library would groan beneath their weight. Had M. Linstant Pradine been able to continue the useful publication he commenced—a collection of the laws of Hayti—it was his design to have united in a regular series all the laws and decrees by which his country was supposed to be governed.

Though a few young men of good position have studied for the legal profession in France, yet the majority of the members of the bar are chosen among the lawyers, clerks, and others who have studied at home. A board is appointed to examine young aspirants. It consists of two judges and three lawyers; and if the young men pass, they each receive a certificate of qualification, countersigned by the Minister of Justice. After this simple process they can open an *étude* on their own account.

One of the greatest difficulties of the diplomatic and consular officers in all these American republics is to obtain prompt and legal justice for their countrymen. Although the *juge d'instruction* ought to finish his work at the utmost in two months, prisoners' cases drag on, and as the law of bail is unknown, they may be, and have been, confined for years before being brought to trial.

The President of the republic names the justices of the peace and their deputies, the judges of the civil and criminal courts, the courts of appeal, and the members of the court of cassation. All but the first-named judges are irremovable according to the constitution; but revolutionary leaders are not apt to respect constitutions, and during President Domingue's time his Ministers upset all the old legal settlements. The last constitution, that of 1879, permitted the President to remove judges for the space of one year, in order that the friends of the Administration should be appointed to carry out their destined work.

It would be perhaps useless to describe in detail the other legal arrangements in Hayti, as they are founded on French precedents.

CHAPTER VIII
ARMY AND POLICE

The Army

A large portion of the revenues is spent in keeping up a nominally numerous army, but in reality the most undisciplined rabble that ever were assembled under arms. With the exception of a few hundred tirailleurs, who were, in the time of President Geffrard, disciplined by an intelligent officer, Pétion Faubert, a man who had seen service in the French army, the regiments have been always composed of the peasantry, without any discipline, and officered by men as ignorant as themselves. I have seen a battalion on parade numbering thirteen privates, ten officers, and six drummers—the rest of the men thinking it unnecessary to present themselves except on pay-day.

A French admiral asked permission to see a Sunday morning's review. On approaching a cavalry regiment equally low in numbers with the battalion mentioned above, the President gravely turned to the Frenchman and said, "Beaucoup souffert dans la dernière guerre."

A more motley sight can scarcely be imagined than a full regiment marching past. Half the men are in coats wanting an arm, a tail, or a collar, with a broken shako, a straw or round hat, a wide-awake, or merely a handkerchief tied round the head; officers carrying their swords in their right or their left hands according to caprice; the men marching in waving lines, holding their muskets in every variety of position; whilst a brilliant staff, in all the uniforms known to the French army, gallops by. President Geffrard used to look on with a smile of satisfaction on his face, and gravely ask you whether there were any finer troops in the world. As I have elsewhere related, the Treasurer-in-chief, who had passed some time in Paris, assured him that although the soldiers there were more numerous, they had not the *tenue* of the Haytian, and suggested that it would be as well for the President to send some of his officers to France as models for the French army to imitate. This is no exaggeration. I have myself heard similar observations. The negro is generally an ill-made shambling fellow, who rarely looks well in uniform and detests the service; but in order to render the work less fatiguing for the poor fellows, the sentries are provided with chairs!

It was after watching such a march-past as I have described above that a French naval officer asked me, "Est-ce que vous prenez ces gens au serieux?" And yet they look upon themselves as a military nation, and constantly boast that they drove the English and French out of the island; forgetting the part taken by their most potent allies, climate and yellow fever; and until disease had carried off the mass of their oppressors, and the renewal of the war in Europe enabled the English to lend their aid, they were crushed under the heel of the French.

The Haytian army has greatly varied in numbers. In the early years (1825 to 1830) of General Boyer's Presidency it was calculated at 30,000 men, with only a fair proportion of officers. Some months after the fall of General Geffrard (1867) an account was published stating that the army in round numbers consisted as follows:—

General officers and staff	6500
Regimental officers	7000
Soldiers	6500
	20,000

It is never possible to say what is the exact force of the army; in a late return it is stated at 16,000, and among the non-effectives are about 1500 generals of division. However, the old system continues, and to most of the battalions the President's observation, "Beaucoup souffert dans la dernière guerre," could be aptly applied. As Gustave d'Alaux somewhere remarks, "Tout Haïtien qui n'était pas général de division était au moins soldat."

The cause of the great superabundance of general officers arises from nomination to a superior grade being a form of reward for political services which costs little. Every successful revolution brings with it a fresh crop of generals and colonels, as a lesser rank would be despised. I know a general who kept a small provision shop, and have seen him selling candles in full uniform. A counter-revolution made him fly the country, and for some time after he was acting as groom in some French seaport.[18] A Minister of War wishing to please a courtesan, gave her a commission in blank, which she sold for about five pounds.

President Salnave raised a common workman to the rank of general of brigade. As he had no money to buy a uniform, he began by stealing a pair of gold-laced trousers from a tailor's shop, but did not do it unobserved. Chase was given, and the culprit fled to the palace, and took refuge in Salnave's own room, who, however, handed him over to the police. The stolen trousers were then fastened round his neck and a rope secured to one ankle, and in this manner the new general was led round the town, receiving every now and then blows from the clubs of the soldiers. When he was quite exhausted, they mounted him on a donkey with his face to the tail, a placard with the word "Thief" fixed on his breast, and the gold-laced trousers still tied round his neck.

The great majority of the officers are in reality civilians, without any military training whatever, but they have a hankering for wearing a uniform, which is partly excusable on account of the respect with which the lower classes regard an officer.

The blacks laugh a little at their own love of gold lace. One day, whilst entering the cathedral with the diplomatic and consular corps in full uniform, I heard a negro say to his companions, "Gardé donc, blancs là aimé galon too!" ("Look, the whites also like gold lace!"), and a grunt of acquiescence showed that they were not a little pleased to find that the whites shared their weakness. "Too," by the way, is almost the only English word which remains to testify to our former presence in the island.

Military honour has never been a distinguished feature in the Haytian army,—I mean that military honour which implies fidelity to the Government that they have sworn to serve. This was most marked in the revolution which broke out at Cap Haïtien in 1865 under Salnave and Delorme. Nearly every superior officer appeared more or less to have betrayed General Geffrard; but as they hated Salnave more, their treachery consisted in plots, in preventing successes, but not in aiding the enemy. Geffrard knew this, and so put over the army General Nissage-Saget, an ex-tailor, I believe, who was utterly incapable and as unsuccessful as the rest. Salnave could not have held his position a week had the officers done their duty; but they appeared to think only of how their personal interests could be best served, and never of the honour or dignity of the Government and country. Some entered into a conspiracy to murder the President, but being discovered, the most compromised fell on his knees before Geffrard and pleaded for mercy, which was somewhat contemptuously granted, with the remark, "You are not of the stuff of which conspirators should be made."

There was no want of personal courage shown by the chiefs during the long civil war between civilisation and barbarism in 1868 and 1869, and some officers showed conspicuous dash and bravery, as Monplaisir-Pierre (negro) and Brice (coloured), (who subsequently were foully murdered by order of their then ally, Septimus Rameau), and Boisrond (coloured), who really merited the epithet of *sans peur et sans reproche* which was given him at a banquet at Port-au-Prince.

Traits of individual courage were constantly occurring, as during the defence of the town of Les Cayes, when young Colonel Lys distinguished himself. He, as all the bravest and best, has lately fallen a victim to the ferocity of the negro authorities; The Haytian, however, is not a fighting animal. Roused to fury by the excesses of his French masters, the negro of the time of the Revolution fought well, but since then many of his military qualities have departed. He is still a good marcher, is patient and abstemious; but Soulouque's ignominious campaigns in Santo Domingo showed that the Haytian soldier will not fight. There has been little or no real fighting since; overwhelming numbers would sometimes endeavour to capture a post, but no battle took place during the civil war of 1869. The only really daring act performed by numbers was the surprise of Port-au-Prince in December of that year, and the chiefs of the expedition were Brice and Boisrond-Canal, supported by a land force under General Carrié.

The ignorance of the officers often leads them into ludicrous mistakes. A general commanding at Port-au-Prince saw a boat entering the harbour with the Spanish flag flying, and he instantly went down to the wharf. "Who are you?" said he to the officers. "Spaniards," was the reply. "Paniols!" exclaimed he, "then you are enemies!" and proceeded to arrest them, under the mistaken idea that all Spaniards must be Dominicans, with whom Hayti was at war. It required the most vigorous language, and some emphatic gestures with his foot on the part of the French Consul-General, to prevent the Spanish officers being thrust into the common jail. The negro had never heard of Spain, although Cuba is within sight of Haytian shores.

An English admiral came into the harbour of the capital, and President Salnave sent an officer on board to welcome our naval chief. This was a black general, who, when he got on board, was so tipsy that he commenced making formal bows to the mainmast, under the mistaken idea that it was the admiral, who, hearing of his maudlin state, came to receive him on deck, and soon dismissed him. I heard that he afterwards declared he had seen two admirals on board. I knew this man well, and though a tipsy savage, was intrusted with a most important military command.

The army is legally recruited by conscription, the term of service being seven years, though volunteers serve only four; this, however, is purely nominal. During my stay, the invariable practice was for a colonel of a regiment to send out parties of soldiers, who seized in the streets any man whom they thought would suit. As this only occurred in times of danger, or when the President's body-guard had to be completed, these captured volunteers had the greatest difficulty in getting free from the clutches of the recruiting sergeant. I have seen even deputies and senators walked off to the barracks.

As soon as it is known that the recruiting parties are about, men begin to stay at home, and only women come in from the country. This brutal system of enlistment was one of the causes of the fall of President Geffrard. To punish the inhabitants of Cap Haïtien for their unsuccessful insurrection in 1865, the President had recruiting parties sent out into that town, and the respectable young men were captured by dozens, transferred to Port-au-Prince, and forcibly incorporated into the battalions of tirailleurs. It was they who in 1867 gave the signal for those revolutionary movements which finally upset the President. The brutality shown by these recruiting parties is revolting, as the men are armed with clubs, and permitted to use them at discretion.

General Geffrard used to harangue these unhappy volunteers as if they were burning with enthusiasm to join the army, whilst, bleeding, tattered, and torn, they listened sulkily to his words, all the time carefully guarded by their brutal captors. Their chief pretended not to see their state.

This reminds me of an incident which occurred during the late war between Chili and Peru. Some hundreds of Indians had been lassoed in the interior, and brought down to Lima to fill up the regiments. President Prado was urged to address them, and they were collected under one of the windows of the palace. The general approached with his staff, and leaning out of window began—"Noble volunteers," when he perceived that the men were tied together, and that a dozen pairs were secured by a long rope. He drew back hastily and said, "Noble volunteers indeed. I cannot lend myself to such a farce;" and no persuasion would induce him to return to continue his speech. President Prado has been deservedly criticised for his conduct during this war; but had his countrymen listened to his advice, there would have been no war between Chili and Peru.

The pay of the Haytian army is nominally as follows:—

General of division	£140	a year.
General of brigade	105	"
Adjutant-general	75	"
Colonel	40	"
Commandant or major	20	"
Captain	12	"
Lieutenant	10	"
Sub-lieutenant	7	"
Non-commissioned	from £3 to £5	"
Private	£2 10	"

The rations of a foot-soldier on duty are about two shillings a week, whilst that of a cavalry-man are three shillings. As the soldiers not on duty are allowed to work, they receive no rations. The President's guard, consisting of several battalions, was composed principally of the mechanics and respectable labourers of the town and neighbourhood, who often paid the colonels so much per week to be exempt from active service.

The ordinary battalions are recruited among the country people, and these rarely present themselves except on pay-day. Even for this there is little encouragement, as if they do not present themselves at the appointed time, the officers divide the balance of the pay amongst themselves. If any man persistently comes to receive his dues, he is detained to do active duty for a month or two, which effectually checks his zeal and his love of dollars.

When the pay of officers is so trifling, it is to be supposed that the better classes do not enter the army as a profession. The higher grades are generally named for political services, whilst the lower are filled by men raised from the ranks. Except in a few special cases, it is rare for a man to have gone through all the grades of officer.

The generals are a power in the State, and have to be conciliated. The most ignorant blacks, as I have mentioned, are given the most important commands, from their supposed influence among the lower orders, whom they perfectly resemble in everything but uniform. They supplement their inadequate pay by every illegitimate means.

President Geffrard had really a desire to form an army, but the materials at hand were poor. His lower officers were as usual taken from the ranks, and inclined to pilfering. A captain was detected in the act of robbing the custom-house. As he had charge of the guard, the President determined to make an example. I find the incident recounted in my journal written at the time, and as the incidents are very characteristic of the people, I will tell the whole story. The danger of not knowing the connections of those to whom you are speaking may be exemplified by the following:—During the inevitable quarter of an hour before dinner, I was sitting next a charming Haytian lady, educated in England and married to an Englishman, when she began to tell me the news of the day. At the parade that morning the President had ordered the epaulettes of an officer to be torn off his coat on account of a petty theft he had committed at the custom-house. After he had given the order, the President turned away his head, but presently remarked, "Is he dead yet?" "Dead! your Excellency," exclaimed an aide-de-camp. "Yes, dead. I thought that an officer of my army so publicly disgraced would instantly have put an end to his existence." The lady's anecdote produced a hearty laugh, first at the acting of the President, and then at the idea of any Haytian officer having a notion of such delicate honour. I remarked to my companion that the President would have done better, instead of only punishing the petty thieves, to lay a heavy hand on the great robbers, as for instance Mr. — —. The lady quietly turned to me and said, "I am sure you do not know that Mr. — — is my brother." The start I gave convinced her that I did not; but I felt uncomfortable until, during dinner, with a nod and a smile, she asked me to take wine with her. Mr. — — had been engaged with some others in a *détournement*, as it was delicately called, of about seventy thousand dollars, but when I knew him afterwards, he was Secretary of State for Foreign Affairs, and a more unworthy man it would have been difficult even for Hayti to produce.

President Salnave had a favourite regiment that he kept up to its full strength, and the men were fairly well disciplined. They were the only men in his pay who really looked like soldiers, but they were most insolent and overbearing. In order to strike terror into the town, Salnave ordered their colonel to march them down to the "Rue des Fronts Forts," where the retail shopkeepers live, and there gave them leave to plunder. His little speech on this occasion has become a proverb in Hayti—"Mes enfans, pillez en bon ordre." Whenever there were any political executions, the shooting squad was chosen from among them, and they have the discredit of having been employed to murder all the political prisoners confined in the jail at Port-au-Prince in December 1869.

The only battalions which, in time of peace, are kept up to their full strength, are those which are sent from their own districts to garrison distant towns, where those not actually on duty are allowed to look for work.

The Police

Of all the institutions in Hayti, the police is certainly the worst conducted. There are regular commissaries employed under the prefects, but ordinary soldiers do the work of constables. In my time they went about the streets with a thick stick of heavy wood in their hands called a *cocomacaque*, and they used it in such a way as to confirm the remark that cruelty is an innate quality with the negro. Never did I see a Haytian of the upper classes step forward to remonstrate—probably he knew his countrymen too well—whilst the lower orders simply laughed and enjoyed the sight of punishment.

Every one arrested accused of a crime is immediately treated as if he were guilty, and the *cocomacaque* is brought to play on his head and shoulders. As an observer remarked, "In Hayti no prisoner has any right to be considered innocent." A woman was arrested near my house accused of having killed the child of a neighbour from motives of jealousy. They said she was a *loup garou*, and as soon as the soldiers seized her they began to beat her. Before she reached the prison she was covered with wounds, and a relative who endeavoured to interfere shared the same fate.

One day, whilst at the American Consulate, I heard a disturbance outside. I took no notice at first, but presently looking out, saw the police raising a prostrate man. He had been insolent to his overseer, and a passing general ordered him to be taken to prison by the soldiers who were following him. They fell upon the man, and in a few moments he was a mass of bruises, and died before he reached his destination. A few weeks after, I saw a body of a negro lying near the same spot; this was that of a thief, on whom the police had executed summary justice with their clubs.

An English merchant saw two soldiers arrest a man accused of murder. As he resisted, they tied his feet together and dragged him along the streets, his head bumping against the stones. The Englishman remonstrated, but he was threatened with the same treatment. A negro arrested for stealing fowls had his arms bound behind him and a rope attached to one ankle, which was held by a policeman, while another kept close to the prisoner, beating him with his club, and as he darted forward to avoid a blow, the other would pull the rope, and the unfortunate accused would fall flat on his face. And all this done in public before the authorities, both civil and military, and no man raising his voice to stop such barbarous work! I have myself seen so many of these brutal scenes that I feel convinced that no account can be exaggerated.

As detectives these soldier-police are quite useless, and crime, unless openly committed, is rarely detected. Robbers have continued in their profession for years though perfectly well known, and no attempt has been made to capture them. There was one who was notorious for the impunity with which he had committed a long series of crimes. When he entered a house he intended to rob, he stripped, rubbed his body with oil, and crawled in, knife in hand. Unluckily for him, one night, being disturbed in his operations, he stabbed his assailant, who proved to be a Senator. It was all very well to rob and stab common people, but a Senator could not be thus treated with impunity; and the man, fearing no pursuit, was quietly captured in bed. The commissary of police, thinking that the fellow had had rope enough given him, and being sure that he would again escape from prison if sent there, had him taken out of town, and he was promptly shot, under pretence of having attempted to escape—*la ley de fuga*, as the Spaniards call it.

General Vil Lubin was, during the time of the Emperor Soulouque, in command of the arrondissement of Port-au-Prince; he proved efficient in his post, but he was a hard man, and one day ordered two soldiers to be beaten. Their comrades carried out the order so effectually that in a short time two bruised corpses were lying at the barrack door. Soulouque heard of it, and, furious at the treatment of two of his own guard, bitterly reproached Vil Lubin, and for months could not meet him without using the expression, "Rendez-moi mes soldats." Yet how many hundreds met their death by his order! In both the civil and military administration brutality is the rule, not the exception.

There has been much talk of establishing a rural police, but nothing effective has come of it.

The Government rely for the detection of conspiracies more upon informers than on the police, and as they are to be found in all ranks, friendship is often used for the purpose of obtaining information. President Geffrard sometimes referred to conversations to which members of the diplomatic corps had been parties, and perhaps too often, as, on comparing notes, they were enabled to fix on their communicative friends, and were thus free to let the President hear their real opinion about his measures, only so far, however, as it suited their purpose. Under Soulouque the system was carried to a greater extent, and his suspicious mind made him treat as truth every assertion of a spy. One day an old beggar-woman, passing before the palace, asked alms of some officers who were conversing together; on being refused, she ran under the Emperor's window and began to shout, "Emperor, they are conspiring against you!" and made so great a disturbance that the guard turned out. The officers were too happy to get rid of the old woman by giving her money; she went off laughing, with her hands full of notes.

Under Salnave and Domingue the spy system was much employed, and it appears likely that, under the present Government, it is rampant, if we may judge by the series of military executions which have marked this Presidency.

The jails, as might be expected in such a country, are filthy places. I have often visited that of Port-au-Prince; it is a cluster of low buildings, surrounded by a wall perhaps ten feet in height, so insecure that no European could be kept there a night except by his own good-will. The ordinary negro prisoner, however, has no enterprise, and, rather liking the lazy life, lies down to sleep out his sentence.

Prisoners condemned to death, and too often political suspects, are confined in cells, and are manacled to a bar running across the room. I looked into one, and saw five men fixed to the same bar. As I knew that there were only four condemned to death, I asked what was the crime of the fifth. "Oh, he is a military defaulter, and we did not know where else to put him."

In President Geffrard's time a little attention was paid to the cleanliness of the jails, but during Soulouque's reign and after Geffrard's time everything was neglected. A friend once visited the prison, to find nine negroes manacled to the same bar, lying naked on the floor on account of the stifling heat, and the jailer admitted that he had not freed them from the bar for above a week, nor had he thought of having the cell cleaned out. The horrible odour issuing from the place when the door was opened fully confirmed the latter assertion.

I knew a general, still living, who had been confined from political motives in one of these cells, I believe for seven years, and his manacles were only occasionally secretly removed by the jailer. Murderers serving out their sentences, thieves, unimportant political prisoners, imprisoned sailors, are all indiscriminately confined in regal rooms opening on a court, and receive their food from friends or relatives. Unhappy would be the wretch who had no one to care for him, as the pitiful allowance for the prisoners, irregularly paid, rarely if ever reaches them.

Female prisoners are confined in the same building, but their rooms open on a separate court. The wife of a revolutionary general was imprisoned there in 1869. She was for a long time kept in irons, but at length heed was given to our remonstrances, and her irons were removed. She was a handsome negress, and took the jailer's fancy, who tried to violate her, but the powerful woman thrust him from her cell. He threatened vengeance; but a few nights after she escaped from prison, and fled to our Legation, where she remained over three months, and it required the vigorous remonstrances of Lord Clarendon to enable us to embark her for Jamaica. On the day that we did so, as we approached the wharf, we noticed a crowd of negroes assembling with the object of insulting their countrywoman, but on my giving my arm to the black lady, an old negro remarked in their jargon, "Consite specté negresse-çi-là" ("The Consul shows respect to that negress"), and allowed us to pass without a word. This lady was from Cap Haïtien, and I may add that she was the only refugee out of many hundreds that I can remember who ever showed any gratitude for the services rendered them.

All the members of the diplomatic corps, since the first acknowledgment of the independence of Hayti, have at various times attempted to persuade successive Governments to look to their prisons, but never with much result. The prisons are indeed thoroughly bad, as might be expected among such a people. The worst on the island, however, is probably at Puerto Plata, in the Dominican republic.

Murder is sometimes punished with death, but that punishment is generally reserved for political opponents. I remember an instance which is worth relating, as it displays the Haytian character in the form it assumes when excited by political passion. In the autumn of 1868, five merchants of the southern province were captured and brought to Port-au-Prince. As they were connected with members of the revolutionary party then in arms, the mob clamoured for their lives, and they were ordered by President Salnave, to be shot. As we knew that these men were perfectly innocent, the French, Spanish, and English representatives made an effort to save them, and called on the Foreign Minister to ask him to accompany us to the palace to see the President. We were told that he was ill in bed, and could not accompany us. We insisted upon seeing him, and found this functionary covered up and trembling, not with ague, but fear. We begged him to get up, but he obstinately refused, declaring he was too unwell. We could not waste further time, as the execution was to take place within an hour. So we left, but I could not refrain from saying to this bedridden gentleman, "In such times as these, sir, a Minister has no right to be ill." He never forgave me.

We went to the palace, but were refused admittance, and only got back to the French Legation in time to see the five prisoners pass to execution. Presently one returned whom the President had pardoned.

When the procession arrived at the place of execution, there was a mob collected of several thousand spectators, principally ferocious negresses. A shout arose, "We were promised five! where is the fifth?" and the crowd closed in on the procession, with knives drawn and pistols ready. The cowardly officers replied, "The fifth is coming," and sent word to President Salnave. He, unwilling to disappoint his most faithful followers, looked over the list of those in prison, and finding that there was a parricide, whom he had pardoned but the day before, ordered him to execution. In the meantime, the four others had been kept waiting, exposed to the insults of the people—particularly one prisoner, whose long white beard and hair and white skin made him particularly obnoxious.

The arrival of the fifth prisoner pacified the crowd. The five were clumsily shot, and then the spectators rushed in with their knives and mangled the bodies under every circumstance of obscenity. Such are the negresses when excited by political leaders, and such are evidently the most devoted followers of President Salomon, if we can place any faith in the accounts of the fearful atrocities perpetrated by them during the massacres of September 1883.

The chief of this ferocious band was a young negress who went by the name of Roi Petit Chout, to whom President Salnave gave a commission as general. She used to come in front of the Legation with some of her companions, knife in one hand and pistol in the other, and utter ferocious threats, on account of our having received some political refugees. These women were used as a high police to keep down disaffection, and horrible stories are told of the murders and cruelties practised by these wretches. When the revolution triumphed, Roi Petit Chout was arrested, but though murder could readily have been proved against her, she was soon restored to liberty.

As all the police department is most inefficiently paid, its members are generally open to bribes, and are accused of levying black-mail on the poorer inhabitants. During the time of Salnave they were unbridled in their savage acts, and every man they met in the streets, foreign or native, was liable to be seized and sent to the forts as a recruit. As regular police commissaries accompanied these groups, these arrests were made in a spirit of wanton mischief; at other times it was to obtain a pecuniary recompense for their good-nature in letting a foreigner go.

To show how ordinary police affairs are managed in Hayti, I must give an account of an incident which occurred to the Spanish *chargé d'affaires* and myself. A dishonest servant forced open the window of our wine-cellar and stole eighteen dozen of claret, and then fled. We gave notice to the police, who were very energetic in taking up the case, and every now and then brought us information of their proceedings. At last they recovered some of the wine, and in triumph brought us two dozen and seven bottles. A few days passed, and a Haytian friend happening to breakfast with us, took up a claret bottle and saw the mark, "Château Giscours, De Luze, Bordeaux." He laughed and said, "Now I understand a remark made by the Minister of the Interior, when he said what capital wine the English Minister imported." On further inquiry, we found that the police had recovered fourteen dozen of our wine (the other four had been bought *knowingly* by our most intimate friend), and that they had divided eleven dozen and five bottles among various high officials. The only observation my colleague made was, "Quel pays!" but I felt inclined to agree with the people when they say of the officials, "Quel tas de voleurs!" The robber was afterwards arrested for another offence, and I could not but pity him, when I saw him tied, bleeding and stumbling under the blows of a policeman's club.

During the siege of Port-au-Prince in the civil war (1868) my French and Spanish colleagues and I were walking through the town, when we were startled by the sound of firing in the next street. On arriving at the spot, we found that the police had arrested a young Frenchman. As he objected that he was a foreigner and not liable to conscription, a crowd soon assembled, and a follower of Roi Petit Chout's band, a ferocious negro, raised his carbine and shot the lad through the body, and my French colleague had barely time to catch his last words before he expired.

Nothing that the French representative could say had any effect on the Haytian Government; the murderer was promoted to be a sergeant, and sent to the army to get him out of the way; but he soon came back to Port-au-Prince, to be more insolent than ever. We had, however, the satisfaction of knowing that, when the revolution triumphed, this man was condemned to death for his other crimes and shot, my French colleague taking care to be present at the final ceremony, to see that the sentence was not evaded. For killing a white he would never have been executed.

It must not be supposed, because I generally refer to my own experiences, that things mended afterwards. Probably during the presidencies of Generals Nissage-Saget and Boisrond-Canal the police, though as dishonest, were less insufferable; but under Domingue and Salomon they were worse than ever, as they always are under the government of the black section of the community.

Under the present regime neither the white nor the coloured man has any rights which the black is bound to respect.

CHAPTER IX
LANGUAGE AND LITERATURE

There are two languages spoken in Hayti, French and Creole. French is the language of public life and of literature, whilst Creole is the language of home and of the people. President Geffrard, among other eccentricities, used to extol the Creole as the softest and most expressive of languages, and his countrymen are unanimously of his opinion; but no Frenchman can accept as a language this uncouth jargon of corrupt French in an African form.

No doubt, African languages, like those of other savages, are very simple in their construction, and the negroes imported into Hayti learned French words and affixed them to the forms of their own dialects. Mr. J. J. Thomas of Trinidad has published a very painstaking grammar of the Creole language as spoken in that island. I gather from it that this patois is much the same as that spoken in Hayti; but in our colony it holds the position of the Saxon in the Norman period, and interpreters are required in our law-courts to explain the language of the people. It shows also that in the French colonies of Martinique and Guadaloupe, as in our French-speaking colonies, wherever the negroes attempt to speak French, they do so in the same way that the Creole is spoken in Hayti. I may add that the patois of the inhabitants of the interior is so corrupt and African, that those who can converse freely with the negroes of the coast are often puzzled when they visit the mountains, and require an interpreter.

As this Creole language is spoken by about a million and a half of people in the different islands of the West Indies, it merits the attention which Mr. Thomas has bestowed upon it; and I would refer those curious on the subject to this elaborate work, in which everything possible is done to raise the status of a patois which remains still, in my opinion, but an uncouth jargon.

There is naturally no Creole literature, but there are many songs and proverbs, some of which may serve to show the kind of language spoken by the Haytians.

The only songs which I can quote are written by persons familiar with the French language, and therefore do not sufficiently represent the pure Creole. The proverbs, however, are genuine, and are therefore the reflex of popular ideas.

Moreau de St. Méry, who lived in Hayti during the latter part of last century, quotes a song written about the year 1750, which, though often reprinted, I will insert here, with a translation made by a Creole some years later. St. Méry has all Geffrard's admiration for the Creole language, and thinks that the inarticulate sounds, which cannot be rendered on paper, are the most admirable part of the language of the Haytians, and perhaps it may be so:—

Creole.	French.
Lisette quitté la plaine,	Lisette tu fuis la plaine,
Mon perdi bonheur à moué,	Mon bonheur s'est envolé,
Gié à moin semblé fontaine,	Mes pleurs en doubles fontaines
Dipi mon pas miré toué.	Sur tous tes pas out coulé.
La jour quand mon coupé canne,	Le jour moissonnant la canne
Mon songé zamour à moué,	Je rêve à tes doux appas,
La nuit quand mon dans cabane	Un songe dans ma cabane
Dans dromi mon quimbé toué.	La nuit te met dans mes bras.
Si to allé à la ville	Tu trouveras à la ville
Ta trouvé geine candio,	Plus d'un jeune freluquet,
Qui gagné pour trompé fille	Leur bouche avec art distille
Bouche doux passé sirop.	Un miel doux mais plein d'apprêt.
To va crér yo bin sincère,	Tu croiras leur cœur sincère,
Pendant quior yo coquin ho,	Leur cœur ne veut que tromper:
C'est serpent qui contrefaire	Le serpent sait contrefaire
Crié rat, pour tromper yo.	Le rat qu'il veut dévorer.
Dipi mon perdi Lisette,	Mes pas loin de ma Lisette
Mon pas souchié Calenda,	S'éloignent du Calenda,
Mon quitté bram bram sonnette,	Et ma ceinture à sonnette
Mon pas batte bamboula.	Languit sur mon bamboula.
Quand mon contré lant' négresse	Mon œil de toute autre belle
Mon pas gagné gié pour li,	N'aperçoit plus le souris,
Mon pas souchié travail pièce	Le travail en vain m'appelle
Tout qui chose à moin mourri.	Mes sens sont anéantis.

Mon maigre tant com 'guon souche,	Je péris comme la souche,
Jambe à moin tant comme roseau,	Ma jambe n'est qu'un roseau,
Mangé na pas doux dans bouche,	Nul mets ne plaît à ma bouche,
Tafia même c'est comme dyo.	La liqueur se change en eau.
Quand mon songé toué Lisette,	Quand je songe à toi, Lisette,
Dyo toujours dans gié moin,	Mes yeux s'inondent de pleurs,
Magner moin vini trop bête	Ma raison, lente et distraite,
A force chagrin magné moin.	Cède en tout à mes douleurs.
Liset' mon tardé nouvelle,	Mais est-il bien vrai, ma belle,
To compté bintôt tourné,	Dans pen tu dois revenir:
Vini donc toujours fidèle,	Ah! reviens toujours fidèle,
Miré bon, passé tandé.	Croire est moins doux que sentir.
N'a pas tardé davantage,	Ne tarde pas d'avantage,
To fair moin assez chagrin,	C'est pour moi trop de chagrin,
Mon tant com 'zozo dans cage,	Viens retirer de sa cage
Quand yo fair li mouri faim.	L'oiseau consumé de faim.

    It will readily be remarked that every word is a corruption of a French one, and as no standard of spelling can exist in what may be called an unwritten language, every writer has a distinct system of representing Creole sounds. The seductive beauty of this language can only be for the initiated, as the beauty of the native women is rarely remarked except by those who have made a long voyage, and have almost forgotten what beauty is. The versified translation of the song does not give an exact idea of the construction of the Creole sentence, I may therefore insert one verse with an interlined literal translation:—

    Lisette, quitté la plaine,
    Lisette, quitta la plaine,
    Mon perdi bonheur à moué,
    Je perdis mon bonheur,
    Gié à moin semblé fontaine
    Mes yeux semblaient une fontaine
    Dipi mon pas miré toué.
    Depuis je ne te vois pas.
    La Jour quand mon coupé canne
    Le jour quand je coupe la canne

Mon songé zamour à moué;
Je pense à mes amours;
La nuit quand mon dans cabane
La nuit quand je suis dans ma cabane
Dans dromi mon quimbé toué.
Dans un songe je te tiens.

It is very difficult to find any very definite rules of grammar in this song—

Lisette quitté (Lisette has left or left),	Past.
Mon coupé canne (I cut the cane),	Present.
Si to allé (if thou shouldst go),	Subjunctive.
Ta trouvé (thou wilt find),	Future.
Qui gagné (who possess),	Present.

Absolutely the same form is preserved in all tenses and moods, and in conversation various expedients are adopted to render the meaning clear.

A. M. L'Hérison, a Haytian, has written a song, which is quoted in Mr. Thomas's grammar, and as it represents the *cultivated* Creole of the present day, it is worth while inserting it:—

Badinez bien avec Macaque

Grand 'maman moïn dit: nans Guinée
Grand mouché rassemblé youn jour
Toute pêpe li contré nan tournée
Et pis li parlé sans détour:
Quand zôt allez foncer nan raque
Connain coûment grand moune agi
Badinez bien avec Macaque,
Mais na pas magnié queue à li
Grand 'maman moïn, dit moïn bon qui chose
Lô li prend bon coup malavoume.
Li dit moin you ça, "Mourose,"
Nan tout 'grand zaffaires faut dit "Houme"
Mais peut-on flanqué moin youn claque
On pilôt terminer ainsi;

Badinez bien avec Macaque
Mais na pas magnié queue à li.

To get the true ring of popular Creole it is necessary to examine their proverbs. M. J. J. Audain, a well-known Haytian, whose first literary efforts brought him into trouble, has published a collection which is very complete. [19] As Hayti becomes older as a nation and loses its French element, we may have a distinct Creole literature. There are many proverbs in M. Audain's collection that would be quite incomprehensible to an untravelled Frenchman: —

16. Soufflé fatras pou ou bonais d'lo.

17. Bonais d'lo, ranne couie.

124. Quand digdale vernis piquée, cale basse vide douée pringa corps li.

The following are easy enough to understand: —

174. Bouré empile pas allé avec piti figu.
(Too much hair does not suit a little face.)

60. Gé ouait, bouche pé.
(The eyes see, the mouth speaks.)

73. Chique pas jaimain respecté pié grand mouché.
(Jiggers never respect the feet of the gentry.)

Some are so simple that they do not require translation, as—

Moune qui rond pas capable vini carré zafaire mouton, pas zafaire cabrite.

Calle pouésson, pas l'agent.

Toute bois cé bois, main mapon pas cajou.

Cé soulier qui connain si chanssons gangnain trou.

Quand ravette fait dause li pas janmain invité poule.

Pas janmain couri deux chimins à la fois.

Toute pouésson mangé moune, cé requin seul qui pôté blâme.

La fimée pas janmain lévée sans difé.

M. Audain's collection contains one thousand and eleven proverbs; they are constantly quoted by the people, who interlard their conversations with them as much as ever Sancho Panza did. When speaking of a very talkative person, they say, "Bouche li pas gagné dimanche" (his mouth has no Sunday or day of rest).

It is scarcely necessary to multiply specimens of Creole proverbs or translations. The former certainly convey a better idea of the language spoken by the negroes than the latter, though, as written, it is much more easily understood than when it is spoken. The negroes appear often to clip their sentences, and leave it to the intelligence of the hearer to divine their meaning.

Official documents are always written in French, more or less correct; it is therefore unnecessary to refer particularly to them; but I may remark that they have a set stock of phrases which are constantly repeated. I will, however, quote a short official letter which amused us.

A Haytian had committed, or was supposed to have committed, a crime, and instead of being arrested and tried, he was ordered to be banished. The letter addressed to him was as follows:—

Liberté, Égalité, Fraternité.
République d'Haïti.

No. 392.

Quartier-Général de Port-au-Prince,
Le 30 Avril 1867,
An 64e de l'Independance.

Le Général de Division, Chef d'éxécution de la volonté du peuple souvrain, et de ses résolutions, et Vice-Président du Governement Provisoire,

Au Citoyen Jules C— —.

Monsieur,—Dès la présente reçue, vous aurez à chercher une occasion pour les plages étrangères, afin que vous partiez du pays qui a reconnu en vous l'homme qui cherche à pervertir la société haïtienne.—Je vous salue.

(Signed) V. Chevalier, G.

This Monsieur Chevalier had been educated in France, and was shrewdly suspected of having had a hand in drawing up the *Acte de déchéance* launched by the revolutionary committee of St. Marc in 1867 against President Geffrard. Amongst the different articles are the following:—

"Attendu que le Général F. Geffrard assassine et empoisonne les citoyens les plus éminents d'Haïti: attendu qu'il entretient à l'étranger un très grand nombre d'espions et d'empoisonneurs *à un prix exorbitant*: attendu que toutes les écoles de filles de la république, notamment celles de Port-au-Prince, ont pour maîtresses des femmes d'une vie dissolue, afin de faire de ces établissements des maisons de séduction à son profit," &c., &c.

A Frenchman inquired, "Etait-il indispensable pour incriminer Geffrard sur ce dernier chapître de faire tort à toutes les demoiselles du pays?"

Among the most remarkable works published in Port-au-Prince may be noticed the History of Hayti by Thomas Madiou (clear mulatto). As it was written in the republic by a Haytian for Haytians, it may be judged from that point of view. I have read it with great care and with considerable interest, and some of the descriptions have been much admired, as the detailed account of the attacks of the French on the Crête-à-Pierrot. As an historical production it is a work of considerable value and merit, for although full of prejudiced statements, and with a strong leaning against foreigners, there is, as far as local politics are concerned, an apparent desire to be impartial. This, however, is not the general opinion. St. Rémy, in his Life of Toussaint L'Ouverture, speaking of Madiou's history, says, "Du reste qu'il soit dit en passant que tout le livre de Monsieur Madiou n'est qu'un tissu de faits érronés et de fausses appréciations." The French condemn it as a false account of the war of independence, and resent the implied defence of Dessalines' massacres. His partiality may be proved by his asserting that the French Governor Blanchelande was the instigator of the black insurrection. Madiou wrote his history whilst in Hayti, and after searching for materials among the old survivors of the war, whose prejudices were still warm. No doubt he was influenced by them, but the industry shown is undoubted. The friends and admirers of Toussaint had, however, a right to complain of the evident wish to depreciate the qualities of almost the only black Haytian who rose above mediocrity.

Occasionally M. Madiou's style is very extravagant, as in the description of a battle (see below[20]) which took place between the coloured men of Jacmel and their black antagonists. Never was there such desperate fighting since the days when—

> "For Witherington needs must I wayle,
> As one in doleful dumps,
> For when his legs were smitten off,
> He fought upon his stumps."

M. Madiou is a mulatto, who has played a prominent part in the history of his country, and his leanings are evidently in favour of his own colour, and, as I have observed, he is severe on Toussaint L'Ouverture for his endeavours to crush the attempts at independent command made by Rigaud.

Another work of inestimable value for the students of Haytian history is the one written by M. Beaubrun-Ardouin (fair mulatto). It is entitled "Études sur l'Histoire d'Haïti." M. Ardouin attempted to collect in this work all the documents that could illustrate the history of his country, and, at the time of his death, ten volumes had already been published. He was for many years Haytian Minister in Paris, which gave him full opportunities for examining the French archives. I only knew him slightly; he was evidently a man of talent and industry, but as he was justly credited with a prejudice against the whites, he was generally avoided by them.

A Monsieur St. Rémy of Les Cayes wrote a Life of Toussaint, which is but a poor production, and is full of prejudice and virulence against both black and white.

A Frenchman, M. Edgar la Selve, has published a work called "L'Histoire de la Littérature Haïtienne." It is a volume of some interest, containing as it does a collection of poetry written by natives, but it is considered to be inferior in point of style and extravagant in its appreciations. When you find M. La Selve ranking the crude productions of a rude school with the writings of the most distinguished among ancient and modern authors, one may readily feel that this work is an offering to the vanity of acquaintances.

It is to be regretted that a person like M. La Selve should have undertaken this task, as, instead of real criticism, which might have proved of value, he puffs up the vanity and presumption of Haytian writers by such observations as the following:—"Rapelle l'invotion de Pindare"—"La grande éloquence et la magnificence des images"—"Sa plume magique"—"La délicatesse de Charles Dovalle combinée avec la grâce de Lamartine"—"Le nom modestement glorieux"—"Esprit vraiment prodigieux et universel"—"Trois génies supérieurs"—"Cet autre Augustin Thierry"—"Comparer aux dialogues de Platon."

What more could be said of the best classics? No wonder this work was unable to command any attention.

In the collection of poetry, it will be noticed that although there are some very pretty verses, there are none of any remarkable merit. It is not a special literature; there is seldom much local colouring: it is rather a reflection of French productions where Lamartine holds the place of honour.

It has been remarked by a French critic that the further we recede from the time of the Declaration of Independence the worse the poetry. The expressions become less exact, the phraseology common, the style incorrect, with less cadence in the verses. The versification is seldom accurate throughout any of these poems. It is but another proof of what I have elsewhere stated, that Hayti is in a state of decay.

I may mention a few pieces that have struck a French friend as being among the best. I prefer his judgment to my own, as I am one of those who believe that no one can appreciate fully the poetry of another nation; but as, in this case, my own opinion agrees with that of my friend, I can take the responsibility of the judgment.

Coriolan Ardouin (mulatto) has written a very charming piece called "Alaïda," beginning thus:—

> "Sur la natte de jonc qu'aucun souci ne ronge,
> Ses petits bras croisés sur un cœur de cinq ans,
> Alaïda someille, heureuse, et pas un songe
> Qui tourmente ses jeunes sens."

There is no local colour in this sonnet beyond, perhaps, the *natte de jonc*. Only in the tropics are children to be seen sleeping on mats.

Dupré has written a patriotic hymn which might pass muster among many others of the same kind. It closes with the following ferocious sentiment:—

> "Si, quelque jour, sur tes rives
> Osent venir nos tyrans,
> Que leurs hordes fugitives
> Servent d'engrais à nos champs."

Pierre Faubert (mulatto) has written several pieces which might be quoted:—

La Negresse

> Le suis fier de te dire, O négresse, je t'aime,
> Et la noir couleur me plaît, sais-tu pourquoi?
> C'est que nobles vertus, chaste cœur, beauté même
> Sont ce qui charme enfin, le ciel a mis en toi.

These lines might have been addressed to the pretty negress of Pétionville of whom I have elsewhere spoken.

Another, "Aux Haïtiens," is an appeal to union among blacks and coloured.

There is a pretty song by Milscent (mulatto), in the style of Béranger, commencing:—

> "J'entends en mainte occasion
> Prêcher contre l'ambition;
> Mon âme en est ravie—(bis.)
> Mais ceux qui nous parlent si bien
> Regorgent d'honneurs et de biens
> Cela me contrarie"—(bis.)

Ignace Nau (mulatto) contributes a very attractive piece called "Le 'Ttchit' et l'Orage:"—

> "Voici, voici l'orage,
> Là bas dans le nuage;
> Voici le vent, le vent
> Tourbillonnant au champ,
> Et disant au feuillage
> Repliez votre ombrage.
> Au lac, à ses bambous,
> 'Roulez, agitez vous.'
> Au parfum ses délices
> 'Refermez vos calices;'
> Au palmier haut dans l'air,
> 'Gardez-vous de l'éclair.'
> Pauvre tchit égaré, chétif oiseau des champs!
> Le mont a disparu sous les rideaux de pluie.
> Hâte-toi, cher oiseau; viens t'abriter du temps,
> Déjà l'eau du lac est ternie."

And many more verses equally good.

Perhaps the most poetic piece in the collection is that written by a Haïtienne, Virginie Sampeur, "L'Abandonnée," which I will quote entire:—

> "Ah! si vous étiez mort, de mon âme meurtrie,
> ferais une tombe, où, retraite chérie,

Mes larmes couleraient lentement, sans remords:
Que votre image en moi resterait radieuse.
Ah! si vous étiez mort.[21]

Je ferai de mon cœur l'urne mélancolique
Conservant du passé la suave rélique,
Comme ces coffres d'or qui gardent les parfumes;
Je ferais de mon âme une riche chapelle
Où toujours brillerait la dernière étincelle
De mes espoirs défunts.

Ah! si vous étiez mort, votre éternel silence
Moins âpre qu'en ce jour aurait son éloquence,
Car ce ne serait plus le cruel abandon.
Je dirais, il est mort, mais il sait bien m'entendre;
Et peut-être en mourant n'a-t-il peut se defendre
De murmurer:—Pardon.

Mais vous n'êtes pas mort! Oh! douleur sans mesure,
Regret qui fait jaillir le sang de ma blessure:
Je ne puis m'empêcher, moi, de me souvenir,
Même quand vous restez devant mes larmes vraies
Sec et froid, sans donner à mes profondes plaies
L'aumône d'un soupir.

Ingrat! vous vivez donc, quand tout me dit vengeance!
Mais je n'écoute pas! à defaut d'espérance
Une fantôme d'idole est mon unique port,
Illusion, folie, ou vain rêve de femme,
Je vous aimerais tant, si vous n'étiez qu'un âme.
Ah! que n'êtes vous mort."

There is something superior in the tone and sentiment of this piece, the only one of the author that M. La Selve publishes. I may notice that Virginie Sampeur is a lady of colour. As she is still living, I will only add that her poem tells her own story. As a rule, these Haytian poets express fairly well all tender sentiments, but they are wanting in a careful literary education, and they have not a very exact appreciation of the genius of the French language.

In miscellaneous literature there are many publications of merit. Emile Nau wrote an interesting book called "Histoire de Casiques," although a critic might fail to discover in it "une mine immense d'érudition." It is seldom that a Haytian writer dedicates himself to anything useful, so that the efforts of Eugène Nau to bring superior agriculture into vogue have a double merit. He is best known for his two productions, "L'influence de l'Agriculture sur la Civilisation des Peuples" and his "Flore Indienne." I knew Eugène Nau very well. He was married to a very charming woman, a sister of Auguste Elie, and no one who has passed a few days at their estate in the plains of Cul-de-Sac will ever forget the pleasant gaiety that reigned in that house. Civil war has, however, devastated that portion of the country, and I fear that even the inexhaustible spirits of Eugène Nau will scarcely be able to bear him through such accumulated misfortunes. The small diplomatic corps were ever welcome guests at Digneron, and I recall with pleasure the evenings spent there with my French and Spanish colleagues. He had a fund of intelligence and good sense; and his steady advocacy of a metallic currency did honour to his perspicacity.

As might have been anticipated, the black portion of the population has shown no literary aptitudes. Occasionally an Edmond Paul has written a political essay which has fallen flat, or a Salomon has indited a vigorous defence of his policy; but, as a rule, the coloured portion of the population has produced the historians and poets of Hayti.

CHAPTER X
AGRICULTURE, COMMERCE, AND FINANCE

Agriculture

M. Eugène Nau, in his pamphlet on the influence of agriculture on civilisation, endeavoured to bring his countrymen to look with favour on the principal source of prosperity in all tropical countries; but the seed he sowed fell on revolutionary soil, and agriculture is more neglected than ever.

And yet in all the wide world there is not a country more suited to agriculture than Hayti; not one where the returns for labour are more magnificent; a rich, well-watered soil, with a sun which actually appears to draw vegetation towards itself with such energetic force that the growth of plants, though not actually visible to the eye, may be almost daily measured.

The system of cultivation varies greatly. In the north an effort was made by King Christophe to keep up large estates, whilst in the west and south President Pétion encouraged the division of the land among peasant proprietors. Large estates still remain, however, in these provinces, which are cultivated under different arrangements, to which I will hereafter refer. The general rule is that large estates obtain mostly in the plains, whilst in the mountains the land is practically in the hands of the peasantry, though many large estates exist nominally.

In 1877 a law was passed for regulating the management of the State domains, for selling them or leasing them for nine years. A longer lease would require a special authorisation of the Legislature. This last clause is principally aimed at foreigners, whom the Haytians desire to keep away from all interest in land.

The national estates lie in different parts of the country, and the extent of them in the aggregate is but imperfectly known, owing to careless administration. According to an official return published in 1877, there were under lease 2105 farms of national land, containing about 230,000 acres, let on an average at the rate of two shillings per acre.

The laws on the tenure of real estate are, with some modifications, the same as the agrarian laws that were framed by the French during their possession of the country, and are remarkable for that minute accuracy and definition of right which characterise French laws in general.

For the better elucidation of the subject a few retrospective notices are necessary.

Going back to 1804, the year of independence, one of the first acts of Dessalines was to create a national domain out of the following elements:—

All the real estate which constituted the State domains during the French period.

All the real estates of the whites which had not been legally transferred.

All land without owners.

Confiscated lands.

In furtherance of his project to get the best part of the land into the hands of Government, Dessalines is accused of resorting to every kind of arbitrary and cruel act, and did not even disdain to encourage forgery in order to dispossess those proprietors who stood firm to their rights. This attack on private property was one of the main causes of the successful plot against his life.

Of the national estate thus formed a great part was subsequently parcelled out by Pétion in donations to those who had deserved well in the war of independence, whilst other lots were sold in fee-simple.

Of the class of large proprietors created under the republic of Pétion, but few undertook the cultivation of their own lands. The usage at once came into favour of letting them out in small lots to working men on the Metayer system, the landlord to receive half the produce, on the condition of furnishing, on sugar-cane estates, the mill and the other necessary appliances. With regard to produce, there are two classes recognised and kept distinct by law, namely, "la grande culture" (large farming) and "la petite culture" (small farming). The first consists in the cultivation of sugar-cane and similar articles; the second in the cultivation of provisions for the market. As in the "grande culture" half went to the proprietor, the tendency has been for some years to encroach with the "petite culture" on the lands reserved for the former. Each peasant is allowed a patch of ground near his portion of the cane-field on which to grow vegetables, and it has been found that his attention is more directed to this than formerly. As long as the sugar-cane is reserved for the manufacture of cheap rum to keep the population in a continued state of intoxication, the falling off in its culture is not to be regretted. In fact, the "great" and "little" culture did very well when anything exportable was cultivated, but now are of little practical importance, as they do not so much affect the great stay of the country, the coffee crop.[22]

I may repeat that the first thing in point of importance in Haytian agriculture is the coffee-tree, which grows almost wild in every mountainous part of the country and around the cottages of the peasantry at elevations of from 500 to 7000 feet above the level of the sea—wild in the sense that the plants appear to spring from the seeds that have fallen from the parent trees, though occasionally I have seen them carefully planted round the cottages.

There is a notion in Hayti that the coffee crop will come to an end by the old trees dying out. I was told this twenty years ago, and the story is still repeated; but any one who observantly travels in the interior would find the old trees surrounded by younger ones that spring from the teeming soil from seeds scattered by the wind or rain. The idea, also prevalent among many foreigners in Hayti, that the coffee collected now is taken from the original trees planted by the French, is untenable. As soon as the civil war caused by King Christophe's assumption of power ceased (1820), a marked progress took place in the production of coffee. There is another fact which is also forgotten; coffee-plants in wet tropical countries generally bear from twenty to twenty-five years; therefore their age may be taken at about thirty years. If this statement be correct, the trees must have been renewed three times since the old colonial days. Most of the coffee plantations I saw in Hayti contained shrubs that have seldom exceeded from seven to ten feet in height, though on the way to Kenskoff I noticed many from twelve to fifteen feet. At Furcy and at La Selle we saw some very good plants, properly cleaned and attended to, and kept at a suitable height for picking the berries. Mackenzie noticed, in 1827, whole sides of mountains covered with coffee-trees of spontaneous growth, two-thirds of the produce being lost for want of hands to gather it. So prolific, he says, were the bushes, that many which were carefully tended produced from five to six lbs. and some were known to give nine lbs.

I have never noticed the peasantry use more than the *mauchette*, a sort of chopper almost as long as a sword, whilst cleaning their coffee plantations. They simply cut down the weeds and creepers, but never stir the soil around the roots with a hoe. The use of manure is unknown.

The only preventable cause for any decline in the coffee crop would be the neglect following the withdrawal of the peasantry to take part in civil wars and revolutions, and the lazy habits engendered by camp life. When riding through coffee plantations after the civil wars of 1868 and 1869, I noticed a marked deterioration from 1864. Creepers of every description were suffered to grow over and almost choke the plants, and poor crops were sometimes the result. In Geffrard's time, though the cultivation was slovenly, efforts were made to keep the plants clean, and during the quiet four years of Nissage-Saget's presidency the peasantry returned to their old habits.

Notwithstanding this occasional neglect, there appears no progressive falling off in the crops; they vary as before, but on the whole keep up to the average.

The quality of Haytian coffee is excellent, but its price in the market is low, from various causes. Sometimes the crop is gathered hastily, and ripe and unripe seeds are mixed; and then it is dried on the bare ground, regardless of the state of the weather; and when swept up into heaps, it is too often intermingled with small stones, leaves, and dirt; and fraudulent cultivators or middle-men add other substances to increase the weight. I have known carefully-selected parcels sent to France marked Mocha, and there realising full prices. Nowhere is coffee made better than in Hayti; it is roasted to a rich brown, ground and prepared with a sufficient allowance of the material, all on the same day, and the result is perfect.

As with other crops in the world, there are good years and bad years; but with neglected plants, the bad come oftener than they would if due attention were paid to their cultivation.

In 1789, when the French possessed the island, the amount produced greatly exceeded anything seen since, with the exceptions of 1863, 1875, and 1876. In those years above 71,000,000 lbs. passed through the custom-house, and it is calculated that about 15,000,000 lbs. were smuggled.

The variations have been as follows:—

	Lbs.
1789	88,360,502
1818	20,280,589
1824	46,000,000
1835	48,352,371
1845	41,002,571
1860	60,514,289
1861	45,660,889
1863	71,712,345
1864	45,168,764

1873	64,786,690
1874	54,677,854
1875	72,637,716
1876	72,289,504
1877	52,991,861
1878	63,255,545
1879	47,941,506
1880	55,562,897

This striking increase in the amount of coffee produced since the great war would appear somewhat to contradict the theory of the degeneracy and idleness of the Haytians, but it must be remembered that the women and children are very hard-working; that the women are in a majority, and that the work is mostly done by Nature; the men, also, are not very light-handed taskmasters. If a space be cleared round the bushes with a *mauchette*—easy work that a child can do—the increase in a plantation will continue, as I have remarked, by the beneficent hand of Nature; the heavy rains knock off the ripe berries and scatter them down the mountain-sides, and give rise to those matted undergrowths of coffee-bushes whose fecundity often surprises the traveller. It is not likely that the produce of the coffee-plants will decrease.

During the French colonial days the principal product was sugar, and in the year 1789 they exported 54,000,000 lbs. of white sugar and 107,000,000 lbs. of brown. As the slaves left the estates, so production decreased, and was fast disappearing when Christophe in the north forced the people by severe measures to resume its manufacture. He gave the great estates of the old colonists to his generals and courtiers, with an order that they should produce a certain amount of sugar under pain of forfeiture. As they had the population under their command, and an unrestrained use of the stick, they succeeded fairly; but as soon as this pressure was removed, the manufacture of sugar ceased, and it is no longer found in the list of exports, except as a fancy article to obtain bounties.

In 1818 the export of sugar had fallen from 161,000,000 to 1,900,000 lbs., and in 1821 to 600,000 lbs., then to disappear from the custom-house lists.

The prejudice against sugar-making is still strong, though, could the owners of estates prove to their people that large profits would accrue to them from its manufacture, it is very probable that the prejudice would die out. A friend of mine tried to persuade one of his cultivators to aid him in a sugar-making project, but the man answered sulkily, "Moué pas esclave"

("I'm not a slave"), and walked away. The negroes do not like a bell to be used to ring them to work, as it reminds them of colonial days, but some bold innovators have introduced and continued the practice, without producing any other effect than occasional grumbling.

Sugar-cane, however, is still very extensively cultivated, and succeeds admirably, the soil appearing peculiarly adapted to it. The cane is now grown for making tafia or white rum, and for molasses, which the people use instead of sugar. Most of the factories built by the French were destroyed, and inferior buildings have been erected in their stead. Watermills are generally used, as being economical, and the never-failing streams from the hills afford abundant power. A few proprietors have put up extensive machinery for sugar-making, but their success has been so doubtful as not to encourage others. A Haytian knows that during a revolution his property would not be respected, and, if a defeated partisan, would be either confiscated or destroyed: so no encouragement is held out to agricultural enterprise; and, what adds to his difficulties, a dangerous spirit of communism has spread among the people, and in many districts the peasantry begin to regard the estates as their own.

Of cotton 8,400,000 lbs. were exported in 1789. This amount, however, soon decreased under independent rule:—

In	1835	there were exported	1,649,717	lbs.
"	1842	"	880,517	"
"	1853	"	557,480	"
"	1859	"	938,056	"
"	1860	"	688,735	"

to rise, on the outbreak of the civil war in the United States, to—

| In | 1861 | 1,139,439 | lbs. |
| " | 1862 | 1,473,853 | " |

increasing until 1865, when the crop was over 4,000,000 pounds; but the fall of prices, occasioned by the collapse of the civil war in the States, from 2s. 6d. to 11d. in the course of a few months, discouraged the agriculturists, and cotton was again neglected. In the last commercial reports the amount of cotton exported from the whole republic is not given.

During the Great Exhibition held in London in 1862, the report on the cotton exhibited there by Hayti mentioned very favourably the two bales which were sent as specimens, and it remarked that England required at least 2,000,000 bales of each of the qualities exhibited. It has been calculated that there is sufficient suitable land in Hayti to furnish half the quantity required. This, however, appears to me an over-estimate.

President Geffrard was fully aware of the importance of taking advantage of the opportunity offered by the civil war in the United States, and supported two measures to encourage cotton cultivation. The first was the immigration of free blacks from America, and the next the offer of bounties.

The immigration was badly managed, as blacks from the North were sent, instead of Southern cultivators. Most of those who arrived, being unfitted for field-labour in a tropical climate, added but little to the production of cotton. A few kept to the work, but many died, and most of the others either migrated to the towns or left the country. As might have been expected, the Haytian arrangements were as bad as they could be. Settlers were given ground without any water, but were told that a canal should some day be cut; food and money were distributed irregularly, and malversation added to the other difficulties.

Bounties were scarcely required, as the price rose from 4d. in 1859 to 1s., 1s. 2d., and 1s. 5d. in 1863, and 2s. 6d. in 1864; and many Haytians tried to do something in order to win a portion of this harvest. Field-hands, however, were scarce, and in order to get in their crops the proprietors had to offer half the amount to those who would come and gather it for them. One peasant proprietor, in 1863, managed with his family to secure 8000 lbs. of cotton, which he sold for £500, a sum to which he was wholly unaccustomed. The comparative large amounts to be received would have had a very great effect on the prosperity of the country had there been the necessary hands ready to take advantage of the opportunity offered. The industrious, however, were few, and many proprietors had to leave a portion of their crop to rot on the plants.

When the prices rose to three or four times the former value, the Government abolished the system of bounties, and imposed a tax of one penny a pound, but had to abolish it in 1865 on the sudden fall in prices. The cultivation is now again neglected, as Haytian cotton has returned to its old level in price, and the land must be more valuable for provision crops. With the uncertainty which characterises the supply of labour in Hayti, it is not likely that cotton will again become an important export.

The French appear to have paid but little attention to the cultivation of the cacao-tree, and in 1789 only exported 600,000 lbs. Even this small quantity decreased, and the amount that passed through the custom-house in 1821 fell to 264,792 lbs. The crops have since much varied, but the export rose gradually, until, in 1863, the amount was 2,217,769 lbs. As far as I have been able to ascertain, no subsequent year has produced so abundant a crop.

Cacao is principally grown near the farthest point of the peninsula, west of Jérémie, amid a population rarely visited, and reported as among the most barbarous of the island.

Tobacco is not mentioned in the list of exports during the French period, and only appears in those returns which were published when the Dominican end of the island formed part of the Haytian republic. A little has been occasionally grown for home consumption, as at the Fonds-aux-Nègres.

Logwood is found in all parts of the country, and is a very important article of export.

There is nothing else grown in Hayti which can be called an article of commerce, but the peasantry cultivate large amounts of garden produce, and some rice and Indian-corn, but they do not do so in sufficient quantities to supply the market. Bananas for cooking purposes are a valuable crop, as they take the place of bread in the daily consumption of the people. Fruit-trees abound, particularly mangoes, sour oranges, and the avocado (alligator pear). The last fruit comes to great perfection, whilst the mango is inferior except in a few localities, and is not to be compared to the "number elevens" grown in Jamaica.

The markets of the capital are well supplied with European vegetables, which are grown in the mountains at the back of La Coupe, the old summer resort of the people of the capital. When staying there, I have often walked to the gardens at the foot of Fort Jaques, where not only vegetables may be found, but many orchards full of peach-trees—sadly neglected, however—with their branches covered with long moss, to the exclusion of leaf and fruit. A few apples and chestnuts are occasionally brought to market. Fort Jaques is situated about 6000 feet above the level of the sea. I may notice that the peaches are usually picked before they ripen, on account of the pilfering habits of the people.

There is little to be said about the domestic animals. The horses are generally small, but strong and full of endurance, and are of Spanish breed. Mules and donkeys are plentiful, as no person is satisfied unless he possesses some beast of burden. The cattle are supplied from the Dominican part of the island, and are much used for traction. Good beef may often be found in the markets. Sheep and goats are plentiful, but of inferior breeds, whilst pigs wander about untended, and are generally so lean that they warrant the reproach that the Haytians cannot even fatten a pig. Poultry are thought to be getting scarcer than formerly: they are generally of an inferior kind.

Commerce

Hayti has for many years carried on a very fair commerce with Europe and America, though probably not a quarter of what she might have if her inhabitants were industrious. In the colonial days, the exports were valued at from £6,000,000 to £8,000,000 a year, and in 1790 had reached nearly £11,000,000 with a less numerous population, whilst the highest since the independence has probably not exceeded £2,300,000.

Notwithstanding foreign wars, civil wars, insurrections, and those continued conspiracies which have almost every year disturbed the country, the productive powers of the soil are so great, that nothing appears permanently to depress the exports, and therefore the imports.

The export trade of Hayti in 1835, which then included the whole island, was as follows:—

	Lbs.	Value.
Coffee	48,352,371	$6,812,849
Logwood	13,293,737	86,409
Cotton	1,649,717	247,457
Mahogany, feet	5,413,316	405,998
Tobacco	2,086,606	125,196
Cacao	397,321	47,678
		————
		$7,725,587

At the exchange of the day this represented just £1,000,000 sterling. The last year in which the statistics refer to the whole island is 1842.

M. Madiou, in his "History of Hayti," vol. i. p. 31, gives the amount of the produce exported in the years 1842 and 1845, but does not affix a value to them:—

1842

Coffee	40,759,064	lbs.
Cotton	880,517	"
Logwood	19,563,147	"
Tobacco	2,518,612	"
Cigars	700,000	No.
Mahogany	4,096,716	feet

and various small amounts of miscellaneous articles.

It will be remarked that in the returns for 1845 tobacco has ceased to appear, as Santo Domingo had by this time separated from Hayti. M. Madiou considers that about 5,000,000 lbs. of coffee are consumed in the island, which is probably an under-estimate, considering the lavish manner in which it is used, and that 20,000,000 lbs. are exported as contraband, to avoid the heavy duties. This calculation appears too high. Whilst I was in Hayti, the illicit trade was considered to represent from 15 to 20 per cent of the acknowledged exports. Much, however, depends on the character of the men in power.

1845

	Lbs.
Coffee	41,002,571
Cotton	557,480
Logwood and other woods	68,181,588
Mahogany, feet	7,904,285

The other woods consist of lignum vitæ, &c. It is curious that he makes no mention of cacao.

In the next returns it will be noticed how mahogany decreased—the cuttings near the coast were beginning to be exhausted—whilst the exports of logwood were greatly increased. This is work that just suits the negro; it can be done by fits and starts, and never requires continuous labour. The following tables may appear superfluous, but they show the effect of comparatively orderly government. These six years were free from any serious civil trouble, and no foreign complications prevented all development that was possible. The war in the States gave trade considerable impulse.

1859

Coffee	41,712,106	lbs.
Logwood	88,177,600	"
Cotton	938,056	"
Cacao	1,397,364	"
Mahogany	2,690,044	feet

1860

Coffee	60,514,289	lbs.

Logwood	104,321,200	"
Cotton	668,735	"
Cacao	1,581,806	"
Mahogany	2,264,037	feet

1861

Coffee	45,660,889	lbs.
Logwood	105,757,050	"
Cotton	1,139,439	"
Cacao	1,304,561	"
Mahogany	1,659,272	feet

1862

Coffee	54,579,059	lbs.
Logwood	167,005,650	"
Cotton	1,473,853	"
Cacao	1,743,853	"
Mahogany	2,441,887	feet

1863

Coffee	71,712,345	lbs.
Logwood	116,669,400	"
Cotton	2,217,769	"
Cacao	2,338,400	"
Mahogany	2,016,557	feet

1864

Coffee	45,168,764	lbs.
Logwood	153,235,100	"
Cotton	3,237,594	"
Cacao	1,399,941	"
Mahogany	2,369,501	feet

No trustworthy statistics could be obtained for the time of Soulouque, on account of the monopolies and the various interferences with commerce. In 1865 the siege of Cap Haïtien, and the disturbances which followed in 1866, the fall of Geffrard in 1867, and the civil war of 1868 and 1869, completely disturbed trade, and no reliable statistics can be obtained.

The latest trade return which I have seen is of the year 1880:—

	Lbs.
Coffee	55,562,897
Logwood	321,729,801
Cacao	2,729,853
Cotton	957,962
Mahogany, feet	71,478
Sugar	2,397

Mr. Mackenzie, who was English Consul-General at Port-au-Prince during the years 1826 and 1827, gives a table of the commerce of Hayti in 1825, which includes the whole island.

Imports.

	Vessels.	Tonnage.	Value of cargoes.
American	374	39,199	£391,784
British	78	11,952	291,456
French	65	11,136	152,681
German	17	3,185	85,951
Others	18	1,328	10,162
			£932,034

The large amount of American vessels will be noticed, and the comparative extent of their trade. In 1864 English-sailing shipping rose to 281 vessels (of 41,199 tonnage) and 74 steamers, against those under the American flag, 88 sailing vessels (of 16,316 tonnage) and two steamers. This, however, was only nominal, the ravages of the *Alabama* having induced American shipowners to transfer their vessels to the British flag.

In 1877 the tonnage of vessels calling at the three chief ports of Hayti (Port-au-Prince, Cap Haïtien, and Les Cayes) was as follows:—

Flag.	Tonnage.
British	184,331

French	91,562
German	80,561
American	22,350

It must be noticed, however, that the English, French, and German tonnage consists principally of steamers, which have ports of call on the island, whereas the Americans have two-fifths of the sailing tonnage.

In 1863 the imports into Hayti amounted to £1,743,052, and in 1864 to £2,045,333. The United States then held the first place, having sent £762,724 and £994,266, their imports, as usual, being principally provisions and lumber. England occupied the second position with £503,630 and £626,624; France, £255,747 and £273,778. Both in the years 1863 and 1864 there was a great decrease in the amount of provisions grown in the country, partly on account of the increase of cotton cultivation; hence the very heavy imports of provisions from the United States.

The exports in 1863 and 1864 were valued at £2,458,000 and £1,895,000, the decrease arising from the inferiority of the coffee crop, and the fall in the price of goods. The average value of the principal articles of export varied as follows:—

Articles.	1863.			1864.		
Coffee, per 100 lbs.	£2	9	3½	£2	5	0
Logwood, per 1000 lbs.	1	2	9	0	17	10
Cotton, per lb.	0	1	4	0	2	0
Cacao, per 100 lbs.	1	9	4	1	6	0

Present Prices

Prices have fallen lately to an unprecedented extent. During the autumn of the year 1882, coffee was once quoted as low as 16s. per 100 lbs., but rose afterwards to 24s.; and all other produce was also depreciated in value.

In 1876 the total imports into the island were £2,110,000; the total exports, £2,200,000.

In 1877 the total imports were £1,594,200; the total exports, £1,694,800, which was below the average.

In 1877 the imports into the capital were as follows, which shows a marked change in the position of the importing countries:—

Great Britain	£619,900
United States	110,200
France	103,100
Germany	36,880

In some of the smaller ports the position of the trade of the United States was relatively better. In Les Cayes, for instance:—

United States	£119,172
Great Britain	23,692
France	22,030
Germany	1,715

A portion of these imports from the United States consisted of manufactures in transit from England. We appear to be holding our own everywhere as regards piece goods and iron, whilst five-sixths of the imports of the United States consist of flour, salt pork, and other provisions. The Haytians are French in their tastes, but the cheapness of our Manchester goods enables our importers to hold their own. The great export, coffee, appears in great part ultimately to reach French ports, as it is not appreciated in other countries, whereas its cheapness and good quality recommend it strongly to the French Government for the use of the army.

When in Port-au-Prince I drew the attention of the Secretary of State for Foreign Affairs to the great discrepancy between their published returns and those of our Board of Trade. In 1865 our exports are set down at £1,163,274, and in 1866 at £1,425,402, for the whole island. Santo Domingo takes but a small amount, whilst the Haytian custom-house did not acknowledge more than half the amount of our returns. Either we overvalue our goods in England, or the smuggling must be large.

The imports from the United States appear to have greatly fallen off since 1864, which must imply that the peasantry are planting more food and consuming a very much smaller amount of imported provisions.

Finance

As in most American republics, the income of the Haytian state depends chiefly on the custom-house. It is said the people will not bear direct taxation, and that therefore the Government must rely on import and export duties. The heavy debt which was imposed on Hayti by France nearly sixty years ago has been the principal cause of the financial embarrassments of the republic.

The mission of Baron Mackau, sent by Charles X. in 1825, had for object the imperfect recognition of the independence of the republic of Hayti, on condition of their paying £6,000,000 as an indemnity to the old colonists—a sum quite out of the power of the country to raise—and only five years were allowed to complete the transaction. One is at a loss to understand how President Boyer could have consented to so burdensome an arrangement. Subsequently the indemnity was reduced to £3,600,000, but although fifty-eight years have passed, a balance still remains due. It was not till 1838 that these arrangements were concluded, and France definitively recognised the independence of Hayti. The republic had effected a loan in Paris in 1825 of £1,200,000 nominal to pay the first instalment due, and even this debt has not been completely settled. The whole transaction proved a cruel burden to the country, and, by introducing heavy export duties and the curse of paper money, greatly injured agricultural and every other interest.

The import duties average about 30 per cent. on the value, whilst the export duties are at so much a quintal on coffee, and have varied according to the exigencies of the moment. Major Stuart's Report for 1877 enters into many details which may be found interesting. I propose to give here only the general results; but I may say that the duties embrace almost every article, and are as high as they can bear.

The progress of the revenue collected in Hayti is another proof to me that the population has greatly increased.

It is not necessary to examine the budgets of many years. In 1821, before the union with Santo Domingo, the income is stated by Mackenzie to have been $3,570,691, and the expenditure $3,461,993. In these sums must be included some exceptional receipts and expenditure, as the revenue of the whole island in 1825 was only $2,421,592. The long and quiet Presidency of Boyer, coupled with his honest administration, enabled him not only to pay off considerable sums to France, but to leave a heavy balance in the treasury. Boyer, however, has the demerit of having introduced the paper currency, and of having put into circulation $2,500,000 more than he withdrew, thus reducing the exchange of the doubloon from 16 to 1 (par) to 40 to 1.

After Boyer came the period of revolutions, and consequent deficits and heavy issues of paper money. In four years they had sent down the exchange to $60 to one doubloon. But the disastrous period of Haytian financial history was the reign of Soulouque, when millions of paper dollars were issued every year, sending down the exchange to $289 to one doubloon.

In 1849 no less than $4,195,400 were issued to meet the expenses of the establishment of the empire.

The budget for 1848, the last year of the republic, is nominally a very modest one (exchange $25 to £1):—

Army	$3,232,238	=	£129,289
Interior	770,395	=	30,815
Finance and foreign affairs	668,814	=	26,752
Justice, education, public worship	303,393	=	12,135
			£198,993

But as 2,200,000 paper dollars were issued during the year, it is probable that this budget was not adhered to.

The budget for the year in which the empire was established is given as follows (exchange $40 to £1):—

Army	$3,810,216	=	£95,255
Interior	735,937	=	18,398
Finance, &c.	2,237,389	=	55,934
Justice, &c.	309,293	=	7,732
	$7,092,835	=	£177,319

But these budgets are not to be trusted, and do not represent the real expenses.

When the accounts were examined subsequent to the fall of Soulouque, it was found that of the coffee monopoly alone £400,000 had been abstracted for the use of the Emperor and some of his Ministers and favourites. The comparative large sums of £40,000, £20,000, and £12,000 were taken at a time, without any account being rendered. During Soulouque's reign over $28,000,000 were added to the currency.

In June 1863, General Dupuy, Finance Minister to President Geffrard, published a very clear financial statement. The total debt remaining due to France was £1,436,000. The custom duties produced:—

In	1860	£511,666
"	1861	463,333
"	1862	566,000

Minor taxes, £26,341.

Deficits.

In	1859	£30,276
"	1860	35,904
"	1861	81,193
"	1862	81,483

These were calculated on the amount of paper money signed to meet them, but at the close of 1862 there was £79,834 in hand.

The budget of 1863-64 was fixed as follows:—

Expenses.		Receipts.	
Finance	£67,776	Duties	£564,050
Foreign Office	171,828	Minor taxes	24,725
War	138,361		————
Interior	171,692		£588,775
Public instruction	44,825		
Justice and public worship	27,714		
	————		
	£622,196		

The deficit was met by adding ten per cent. to the duties.

During the Presidency of General Geffrard the finances were better administered than under Souloque, but millions of dollars disappeared, without any one being found willing to give an account of what had become of them. One coloured and two black generals are supposed to have appropriated the principal portion. On the Chamber of Deputies venturing to make inquiries on this interesting point, it was summarily dismissed, and a packed Chamber substituted.

Civil war ended by General Geffrard resigning and quitting the country. I do not believe, however, that he carried with him more than he could have fairly saved out of his salary. He, moreover, was the only President that I knew who kept up the position of chief of the State with any dignity.

No budgets were procurable during Salnave's time, and the civil war that was carried on during three years caused the Government and insurgents to issue paper money, so that before Salnave's fall this paper currency was to be obtained at 3000 paper to one silver dollar. It was withdrawn by the subsequent Government at 10 to 1 for their own paper.

The finances under General Nissage-Saget were, for Hayti, at first decently administered; but when the bad black element from the south entered into its councils, malversation became the order of the day. But during this Presidency a great change was made in the currency: all paper money was withdrawn at an exchange of 300 to 1, and American silver dollars substituted. This change was much criticised both before and since, as unsuited to the circumstances of the country. On the whole, the balance of arguments was in favour of a metallic currency.

Under President Domingue there were no honest financial measures taken. Everything was done to suit the pleasure of Septimus Rameau, and a loan was raised in France, and the largest portion distributed among the friends of the Minister in a manner which astonished even Haytians. It was a disgraceful transaction, that the next Chamber endeavoured to ignore; but as it was supported by the French agents, the Government of Boisrond-Canal had to yield and acknowledge it.

For the years 1876 and 1877 we have the receipts and expenditure stated in detail. The income from duties, &c., was £805,900; the expenditure, £804,737; including £202,876 to the sinking fund. The army and navy figure for only £167,568, and public instruction was increased to £82,245. In Soulouque's budget of 1849, justice, education, and public worship were credited with only £7732.

Budget for 1876-77

Finance and commerce	£89,558
Foreign relations	46,714
War and marine	167,568
Interior and agriculture	111,931
Justice	36,095
Public instruction	82,245
Public worship	12,586
District chest (communes)	75,160
Sinking fund	202,876
	————
	£824,733

The latest budget I have before me is that of 1881. It is as follows:—

Finance and commerce	£67,610
Foreign relations	48,954
War	214,837
Interior	298,913

Justice	54,565
Public instruction	115,037
Public worship	13,875
	£813,791

The amount of the income to meet this expenditure is not stated.

The circulating medium in the early days of Haytian independence consisted of foreign gold and silver coins, and then some fabricated in the country, of inferior quality and appearance, of both silver and copper. In 1826, President Boyer beginning to feel the pressure of his engagements with France, issued paper notes of different values. Being irredeemable, they soon fell to a heavy discount, 3½ to 1. The succeeding Governments, as I have noticed, continued the same course, until, on the accession of Soulouque to power, the exchange was about 4½ to 1. The unchecked emissions after he ascended the imperial throne gradually lessened the value of the paper, until, in 1858, it was 18 to 1.

Some order having been put into the finances by General Dupuy, the exchange in 1863 was more favourable, being 12½ to 1; the troubles which succeeded in 1865 sent it to 17 to 1; and with the revolutionary Government of Salnave and the civil war that followed it went down like the assignats during the French Revolution,—in 1857, 30 to 1; in 1859, 3000 to 1.

The issues of Salnave's Government were so discredited that they were at one time exchanged at 6500 paper dollars for one of silver. Until lately the American dollar and its fractions, with a plentiful bronze currency, sufficed for all wants. Now, however, a special Haytian dollar is being coined, with the object apparently of preventing its export—a very futile expedient, as experience proves.

A sort of National Bank, managed principally by Frenchmen, was established a few years since, but its operations do not as yet appear to have had much influence on the country. As the bank, however, has some control over the collection of duties, it may introduce a more honest perception of these imports; but I do not think the managers will find that their lines have fallen in pleasant places.

FOOTNOTES:

[1] Ever since the reign of Soulouque, professional authors have been paid by the Haytian Government to spread rose-tinted accounts of the civilisation and progress of Hayti. But twenty-four hours in any town of that republic would satisfy the most sceptical that these semi-official accounts are unworthy of belief.

[2] Mackenzie states that he noticed the thermometer marking 99° every day for considerable periods.

[3] It is a well-known fact that the noise of the approach of an earthquake is generally heard; but in Port-au-Prince there is a curious phenomenon which I have never known explained. A subterranean noise is frequently heard approaching from the plains, and appears to pass under the town without any movement of the earth being perceptible. The Haytians call it "le gouffre," or "le bruit du gouffre," and many fancy the whole of that portion of the island to be undermined, and predict a fearful fate for the capital.

[4] Our unsuccessful attempt to conquer Hayti does not merit to be recorded in detail, but it is humiliating to read of the stupidity of our chiefs at Port-au-Prince, who made our soldiers work at fortifications during the day and do duty at night. No wonder that we find a regiment 600 strong losing 400 in two months, and the 82d landing 950 men, to be reduced in six weeks to 350.

[5] St. Remy, speaking of Toussaint's capture, says, "Embarquement par les *blancs*." How like a mulatto not to say "par les français!"

[6] This biography, as well as the others I have seen, is full of absurdities; talks of Toussaint advancing with an imposing army, which turns out to be of 950 men. At the battle of Verretes 1500 blacks drive 3500 English troops from their intrenchments, and then 6000 English are defeated and cut to pieces by a few squadrons. As far as I can learn, Brisbane had eighty English soldiers and some untrustworthy black and coloured allies, mixed with French planters. Even a moderately sensible Haytian could not accept so absurd a biography.

[7] I am glad to be able to notice that M. Robin (mulatto), in his "Abrégé de l'Histoire d'Haïti," remarks in relating Toussaint's sad death:—"Ainsi fut récompensé de ses longs et éminents services cet illustre enfant d'Haïti, qui pouvait bien se dire le premier des noirs," &c. &c. Dessalines appears to have encouraged Leclerc to arrest Toussaint, and then dishonourably betrayed Charles Belair (black), nephew to Toussaint, and his wife into the hands of the French, who shot Belair and hung his wife.

[8] One thing I wish distinctly to state, that I never heard of any mulatto, except Generals Salnave and Therlonge, who was mixed up with the cannibalism of the Vaudoux, nor of any black educated in Europe.

[9] On the African coast the word is Vodun. Burton mentions that the serpents worshipped at Whydah were so respected that formerly to kill one by accident was punished by death. Now a heavy fine is inflicted. Bosman states that the serpent is the chief god in Dahomey, to whom great presents are made. They are harmless; white, yellow, and brown in colour, and the largest was about six feet long, and as thick as a man's arm. Fergusson, in his introductory essay on "Tree and Serpent Worship in India," mentions that at a place called Sheik Haredi, in Egypt, serpent-worship still continues, and that the priests sacrifice to them sheep and lambs. On the west coast of Africa, women, when touched by the serpent, are said to become possessed; they are seized with hysteria, and often bereft of reason; they are afterwards considered priestesses. The whole essay of Fergusson is exceedingly interesting.

[10] Red, the royal colour at Mdra.—*Bosman.*

[11] Burton, in his "Mission to the King of Dahomey," notices that the fetish priests are a kind of secret police for the despotic king, and exercise the same influence as in Hayti. They are supposed to be able to give health, wealth, length of days, and can compass the destruction of the applicant's foes, all for a fee. Bosman, in his account of the slave coast of Guinea, says that a negro who offered opposition to the priests was poisoned by them, and became speechless and paralysed in his limbs; and that if any woman betrays the secrets of the priests, she is burnt to death.

[12] Barbot states that the common food of the natives of the kingdom of Ansiko (west coast of Africa) is man's flesh, insomuch that their markets are provided with it, as ours in Europe with beef and mutton. All prisoners of war, unless they can sell them alive to greater advantage, they fatten for slaughter, and at last sell them to butchers to supply the markets, and roast them on spits, as we do other meat (date 1700).—Churchill's Collection, vol. v. p. 479. Barbot also notices that the people of Jagos, Congo, and Angola were also cannibals.

[13] Barbot, in his account of the Ansiko kingdom, says: "That which is most inhuman is, that the father makes no difficulty to eat the son, nor the son the father, nor one brother the other; and whosoever dies, be the disease ever so contagious, yet they eat the flesh immediately as a choice dish." — Barbot, in Churchill's Collection, vol. v. p. 479.

[14] I may here notice that the Haytians have chosen the mountain cabbage-palm (*Palma nobilis*) as the tree of liberty in the national arms. It is in nature a beautiful palm, with its dark-green foliage and perfect shape. The cap of liberty stuck on the top of it makes it look rather ludicrous, and the arms around its base are not very appropriate to so unmilitary a people.

[15] "Nous ne sommes plus aux temps où quelques rares curés, repartis dans les principales paroisses de la république faisaient d'énormes bénéfices par des moyens souvent hélas reprouvés par la conscience et par les lois de l'église.... Qu'ai-je besoin d'évoquer dans le passé les lamentables souvenirs de l'église en Haïti. Je suis prêtre, et je voudrais pour l'honneur du sacerdoce pouvoir laver son opprobre de mes larmes et de les plonger dans un éternel oubli. Mais il ne dépend ni de moi ni de personne d'en effacer la triste mémoire." — Monseigneur A. Guilloux, Archbishop of Port-au-Prince.

[16] "Ne suffit-il pas d'ailleurs de parcourir les villes et les bourgades de la république pour rencontrer encore les témoins vivants d'un libertinage sans exemple." — Guilloux.

[17] Military trials have always been a disgrace to Hayti. Even under their model President Boyer (1827) they were as bad as they were under the Emperor Soulouque or the present President Salomon. Mackenzie, in his notes on Hayti, states that no defence was allowed, as that would have been waste of time. Four officers were tried and condemned to death: their arms were tied, and they were led by a police officer to the place of execution. They showed great intrepidity, though the soldiers fired a hundred shots before they killed them. President Geffrard had certainly more respect for the forms of law.

[18] Mackenzie tells a story of a town-adjutant calling on him in gorgeous uniform; he next met him cooking the dinner of his host.

[19] Recueil de Proverbes Creoles. Port-au-Prince, 1877.

[20] Vol. ii. p. 24: — "Les légionnaires au nombre de 800 environ furent enveloppés de toutes parts; ils se trouvaient sans nul espoir; assurés de leur mort, mais résolus de se bien défendre, ils se retranchaient sous la mitraille la plus meurtrière, les uns derrière des arbres renversés, d'autres derrière

d'énormes? pierres; percés de coups de baïonettes, criblés de balles, ils combattaient toujours avec une intrépidité sans égale: plusieurs ayant le bras coupé se défendaient avec celui qui leur restait; ceux qui par la perte de leur sang ne pouvaient plus se tenir debout se trouvaient sur leurs génoux, combattaient encore avec fureur, se faisaient un rempart des corps expirés de ceux qui étaient tombés," &c., &c.

[21] There is a line wanting in this stanza, which the authoress herself has not been able to remember.

[22] I would refer to Major Stuart's excellent Report for 1877 for details on these subjects. I have myself partly founded my observations on this Report.